DATE DUE

NV 28 '90			
FE 8 '01			
JY 10 '01			
SE 10 '02			
JY 30 '02			
SE 21 '02			
MR 24 '03			
JY 9 '03			

FILMMAKERS SERIES
edited by
ANTHONY SLIDE

1. *James Whale*, by James Curtis. 1982
2. *Cinema Stylists*, by John Belton. 1983
3. *Harry Langdon*, by William Schelly. 1982
4. *William A. Wellman*, by Frank Thompson. 1983
5. *Stanley Donen*, by Joseph Casper. 1983
6. *Brian DePalma*, by Michael Bliss. 1983
7. *J. Stuart Blackton*, by Marian Blackton Trimble. 1985
8. *Martin Scorsese and Michael Cimino*, by Michael Bliss. 1985
9. *Franklin J. Schaffner*, by Erwin Kim. 1985
10. *D. W. Griffith at Biograph*, by Cooper C. Graham et al. 1985
11. *Some Day We'll Laugh: An Autobiography*, by Esther Ralston. 1985
12. *The Memoirs of Alice Guy Blaché*, trans. by Roberta and Simone Blaché. 1996
13. *Leni Riefenstahl and Olympia*, by Cooper C. Graham. 1986
14. *Robert Florey*, by Brian Taves. 1987
15. *Henry King's America*, by Walter Coppedge. 1986
16. *Aldous Huxley and Film*, by Virginia M. Clark. 1987
17. *Five American Cinematographers*, by Scott Eyman. 1987
18. *Cinematographers on the Art and Craft of Cinematography*, by Anna Kate Sterling. 1987
19. *Stars of the Silents*, by Edward Wagenknecht. 1987
20. *Twentieth Century-Fox*, by Aubrey Solomon. 1988
21. *Highlights and Shadows: The Memoirs of a Hollywood Cameraman*, by Charles G. Clarke. 1989
22. *I Went That-a-Way: The Memoirs of a Western Film Director*, by Harry L. Fraser; edited by Wheeler Winston Dixon and Audrey Brown Fraser. 1990
23. *Order in the Universe: The Films of John Carpenter*, by Robert C. Cumbow. 1990
24. *The Films of Freddie Francis*, by Wheeler Winston Dixon. 1991
25. *Hollywood Be Thy Name*, by William Bakewell. 1991
26. *The Charm of Evil: The Life and Films of Terence Fisher*, by Wheeler Winston Dixon. 1991
27. *Lionheart in Hollywood: The Autobiography of Henry Wilcoxon*, with Katherine Orrison. 1991

The Films of Oliver Stone

Edited by Don Kunz

Filmmakers, No. 55

The Scarecrow Press, Inc.
Lanham, Md., & London
1997

~~~~~~~~ ~~ ~~~ ~~~~~~ ~~~~~~ ~~ ~~~~~~~a
by Scarecrow Press, Inc.
4720 Boston Way
Lanham, Maryland 20706

4 Pleydell Gardens, Folkestone
Kent CT20 2DN, England

British Library Cataloguing in Publication Information Available

Library of Congress Cataloging-in-Publication Data

The films of Oliver Stone / edited by Don Kunz.
    p. cm.— (Filmmakers ; no. 55)
  ISBN 0-8108-3297-6 (cloth : alk. paper)
  1. Stone, Oliver—Criticism and interpretation. I. Kunz, Don, 1941– .
II. Series : Filmmakers series ; no. 55.
PN1998.3.S76F56   1997
791.43'0233'092—dc21   97-1643

ISBN 0–8108–3297–6 (cloth : alk. paper)

Dedication

This book is dedicated to my mother.
When the great economic depression deprived
her of a college education, she instilled in me
a love for learning.

Contents

Preface

After two decades of work in the motion picture industry Oliver Stone has become the consummate Hollywood insider at age fifty. He embodies the American success story of the apprentice who rises to the top of his profession against astronomical odds through hard work, hard scrapping, and dogged persistence. Stone began as a screenwriter for the industry, seeing his scenarios rejected, rewritten beyond recognition by veterans better positioned than himself, ruined by ego-swollen directors, and put on indefinite hold. Although he made his directorial debut in 1974 with a low-budget horror film, *The Hand*, his first success came as a writer. *Midnight Express* (1978) earned him an Academy Award for best screenplay adaptation. The award permitted him a second chance at directing with *Seizure* (1981). While that film was a rather undistinguished formula performance, his third directorial effort, *Salvador* (1986), displayed unusual courage, inventiveness, and budgetary restraint which caught the attention of the motion picture industry's powerbrokers. It earned Stone the opportunity to make *Platoon* (1986) based on his own original and often rejected screenplay. With *Platoon*, Stone redefined the Vietnam War film and earned four Academy Awards including those for best director and best picture. Such success permitted him to become a producer and deal maker with other Hollywood insiders. All this is to say that success like capital earns interest. In one way Stone has become like one of those insider traders that he treated in *Wall Street* (1987); he has become a player, an extremely well-financed risk taker in a position to call the shots because he has the bankroll, the reputation, and the know-how.

Stone's success has been ironic and even paradoxical; ultimately he became an insider by behaving like an outsider. After his early apprentice work as screenwriter and director, Stone set about redefining what the American film industry could do in the eighties and nineties. He did disturbing spins on Hollywood paradigms, explored controversial subject matter, and challenged the notion that American cinema was primarily entertainment. The Hollywood deal makers did not embrace Stone merely because he was colorful and flamboyant. He was admitted to their company because he proved there was a large paying audience for his work, and if there was the glamour of celebrity and the clamor of controversy about him, so much the better. It was big box office: $250 million gross worldwide for *Platoon* alone. Like a brash, upstart, high roller on a hot streak, Stone emboldened the more conservative players to capitalize on his success.

Of course, they paid a price. By admitting Oliver Stone into the Hollywood establishment as an Academy Award winner, the industry was conceding him the power to continue the revolution he had begun—expanding the Hollywood product line beyond the safety of special-effects extravaganzas and bankable sequels toward serious social problem films with disturbing resolutions which challenged the audience to take action.

Oliver Stone, then, has matured into an auteur. And after a decade of being in a position to show what he can do when in control of a film project with an adequate budget, his cinematic signature is becoming quite clear.

Typically, Stone's films are written or cowritten by him, usually adapted from other literary material, sometimes multiple sources. He seems especially partial to autobiography or biography: *Salvador* was based on Richard Boyle's account of his journalistic career south of the border; *Talk Radio* (1988) drew in part on Stephen Singular's account of Denver talk show host Alan Berg; *Born on the Fourth of July* (1989) adapted Vietnam War veteran Ron Kovic's autobiography; *The Doors* (1990) was based partly on Jerry Hopkins' biography of lead singer Jim Morrison, *No One Here Gets Out Alive*; *JFK* (1991) drew heavily on New Orleans' District Attorney Jim Garrison's *On the Trail of the Assassins* and Jim Marrs' *Crossfire: The Plot that Killed Kennedy*; *Heaven and Earth* (1993) adapted Le Ly Hayslip's autobiographical *When Heaven and Earth Changed Places* and *Child of War, Woman of Peace*. The screenplay of *Nixon* bears extensive footnoting which references historical records. And two of Stone's other films draw more directly upon his own life. Stone's original screenplay, *Platoon*, fictionalized his Vietnam War experience; *Wall Street* seemed to trade on his insider knowledge as the son of a New York stockbroker as well as on the exploits of flamboyant traders like Ivan Boesky. In developing his material on-screen, part of Stone's method is to use many of the same actors from film to film—a kind of repertory company. He has found multiple roles for Tom Berenger, Willem Dafoe, Tony Frank, Kevin Dillon, Tommy Lee Jones, John C. McGinley, Charlie Sheen, Frank Whaley, Michael Wincott, James Woods, and his own son, Sean Stone. But he also has employed major stars like Michael Caine, Tom Cruise, Michael Douglas, Daryl Hannah, Hal Holbrook, Sir Anthony Hopkins, Kevin Kostner, Jack Lemmon, Walter Matthau, Meg Ryan, Martin Sheen, Sissy Spacek, and Donald Sutherland for single performances in both major and minor parts.

In casting his protagonists Stone has been especially adept at eliciting strong performances from previously little known actors who can play nervous, edgy, threatening roles like James Woods (*Salvador* and *Nixon*), Tom Berenger (*Platoon*), Eric Bogosian (*Talk Radio*), Val Kilmer (*The Doors*), and Tommy Lee Jones (*JFK* and *Heaven and Earth*). Or he has deliberately cast against type to catch his audience off guard and throw them off balance: Tom Berenger who plays the evil Sergeant Barnes in *Platoon* turns up as the unscarred Marine recruiting officer who sounds like John Wayne in *Born on the Fourth of July*; Tom Cruise, the gung-ho star of *Top Gun*, becomes the paralyzed veteran Ron Kovic in *Born on the Fourth of July*; the infamous Jim Garrison is assigned the role of his nemesis Earl Warren, while clean-cut Kevin Costner plays the infamous Garrison in *JFK*; Woody Harrelson, the affable bartender of *Cheers*, becomes a demonic murderer in *Natural Born Killers*. Upsetting audience expectations through casting, Stone forestalls hope that the problems his films expose will be corrected by movie-star characters in conventionally upbeat Hollywood endings.

Moreover, Stone is fond of playing a more serious version of Alfred Hitchcock's hide-the-director game by making cameo appearances in his own films: In *Platoon* Stone appears as an officer calling in an air strike while an NVA sapper blows his bunker apart; in *Born on the Fourth of July* he assumes the role of a broadcast journalist interviewing a military officer who is convinced that the United States is winning the Vietnam War. In *The Doors* Stone even crops up as a film-school professor presiding over the screening of a movie by Jim Morrison. In such appearances Stone is self-effacing—playing the little guy in the big scene bearing witness. Of course, this seems more and more ironic as Stone has become the big man behind the camera calling the shots. Nevertheless, he continues to impersonate what he used to be and what most of his audience will remain—the bystander inadvertently glimpsed in the shadows cast by the glare of recent American history's big events. Indeed, his filmed stories seem to comprise an alternative history witnessed from the odd angle on the periphery.

Or his audiences have bought it as such. Beginning with *Salvador*, continuing into his Vietnam-War trilogy (*Platoon, Born on the Fourth of July*, and *Heaven and Earth*), reaching its fullest expression in *JFK*, and extending into *Nixon*, Stone's films have represented controversial reinterpretations of major political events. In each Stone's most formative experience, the Vietnam War, lurks like a ghostly grimace symbolizing the corruption of New Frontier idealism—at once an explanation and elegiac invitation to mourn with him for an America now dazed, lost, confused, and betrayed.

Similarly, *Talk Radio, The Doors, Wall Street*, and *Natural Born Killers* provide a kind of social history of America from the sex-drugs-rock'n'roll sixties through the insider-trading and media-driven eighties into the multiple-murder nineties. Taken together his films comprise a social and political history of America's last thirty years, his generation's experience gleaned from the individual stories of those who helped make it by living it and often as not writing about it—Richard Boyle, Ron Kovic, Jim Morrison, Alan Berg, Jim Garrison, Le Ly Hayslip, Richard Nixon, and Stone himself.

But these are not simply American true confessions realistically recounted by Stone and fit together like pieces of a jigsaw puzzle to spell out a larger composite history of three decades of apocalyptic upheaval. They are stories as much as histories. While Stone seems to walk in his protagonists' shoes, his films fuse the scuffed facts of the participants' experience with the buffed fiction of the auteur's personal vision. As coauthor or director and sometimes producer, Stone has bent each of his adapted sources with his own moral and artistic weight until they conform to his understanding of this generation's experience. Whatever the subject matter, he has tended to tell the same kind of story over and over again. In the words of talk show host Barry Champlain from *Talk Radio*: "This country is in deep trouble, people . . . and somebody better do something about it."

Stone consistently has ignored the conventional Hollywood warning against making films with a message. In fact he has done more to revive the Hollywood social problem film than any director now working. This genre flourished from the beginning of America's Great Depression until the rise of McCarthyism, roughly 1930–55. Those turbulent years of economic breakdown, the rise of fascism, World War II, and postwar idealism fostered concern with social conditions and an impulse toward political change. Similarly turbulent conditions have existed from the mid-1960s until the present: The assassinations of JFK, MLK, and RFK; the decade long Vietnam War, the widespread use of illegal drugs; the ubiquitous and intrusive presence of television; the leveraged buyouts and insider trades; the Watergate and other government scandals. Such events have fueled Stone's interest in making movies about American social problems which other directors seemed eager to avoid.

Of course, he has updated, revised, and re-created the genre rather than merely reviving it. Stone's problem films typically identify and explore some conflict between an individual and a social institution, and they may advocate some change, but they rarely show any amelioration. Richard Boyle may make a patriotic speech about America's corrupting conspiratorial military intervention in El Salvador, but he fails to save anyone other than himself. Barry Champlain may berate and humiliate a nation full of ethnocentric paranoiacs and drug-crazed buffoons in an attempt to enlighten and reform them through talk radio, but he is assassinated. Jim Morrison may try to get his rock and roll audiences to "break on through to the other side," but the revolution he incites turns into ugly self-indulgence, and he escapes to France to die in his bathtub like that other revolutionary, Jean-Paul Marat. Bud Fox helps destroy the greedy Wall Street insider, Gordon Gekko, but goes to jail himself. Jim Garrison has his day in court trying to expose the far-reaching conspiracy that led to the assassination of JFK, but the jury does not believe him; the only thing that moves "back and to the left" is the dying president's shattering skull at moment of impact. Mickey and Mallory escape the law to spawn the next generation of serial murderers in *Natural Born Killers*. Nixon resigns unrepentant after the failure of the Watergate cover-up.

If any positive change rightfully can be expected, apparently Stone feels it is owed to survivors of the Vietnam War. Chris Taylor may have become a murderer in order to survive, but he tries to find or make some goodness in what is left of his life. Ron Kovic may be impotent and paralyzed, but he succeeds in addressing the Democratic National Convention of 1976 to plead for improved treatment of Vietnam veterans. Le Ly Hayslip not only survives the Vietnam War after having been victimized by all sides, but she becomes a prosperous American business-woman solaced by Buddhist teachings. Perhaps these three characters are stand-ins for Stone himself, the Vietnam veteran returned from the brink of the grave to write, direct, and produce the postmodernist horror film called revisionist American history.

Typically, the resolution of Stone's social problem films is not formulaic but problematic. He does not show his audience a social ill being cured by some heroic protagonist played by a likeable movie star. Instead, he entrusts closure to the audience whom he invites to initiate reform. In fact Stone's penchant is for using unsympathetic protagonists who fail to do much more than convey his messages with a special air of desperation. They are almost always young males who are quasi-adolescent risk takers; they seek adventure, are prone to violence, eager to prove their manhood to their fathers, think of themselves as martyrs on a redemptive quest which becomes an obsession, and they seem driven by testosterone. Warrior crusaders like Stone. Even his one female protagonist, Le Ly in *Heaven and Earth*, exhibits some of Western culture's conventionally masculine character traits.

Ironically, the typical Stone protagonist derives his authority from that which makes him unsympathetic; he sacrifices love and family and the traditional values which those things imply in order to pursue his quest for a redemption which is at once personal and national. Repeatedly Stone makes patriotism the sole possession of the courageous individual seeking to bear public witness to a horrifying truth. Consider Richard Boyle fighting with the INS officials who seek to deport the woman he has helped escape the American-backed right-wing death squads in El Salvador, telling them that they don't know what they are doing, that they don't know what it's like down there. Or witness Barry Champlain risking his life to make the facts of the Holocaust real to neo-Nazis. Or hear Ron Kovic rising from his wheelchair at the 1972 Republican National Convention to dispute the official administration view of the Vietnam War. Or see the Lizard-King Shaman Jim Morrison fighting the culture wars against repression on stage in New Haven. Or note the nerdy Jim Garrison trying to expose a shadow government that has brought about a coup d'état through a policy of assassination. Most of Stone's protagonists threaten to self-destruct in a frenzy of righteousness while their families become wounded bystanders. Stone shows his messenger paying a heavy price in order to make us feel the importance of the message.

Those who love such protagonists find that bearing witness to their suffering is a sort of fatal attraction. Perhaps Stone intends that the protagonists' family members act as surrogates for us, his audience. Certainly, these witnesses are more normative characters from whom the protagonists are separated by some terrible truth. In *Salvador* Boyle's wife leaves him in midjournalistic mission to return to Italy with their child. In *Platoon* Taylor's only contact back in the world is through letters he composes to a grandmother who does not reply; talk about a silent majority! In *Talk Radio* Champlain's wife divorces him for infidelity; when he seduces her to return and fall in love with him again, he makes her part of his show by humiliating her on the air. In *Born on the Fourth of July* Ron Kovic's horrifying postwar adjustment alienates his mother and father and girlfriend. In *Wall Street* Bud Fox hurtfully rejects his father's populist values in order to embrace the greedy materialism of Gordon Gekko. In *The Doors* Jim Morrison tells everyone his parents are dead when they are not; his family life is a mutually abusive relationship with a common-law wife. In *JFK* Garrison's spouse repeatedly complains that he cares more about the dead president than his own family which he neglects. In *Heaven and Earth* Le Ly's husband threatens homicide, kidnaps their children, and commits suicide. In *Nixon* Pat sees her marriage destroyed by her husband's drive to seek and retain his presidency.

Often behind the typical Stone story of family disintegration lurks a strained relationship with a parent. In *Born on the Fourth of July* the paralyzed and impotent veteran returns to blame his mother for telling all the religious and political lies that led him to suffer awful and irreversible wounds. In *Wall Street* Bud Fox tries to prove that he is a better man than his honest, working-class father by becoming a fabulously wealthy Wall Street player. In *JFK* Garrison associates himself and the rest of the nation with Hamlet trying to avenge his murdered father/king. In *Heaven and Earth* Le Ly shares a special relationship with her father who guides and counsels her and whom she fears her behavior has disgraced. In *Natural Born Killers* Mickey and Mallory are abused by their parents. And in *Nixon* the President seems warped by trying to live up to his mother's impossible expectations. Although his films are ostensibly about others, Stone's difficult relationship with his own parents seems to be played out in them repeatedly: the attempt to prove himself as a man by going to war and later to Hollywood, the resentment and anger at his parents' divorce when he was a teenager.

In his own story the auteur sees the story of his generation; an adolescent rebel's quest for social reform and personal redemption continued into adult political life has become part of Stone's cinematic signature. His protagonists are uncomfortable to be around. They want so badly to be loved for telling unsettling truths, but their angry, self-righteous, missionary zeal usually makes them offensive, frightening, or tragic. Stone frequently uses a sexual trope to convey this clearly. Richard Boyle's reckless truth telling does not stop American intervention in El Salvador; it only makes him more vulnerable, something Stone renders graphic by the border guards who literally intend to castrate him. Ron Kovic's sexual impotence stands for the political impotence he feels upon his return from Vietnam. Barry Champlain is forced to admit on air that he is very much like a serial rapist that calls his show asking for help. Gordon Gekko promises his former lover, Darien, to Bud Fox as a "perk." Le Ly is forced into prostitution. Garrison is able to resume sexual relations with his wife only after he convinces her of the assassination conspiracy. A strong sex drive serves as an objective correlative for the truth-telling, manhood-proving quest of many of Stone's protagonists. Perhaps it is a lowest common denominator linking their radical experience with that of an American mass audience fascinated by sex at least as much as burdened by the disintegration of the nuclear family.

The celluloid stories Stone tells clearly are designed to convince Americans of the need for social and political change, to shock them, to rouse them from their lethargy, to terrify them, make them angry, incite them to act. His cinematic techniques serve those ends. The Stone directorial signature is technically flamboyant. He claims to regard the camera as another actor in the scene, thus creating for his audiences the immediacy of the eyewitness or even the feeling of participation in the film's story. The fact that the camera is often hand-held and therefore extremely mobile enhances such effects and gives his work a look ranging from cinema verite to a frenetic, invasive, or even assaultive expressionism. His camera work re-creates for us the experience of the protagonists—providing the same alienated, warped, off-center participant's perspective on events, that of being caught up in the swirl and vortex of cataclysmic upheaval. Its effectiveness might be measured by the number of people who fled from the theaters literally sick to their stomachs from watching *Born on the Fourth of July.*

His use of grainy stock, his mixing color with black and white, his penchant for flashback and fantasy sequences, his hyperkinetic editing, his deliberate confusion of simulated and actual historical footage—these confirm the impression of a director who is ready to try any cinematic resource available to convey his vision with authority. But it also seems to capture the fierce pace and assaultive clamor of modern life—the heavy traffic of images bombarding us from the TV and computer screens, the roadside billboards, the printed headlines, the newsmagazine photos, the angry radio talk shows, the chatter of the cellular phones and CB radios as well as the private swirl of memory and fantasy that wash over all of us in an unquiet workplace, home, or automobile shuttling between them. To many this seems manipulative and unsubtle. But Stone is a filmmaker eager to continue learning his craft, willing to risk new ways of persuading audiences to accept uncomfortable ideas about themselves and their nation. And it isn't like he hasn't got a lot of competition for our attention.

Moreover, some of his directorial strategies are subtle, at least by Hollywood standards. In his first mature film, *Salvador,* Stone's theater audience does not always know what his camera is telling them. Are they watching a news program on television from the point of view of a character or are they eyewitnesses to some action as it unfolds? In other words, Stone invites his audience to wonder how much of what it knows about the guerrilla war in El

Salvador is authentic and how much is a mediated reality packaged for them by official sources in order to gain political support for American military intervention. By the time Stone made *JFK* his treatment of this issue had become much more sophisticated because his technical expertise in shot making, editing, and special effects had as well. Without careful study an audience would find it difficult to tell where historical photos and footage end and where Stone's simulation of them begins. The result was the making of a countermyth to the Warren Commission Report which was so compelling that it prompted congressional action declassifying many of the secret documents concerning the Kennedy assassination.

Stone's deliberate cinematic confusion of fact and fiction is precisely what journalists and some historians cannot abide, and yet, ironically, his techniques emulate their own. The New Journalism long ago established by Gay Talese, Jimmy Breslin, and Tom Wolfe; the non-fiction novel reinvented by Truman Capote and George Plimpton; the narrative histories by Natalie Davis and Simon Schama; and even the rigged side-mounted gas tanks on General Motor's pickup trucks exploded by *Dateline NBC*, all seem to make Stone au courant. In truth, many contemporary journalists and historians may share Stone's artistic inclinations if not his vision of American culture.

That Stone has the reputation of being difficult to deal with is one measure of how hard he has worked to perfect his craft and to continue to grow as an artist in a profit-driven and bureaucratic industrial culture. One of his strategies for doing so has been to surround himself with some first-rate talent like Robert Richardson, his longtime cinematographer, as well as musical composers like Stewart Copeland and John Williams, and film editors David Brenner and Joe Hutshing. And he has gotten outstanding work from them. *Platoon* earned Academy Awards for best editing and best sound as well as best director and best picture; it also brought Stone Golden Globe and Director's Guild of America awards for best director. *Born on the Fourth of July* won Stone additional Academy Awards for best editing and best director and Golden Globe and Director's Guild of America Awards for best director. *JFK* received Academy Awards for best cinematography and best editing. And under Stone's direction Michael Douglas earned an Academy Award for best actor in *Wall Street*.

By Hollywood standards, Stone's accomplishments and accolades as a director between *Salvador* (1986) and *JFK* (1991) were phenomenal. This is all the more extraordinary because he has not played it safe even with his big-budget films. Instead, he has taken as many risks with flamboyant techniques as with controversial subjects. If the result often seems overpowering, perhaps that is not such a bad strategy with a mass audience in an unsubtle age. Since 1991, Stone's *Heaven and Earth*, *Natural Born Killers*, and *Nixon* have continued the director's penchant for treating serious and controversial subject matter in a provocative and innovative style. And while these films may not have garnered the spectacular profits and cascade of awards earned by his earlier work, they are major artistic achievements by a courageous, independent-minded, and visionary filmmaker.

The essays which follow illuminate various aspects of Stone's craftsmanship as a director and suggest their impact upon American culture. David Breskin's interview, "Oliver Stone," offers an insightful overview of the director's life and work. In an engaging style perfected in writing for *Rolling Stone*, Breskin explores connections between formative events in Stone's life and the rebellious attitude which colors the stories he tells and shapes the flamboyant way he tells them. Then, in "The Hysterical Imagination: The Horror Films of Oliver Stone," David Sanjek explores Stone's early directorial work. Sanjek argues that Stone's characteristic narrative practices, thematic materials, and ideological assumptions are apparent from his directorial debut and that they are rooted in the conventions of the horror film. Thus, beginning with *Seizure* (1974) and *The Hand* (1981), Stone's filmmaking may be understood as a movement from exploring the horrors within (repressed consciousness) to those without (institutions); Stone's films are strikingly modern versions of this genre because they find horror in everyday contemporary life.

The horrors perpetrated by the right-wing death squads in El Salvador are graphically depicted in Stone's first major success as a director. In "Manifestations of Foreign Culture through Paradox in *Salvador*," John F. Stone shows how stereotypical characterizations of Latin Americans are used to depict Salvador as a nascent United States whose rebellious emergence is ironically blocked by American interference. Stone's film depicts members of Salvador's right-wing, militarist government (which is propped up by the

United States) as indolent, unhygienic, intemperate, lawless, violent barbarians—a stereotype based on racist assumptions that historically have been used to justify Euro-American expansion and intervention. At the same time Salvador's left-wing rebels are depicted as hard-working, clean-living, honest, rural folk seeking freedom from oppression by elitists—a populist stereotype which harkens back to the American Revolution. Thus, the film asserts that the United States' foreign policy in El Salvador is tragically misguided; it supports a government which is attempting to crush the very values America was founded upon.

In a companion article, "*Salvador*: Oliver Stone and the Center of Indifference," Richard Keenan argues that Richard Boyle, the partly historical and partly fictional protagonist of Stone's first political film, takes a spiritual journey through what Thomas Carlyle called the "Center of Indifference" to the light of truth which enables salvation. Against a backdrop of facts about Boyle's personal and professional life, about U.S. intervention in El Salvador's civil war during the Reagan administration, and about major television network coverage of that conflict, Keenan highlights Stone's cinematic shaping of a story which is both inventive and truthful. In Keenan's view *Salvador* generally has been interpreted too narrowly by journalists as a film which demonstrates the director's willingness to distort history. Instead, Keenan asserts, the truth of Stone's film is more conceptual and general. Based upon enough facts, Stone's *Salvador* is more than historical in a simply factual sense. The primary truth *Salvador* offers its audience vicariously through Boyle's fictionalized experience is literary, something more akin to a Joycean epiphany or a moment of grace in a Flannery O'Connor story.

The tragic consequences of American intervention in Vietnam is, of course, the subject of the film which won Stone his first Academy Award for best director. While *Platoon* is most often thought of as so realistic as to revolutionize the Vietnam War film genre, two articles in this volume illustrate how clearly Stone draws upon familiar cinematic and literary paradigms. Clyde Taylor's "Colonialist Subtext in *Platoon*" argues that despite its appearance of giving significant roles to African Americans, the film remains very close to a conventional Hollywood treatment of blacks, who remain shadow figures and appendages to the whites—

good niggers or bad niggers whose lineage may be traced back to the paradigm of the colonialist warrior narrative. Vietnam War veteran Don Whaley sees *Platoon* more positively. Examining Stone's own adventurous life as a young man as well as the director's overt references to literary influences upon him, Whaley concludes that "*Platoon* stands, with the writings of Norman Mailer, the performances of The Doors, and the drug narratives of Carlos Castaneda as an important expression of the adventure myth in the late 20th century." Aurally, visually, and structurally the film self-consciously echoes other mythic adventures—Christian, Greek, Egyptian, British, Hispanic, and American. But thematically *Platoon* follows the paradigm of modern adventure stories informed by the philosophy of Nietzsche: the adventure is a quasi-criminal rebellion against domestic pieties, taking the form of a journey into the hero's own psyche from which he returns reborn and possessed of self-knowledge.

Wall Street, too, owes something to conventional narrative, specifically the initiation story. Nevertheless, Jack Boozer Jr. shows how inventive and thematically sophisticated a filmmaker Stone can be when working with a familiar formula. In "*Wall Street:* The Commodification of Perception," Boozer links Stone's story of insider traders and corporate raiders of the Reagan/Bush years to the pernicious influence of modern communications systems, especially television, which discourages social interaction, isolates the individual, and leads to wholesale confusion over what is real, an event or its mediated image. Boozer sees Stone's film as a political-economic allegory of America in the 1980s in which perception itself becomes the primary commodity for sale in a culture driven by mass consumption.

Mediated reality is a phenomenon which Stone also treats in *Salvador* and revisits in *Talk Radio, JFK,* and *Natural Born Killers*. *Talk Radio* depicts a shock jock so eager to become a media celebrity that he is willing to incite civil disorder and even criminal activity in his audience in order to win high ratings and sponsor appeal. In "Oliver Stone's *Talk Radio*" Don Kunz describes how—despite a small budget, a short schedule, and two seemingly incompatible literary sources to adapt—Stone creates a small masterpiece. This disturbing drama of conspiracy and assassination which Stone made in Dallas and released on the twenty-fifth anniversary of President Kennedy's murder seems like a preview of coming attractions for *JFK,* which Stone returned to Dallas to make soon afterward.

Stone's second Vietnam War film, *Born on the Fourth of July,* functions as a sort of sequel to *Platoon* because it focuses on the wounded veteran's return home. In "Oliver Stone's Film Adaptation of *Born on the Fourth of July*: Redefining Masculine Heroism," Don Kunz shows how Stone transforms Ron Kovic's biography to form the centerpiece of a Vietnam trilogy. Under Stone's direction Kovic's story becomes one of escape from a spuriously defined masculinity underlying America's fundamental values and myths. After much suffering brought about by his emasculation in the war, the Vietnam veteran evolves into a reformed warrior hero committed to repatriate other disenfranchised citizens as well as himself through political action.

In his next film Stone shifted his attention from telling the story of a fellow Vietnam veteran to depicting the life of a fellow artist/rebel, Jim Morrison, lead singer of The Doors. In her article "Enough to Base a Movie On?" Suzanne E. O'Hop explores Stone's affinity with Morrison, the singer who saw his lyrics as cinematic, the filmmaker who saw his cinema as poetic. Heavily influenced by Morrison's poetry, Stone's *The Doors* becomes a kind of hallucinogenic trip whose images, tropes, and themes derive from Morrison's concept of the artist as shaman and life as movie.

In "*JFK*: Historical Fact/Historical Film" Robert A. Rosenstone defends Stone's most controversial film against the widespread charge that it has twisted history. Rosenstone shows how *JFK* is clearly intended to fit the paradigm of mainstream Hollywood drama and so cannot be judged by the criteria used for written history. Nevertheless, he argues that it serves the broader purposes of historical texts, making us rethink how we got to where we are and just what values we profess to live by. In a companion essay Martin J. Medhurst builds on the idea of Rosenstone and others that history is not discovered already made but rather created and re-created by our shifting perceptions of the past based upon where we stand in the present. Thus, history is a rhetorical construction. In "The Rhetorical Structure of Oliver Stone's *JFK*" Medhurst shows how Stone's interpretation of President Kennedy's assassination as a fascist conspiracy by the military industrial complex works like a parable whose narrative strategy, explanatory paradigm, and ideological implications are all rooted in Adamic myth. Medhurst demonstrates how *JFK* can be viewed as a story of paradise lost through the murder of an Adam-like president and partially regained by an Adam-like district attorney who helps an audience of ordinary citizens to see more clearly, then invites them to redeem America from its lost innocence by their personal involvement.

Wrapping up the chapter on Stone's most provocative film with "*JFK*: The Lesson and Legacy of Vietnam," Jim Welsh reviews the hostile reception accorded it and the ad hominem attacks made on its director by powerful journalists and politicians. Welsh agrees with Rosenstone and Medhurst that *JFK* does not so much rewrite history (as Establishment figures have charged) but compel viewers to rethink it. And he finds cinematic precedent for such cinema in the work of British filmmaker Peter Watkins (*Culloden*, 1964; *The War Game*, 1965). According to Welsh, Stone resembles Watkins in being a passionate moralist with a leftist agenda, in presuming to reconstrue past events to suit his political philosophy, in being obsessively driven to tell the story of ordinary citizens caught up in cataclysmic events, and in being vilified as a polemicist and propagandist. However, Welsh finds an important difference in Stone's principal point of reference—the Vietnam War—which in *JFK* is implicated as motive for presidential assassination.

In *JFK* Oliver Stone asserts the Kennedy assassination was a coup d'état by the military industrial complex which feared the president was compromising its opportunity for war profiteering by early withdrawal from Vietnam. In *Heaven and Earth* he returns to the subject of the Vietnam War, this time attempting to depict that nation-shaking event from the perspective of a Vietnamese woman. In "When Man and Woman Changed Places. . . ." Bryan Marinelli illustrates how that unique perspective gradually erodes as the film unreels. Initially this work promises to revolutionize war films which historically have been by, about, and for men. But the story of the resilient Vietnamese female protagonist Le Ly Hayslip (from whose autobiographical books the film is adapted) is soon overshadowed by the story of her American soldier husband Steve Butler (a composite character created by Stone). Butler's psychic trauma as a result of the war can be glimpsed from his first scene but manifests itself most clearly when the couple relocate to the United States. There he cannot reassume a tradi-

tional patriarchal role and consequently commits suicide. Thus
Marinelli concludes that *Heaven and Earth* fails to live up to its
promise of broadening, deepening, and revising America's understanding of the Vietnam War. He asserts it does more to confirm
than deny that America's Vietnam War films are really about an
American masculine response to changes in gender relations in
recent decades. Once again Stone's own story seems so powerfully
felt that it colors, shapes, and finally overshadows even the most
foreign of the director's artistic material.

In *"Natural Born Killers* and American Decline" Daniel Green
offers a preliminary summing up, showing how Stone's cinematic
depiction of the last thirty years of American history led to his
most self-reflexive and self-critical film to date. He argues that
Stone's body of work challenges any notion of history as authoritative and that *Natural Born Killers* represents Stone's most horrifying depiction of the dissolution of Americans' ties to centers of
authority and the principles they embodied. While Stone's earlier
films traced the unraveling of the fabric of American culture beginning with the shattered idealism resulting from President
Kennedy's assassination, his more recent *Natural Born Killers*
graphically dramatizes the utter nihilism of serial killers turned into
entertainment celebrities by broadcast media. Green argues that in
Natural Born Killers Wayne Gale, the television host of a show
called "American Maniacs" seems to be a stand-in for Stone himself. Both treat sensationally violent subjects voyeuristically in a
hyperkinetic style. According to Green, Stone has found himself
complicit in fostering the decline of the culture whose demise he
meant only to decry. Thus, with *Natural Born Killers* Stone seems
to reach a mature, self-critical awareness.

In this volume's final essay, "'Citizen Nixon'—Oliver Stone's
Wellesian View of a Failed Public Figure," Frank Beaver argues
that *Nixon* owes as much to Orson Welles' *Citizen Kane* as to
Shakespeare's dark historical tragedies with which it more commonly is compared. Thematically both films explore the lives of
enigmatic public figures who are desperate for love but alienated
from the objects of their affection, plagued by self-doubt and mel-
ancholy, burdened by a drive to succeed at all costs, and ironically
lose by winning. Structurally both films employ a mosaic, nonlinear approach in which the protagonist's death (actual or political)
serves as a framework for numerous flashbacks which accumulate

as an investigative psychodrama. Cinematically both films are experimental in design, mixing documentary and simulated footage as well as black-and-white and color stock and employing extreme angles and expressionistic images as well as voice-overs and sound bursts to underscore psychological discoveries. Although Stone clearly pays homage to Welles, Beaver asserts that *Citizen Kane* and *Nixon* remain quite different films in their overall effect. While Welles uses the biographical record of William Randolph Hearst minimally in creating an imaginative story of Charles Foster Kane, Stone bases *Nixon* upon meticulous and extensive research of historical records in order to create an overriding aura of creative authenticity characteristic of docudrama.

Taken together, this collection of essays demonstrates that in his directorial career to date Oliver Stone has displayed a penchant for making films which treat major American political events or social problems, which focus on an angry male protagonist pursuing a redemptive quest that is at once personal and national, and which display technological flamboyance. This is to say that his body of work has been in the public interest, deeply felt on a personal level, and stylishly innovative. As a director he has been a man on a mission. His films testify to the courage, vitality, and creative intelligence which have made him a major force for change in the Hollywood motion picture industry.

Acknowledgments

I gratefully acknowledge the assistance of many people in the making of this book.

The students in my 1994 graduate seminar on the films of Oliver Stone, colleagues in the Literature/Film Association, and the contributors to this volume all enlarged my understanding and appreciation of Oliver Stone's skill as a director.

The University of Rhode Island Foundation and the University of Rhode Island Research Council provided grants which funded initial research as well as final manuscript preparation.

Oliver Stone and his office staff offered assistance in dealing with studios holding the rights to his films, and they located and provided permission to use the cover photo for this volume.

Finally, grateful acknowledgment is made for permission to reprint the following works:

"Oliver Stone" by David Breskin from his book *Inner Views: Filmmakers in Conversation* (Boston and London: Faber and Faber, 1992). Copyright by David Breskin. By permission of the author.

"The Hysterical Imagination: The Horror Films of Oliver Stone" by David Sanjek originally appeared in *Post Script: Essays in Film and the Humanities* 12.1 (Fall 1992): 49–60 and is reprinted with the permission of the journal.

"Manifestations of Foreign Culture Through Paradox in *Salvador*" by John F. Stone originally appeared in *Journal of Popular Film and Television* 19.4 (Winter 1992): 180–85. Reprinted with permission of the Helen Dwight Reid Educational Foundation. Published by Heldref Publications, 1319 18th St. N.W. Washington, D.C. 20036-1802. Copyright 1992.

"The Colonialist Subtext in *Platoon*" by Clyde Taylor first appeared in *Cineaste* 15.4 (1987): 8–10 and is reprinted with the permission of the journal.

"*Wall Street*: The Commodification of Perception by Jack Boozer from *Cultural Power/Cultural Literacy: Selected Papers from the 14th Florida State University Conference on Literature and Film*, ed. Bonnie Braendlin (Gainesville: University Presses of Florida, 1991), 76–95 is reprinted with permission of the University Presses of Florida.

"Oliver Stone's Film Adaptation of *Born on the Fourth of July*: Redefining Masculine Heroism" originally appeared in *War, Literature, and the Arts* 2.2 (Fall 1990): 1–25 and is reprinted with the permission of the journal.

"*JFK*: Historical Fact/Historical Film" by Robert A. Rosenstone originally appeared in the *American Historical Review* 97.2 (April 1992): 506–11 and is reprinted with the permission of the American Historical Association.

"The Rhetorical Structure of *JFK*" by Martin J. Medhurst originally appeared in *Critical Studies in Mass Communications* 10.2 (June 1993): 128–43 and is reprinted with the permission of the Speech Communication Association.

Chapter 1

Understanding
Oliver Stone

Oliver Stone: An Interview with the Director

David Breskin

Born in 1946, the only child of a Jewish stockbroker father and French Catholic mother, Oliver Stone was raised in the East Coast tradition of button-down conservatism. Since then he's spent much of his life in antagonistic conversation with that background: as teacher, seaman, soldier, freak, failed novelist, decorated director and screenwriter, and gangster of Hollywood. Stone dedicated both *Salvador* and *Wall Street* to his father, who died in 1985, but his mother is very much alive, and was hanging Christmas stockings when we met in December 1990 at the Santa Monica home he shares with his second wife, Elizabeth, and their seven-year-old son, Sean.

Stone's work tends to be loud and angry and fast, full of jagged politics and big emotions. Screen his movies in succession and you're left feeling you've survived a cinematic bar fight—a bit dented about the head and heart by the velvet fist of his vision. From his pumped-up screenplays for *Midnight Express, Scarface,* and *Year of the Dragon* to the populist revisionism of *Platoon, Born on the Fourth of July,* and *JFK,* Stone's films again and again show the solitary man's fight for possession of his soul in a world which seeks to steal it, corrupt it, and destroy it. He's a true modernist; a brutish man with the mind of an artist but the soul of a boxer. He wears his heart on your sleeve.

Alan Parker's *Midnight Express,* a xenophobic, scary tale of an American dope-smuggling boy trapped in the dark recesses of a Turkish jail, won Stone his first Oscar and his first real acceptance. His first major directing opportunity, *The Hand,* starring Michael Caine, was a psychological horror film about repression, projec-

3

tion, and evil. It left Stone crushed, pondering the question: does the sound of one hand clapping in a theatre make a noise? He recovered with a screenplay for Brian DePalma's *Scarface*, brayingly displayed the elements that would become trademarks in Stone's own pictures: overdrawn characters, heated action, controversial politics, a flaming arrow of narrative.

Then *Salvador,* his scrappy, leftist take on civil war in Central America, nudged open the door which *Platoon*, after years of waiting, marched through. *Platoon* was not just a movie, but a personal exorcism for Stone, and for many Americans an opportunity to finally mourn a lost war, a kind of filmic national catharsis. It won Stone great fame, and his first Best Director Oscar. He won again for the second piece of his Vietnam trilogy, *Born on the Fourth of July,* an epic of emotional fireworks on the domestic front. For all his heavy-handedness, Stone is hardly a one-dimensional director. Even in his weaker pictures—such as *Wall Street,* his moralistic bromide on 1980s materialism, or *The Doors,* his exuberantly romantic but hollow portrayal of one of his great heroes, Jim Morrison—Stone has the surprising ability to coax absolutely superior performances out of his actors.

For our first session, we talked between his appointments while driving around Los Angeles in his black Mustang convertible and in a barren office at his editing studio, where he was hurrying *The Doors* to completion. We spent our second session, in January 1991, on the patio and in the living room of his home. Stone spoke quietly, in a kind of portentous half-whisper. He complained, repeatedly and good-naturedly, about how much time this was taking, as if four hours of reflection made for a painful wedge in his busy schedule. He seized the upper hand on the patio by suggesting I sit on a chaise longue that, to me, looked and felt wet. I protested. He waved off my complaint and sat himself on a dry one. When I did sit, I was instantly soaked, and though he did allow me the benefit of a towel, it was little help. So I went through the interview feeling as uncomfortable as many feel watching his films. Say what you will; the man is a master of tactics.

A chronological footnote: at the time of our conversations, the controversy over the historical veracity of *The Doors* was already beginning to brew. This proved simply the orchestra tuning up in the pit compared to the onslaught of discord attacking *JFK*, which was in preproduction at the time. At the end of our drive around town, I had asked him when he had last been down to city hall to have his poetic license renewed. He just laughed. And then he laughed some more.

Session One

Let's start at the beginning, really the beginning. What's your first memory?

[Pause. Big, exaggerated laugh.] Oh boy. Beautiful women in trees in a jungle. I had erotic dreams when I was three, four. And they've always stayed with me, throughout my life. Many erotic dreams.

Did you have any understanding of them? Did you report them to anyone?

No, no, I never talked about them. Not even to my mother. [Laughs.]

Were the women blondes?

Yeah, primarily blondes, but there were colored women and a lot of Oriental women, some striking brunettes. Even some redheads. I would say it got liberal. My fantasy is like that Fellini film, what was it, *City of Women*? I don't think it was one of his more successful films, but I loved the idea of having a walled city [laughs] and being the only male in the whole city.

And you were a three year old waking up with a "woody" to these dreams?

Oh yeah, my pecker used to get hard. It was great. I think that eros is the most underrated force in the universe. I think eros carries us through the darkest hours. The deepest, darkest tunnels of the mind are the places you hide in, like Viet Cong warriors did. And the bombs are being dropped by B-52s. The VC used to build caves. I've been down them and seen the maps. There'd be a first layer, then a second layer underneath, like an onion skin. Sometimes these things would go down seven or eight layers deep, and there'd be an R-and-R facility down in the bottom, like a golf course or something, hospitals, schools, video clubs down there.

[Laughs.] Often I'd retreat to this place in my head, where there'd be some kind of sanctuary. And eros was the driving force. Eros, and its correspondent, love.

What did you do with this stuff as a kid?

Oh man, it's secret stuff. It's like Viet Cong tunnels, I told you. I wouldn't reveal more than that, but it's certainly a driving thread to my life. Simone de Beauvoir said, "Sex is the sixth continent." It's the place you can go for free. Everybody can do it. I like that idea. It's a democratic impulse. I think sex is the driving force, the resistance to totalitarianism in our age. The totalitarian spirit is everywhere, in orthodoxy, in politics, in emotions, in TV. Controls, I think, are the keynote of our age. The way people have always fought back through the ages—the medieval ages, the poor people, the worst times of history—has always been through sexual freedom. Sexual impulse. It's going on now with censorship and repression all over the world—in China, in Arabia, what they do to women. We're fighting this on a global front. It's just not the U.S. The American story is minor; the feminists are a minor thing.

Yeah. Sure. [Pause.] Okay—

[Sighs.] I see you got bored.

No, I'm not bored at all.

Yeah, you shifted the subject. I was trying to tell you that . . . I think, well, I think I said what I said. [Quietly] The sixth continent.

    Some of my earliest, fondest, most nostalgic memories were France in the 1950 to 1954 era. My mom took me to France and left me there for the summer with my grandparents in a country house, and I grew up in the French style in the summers, playing around the countryside, riding bikes, hanging out with French kids, in the Algerian War days, the Vietnam days. We'd play soldiers and stuff, and I'd hear about Indochina—little did I know I'd end up in Vietnam. I remember loving my grandfather. He would tell me World War I stories. He was gassed in World War I; he was a French infantryman. And I remember my American grandfather. He was an old, old man, walking around the East River Drive in New

York City. And I remember New York in the late forties and early fifties. I remember the overcoats and the hats and the ties and the cold. I remember going down to Wall Street and being knocked out by all the buildings that were so high, with little windows and no light.

Your dad gets described as distant and negative—

Not at all, not at all. My dad was very loving. Very loving man. That's a partial description of him: he was sarcastic and distant at times, but he was very loving. He was so proud of me; he admired me. I was the only child. He just didn't want me to get spoiled by my mom. He would take a little harder tack with me. He wanted to enforce discipline, he wanted me to learn discipline very early. He said, "Every day you got to do something you don't want to do." [Laughs.] And he made me write by giving me money. He'd encourage me to write a theme a week.

For your allowance?

Yeah, so I could buy comics. And he always would give me math problems to do. He was a very good writer, very intelligent. He had a warm heart, but he had difficulty, as all men, as a lot of men did of that era, the depression era—he had difficulty *expressing* his feelings. He thought it was unseemly.

What did he fear from self-expression?

He was sort of a secret playwright. He had written three or four plays which he kept in the drawer; they weren't good enough to be produced. And he was an unpublished poet. But he thought it wasn't something you do for a living. Also, he thought a man should not be seeking visual distinction. His clothes should be anonymous, the man should be anonymous—short-haired, wear a tie. You see, I suppose I was wildly indulgent to my father.

He accused you of "showing off?"

Well, no, at first I was very conformist in my youth. I wore a tie and a jacket, I wouldn't go out of the house. It was very difficult to live in New York because it was very conformist. But dad would be sarcastic and sometimes he would hurt people's feelings, including my own. You had to understand how to take that kind of humor. He was a loving father.

He was "there" for you?

He was there for me.

I'm thinking of the scene in Wall Street *with Bud Fox [Charlie Sheen] and his father [Martin Sheen] where they're arguing in the elevator and then on the street, and Bud says, "You've never been there for me." I wondered how much of that was autobiographical?*

I probably felt that at times from my dad, because it would be very rare for him to give me any kind of compliment. I was a bum to him, especially after Vietnam, because I was dope-smoking and talking black talk and in jail and had no college education and was writing these kooky screenplays. So he thought I was becoming like his brother Joe, who he said never did anything his whole life.

Your dad was successful with his investment newsletter, wasn't he?

Successful intellectually. And he was respected. But financially, he never became a millionaire. Close. When he died, he left my mother with some money, and I think I got $19,000, after a whole lifetime of making money for others.

You'd think that if a guy is going to be such a Republican he should do better than that.

[Laughs.] I can't fault him. He was worried about money, but he was never ultimately that interested in it. He never had the knack for making it. He was more interested in ideas. Every investment he'd make would go south. He opened a factory in Connecticut to make machetes for Guatemala.

[Jokingly.] Probably some of the same machetes used by the death squads you were dealing with in Salvador!

That's a stretch. He went out of business before the death squads. And then all his stock deals! Everything he'd buy for others would do well, but whatever he'd buy for himself—generally he would get hurt.

I guess that runs in the family. You had a bad experience with stocks just after you filmed Wall Street.

Every investment I've made on Wall Street has gone south. Never again. I'm stopping it. I don't like it. It's all easy money. I don't treat it seriously.

You should have listened to Lou [fatherlike Hal Holbrook] in Wall Street.

What did he say? What was the line?

He said "There's no sure thing. Things take time."

[Laughs hard.] He was like my dad, too.

You should have taken your screenplay's advice! But of course Lou was not as interesting or magnetic as Gordon Gekko [Michael Douglas]. There's probably more of you in Gekko, isn't there?

Gekko's another character. It's not my dad. Gekko is a character out of my mom. Sort of flashy, flashy. My mom is more outward, external, physical in the world—not as abstracted as my dad. She never made enemies; she made friends. Dad would make enemies with his tongue. Mom was a charming woman. To me, she's a bit like a piece of Auntie Mame and a piece of Evita. Just larger than life. Big parties. Loved to travel; loved to tell tall tales. She'd invent anything. She was the best friend of anybody who would come into her mind that moment. She had a tremendous ability for fantasy.

Did you ever feel like a bum at home, before Vietnam?

Oh, I always felt like an outsider at school.

Why?

Just a quality of one's character. It's an existence. It's an anguish that you have.

Do you think that was nature or nurture?

I think it's nurture. I think it comes from being an only child. I think it comes from not having access to easy conversation, or easy living with a sibling—which makes you less important in a way— and I think you get more self-conscious as an only child. I was very self-conscious when I was young. I'd walk down the street and I would feel that people were condemning me, judging me, looking at me.

Back between nine and twelve years old you did a lot of writing . . .

I wrote themes every week. In Paris, I wrote a Balzackian, romantic novel about the French Revolution. I was very influenced by Balzac and Dickens. It was more a romantic image of writing. I didn't get very far. It just seemed that writing was a possible retreat from reality that was acceptable, in the sense that the world of the imagination was a sanctuary from real life. As were movies. I loved being in the dark, and seeing movies. It's an escape. My mom was very much into that.

You played hooky with her?

I'd play hooky with her; she'd take me to the movies a lot. A lot. On Wednesdays they'd change the movies; they'd have double features every week. And we'd go and see double and even triple features some days. It was great. I'd go to the movies with my father, too, and we'd see Kubrick films and David Lean films, and he was always very impressive in his analysis. He'd walk out and inevitably—no matter what movie we'd seen—he'd say, "We could have done it better, Huckleberry." And then he'd tell me what was wrong. He'd analyze the plot for loopholes, and of course, movies always have loopholes. Why didn't so-and-so do such-and-such? It was quite an education.

We saw *Paths of Glory* together, *Strangelove.* I think Kubrick was my favorite in that time, when I was between fourteen and sixteen. And then David Lean, *Lawrence of Arabia. One-Eyed Jacks* I remember seeing and loving. And Fellini made a big impression.

I remember seeing *La Dolce Vita* in '59 or '60 and that just blew me away. It seemed to be doing things in black and white that American films were not doing. That you could just take an ordinary person, an ordinary life, and reexamine that life in mythic terms. I think it was seven days and seven nights that he crosses the city. I loved the theme of that movie.

What kind of reality were you seeking to escape?

Oh, I think the reality of school. Rigid law, orthodoxy, oppression to some degree. I think school was rough. I went to a very strict boarding school, all boys. Had to go to chapel every morning. Four to five hours of homework every day. Five classes. Discipline. The teachers were good. The smell of locker rooms. The dank food. How can I describe the food? It was totally Dickensian.

Perfect for someone named Oliver. Apparently you had the shock of your life when you found out your parents were getting divorced.

Put it this way: the first shock of my life.

The first shock. But the first shock is really the shock in a way.

Well, I had another shock. I had a couple of medical shocks, but I don't want to discuss that.

Why not?

I just don't. My medical records, my tax records, I don't think that's really . . . I had a couple of medical things that happened, I had a few operations that really were hard. Doctors sometimes don't tell you stuff for about ten or fifteen years because they don't think you're old enough to hear it—so sometimes you get some pretty good shocks. But aside from that I think my parents' divorce was major for me.

I had thought they were very contented and that I was rich, and that we had it made. And, basically, my father said that they were unhappy and that they were betraying each other, that she was screwing around and he was screwing around, and that he was broke, in debt. He didn't have money, he *owed* money: that whole concept of debt, I just didn't understand it until that point. And my mother, according to him, was profligate in her expenses and spent everything.

And she had a lover. She took several lovers. It was shocking. It was an interesting time. It was sort of the onset of the sexual liberation of the sixties, and couples from the fifties were starting to play around on each other. It was amazing. My father had been with other women since the forties, and my mother had had other lovers.

You didn't know anything about this?

No, no. It was all delivered to me on a weekend in boarding school, and by *phone*. Nobody even came to tell me. It was delivered to me by the headmaster, and that was really hard to take. My father had talked to him and he thought it was his obligation to tell me. My mother didn't even want to come and see me; she was hiding in Europe. And you can imagine the way the headmaster tells you these things: "Buck up, young man, this is not the end of the world." It was hard.

If you had to put it into a literary hindsight, I would say it was very close to *Catcher in the Rye*. A very depressing novel, but emotionally right on. I felt like shit, like nothing. Everything was metallic. All the surfaces were metallic. All the people, all the adults were dangerous, not to be trusted. The world was a very empty place to me.

I think that set up, basically, a period for me, from sixteen on, until thirty was going through a sort of adolescent thing, especially from sixteen to twenty-two, a sort of revolution in my life. Everything was thrown topsy-turvy. Basically, I ended up in the merchant marine in Vietnam, going through a lot of changes. All the old rules were thrown out.

What was that feeling like at sixteen? You talk about feeling "sheltered and special" before that. Maybe in juxtaposition it was even worse, maybe all of a sudden you weren't so special?

I went to Yale, so I was doing very well, but emotionally I could just not engage myself for four more years. I had to get out of this world. I didn't believe it. I didn't believe anybody at Yale. I didn't believe what they were trying to turn out. It wasn't like I was a genius and knew what I wanted. I just knew what I didn't want.

And I had vague glimpses of the world of the Far East from Conrad, *Lord Jim,* and I'd also read Kipling, and *Red Badge of Courage,* and Hemingway, and I was very romantic in my thoughts. And it was through getting out into the world, getting away from all I knew, pushing out into history—Hemingway used that phrase—that I would have nothing more to do with the East Coast, New York City, that world.

Did you feel like a bum when your parents broke up? I would think that for an only child it would be difficult not to internalize that schism.

Oh yeah. Yeah. My father moved into a hotel, where I lived with him. And my mother was moving into another kind of life, a sixties life—drugs, parties. I was really mixed. I felt I had nothing to do with it: I was an outsider. I had to find a new family in a sense. The family was *over.* It just disintegrated. You don't have a brother or a sister; you don't have any second person you can still be family with. Basically, the triangle splits and we're three people in different places, and I'm sixteen and all of a sudden I'm on my own. Dad said to me, "I owe this and this and this. I will put you through college, and then you're on your own." To me, it was a new world.

As a loner, I just floated out to the Far East, and to this day I think it was an orphan home for me and became for me the means by which I began to see the world with a new family, a new light, the light of the Far East. And then the irony of marrying a girl from the Middle East when I came home from the Far East, and then I spent time in the Middle East. I really sort of journeyed, and I wandered. And through a process over a long time, I got my existence back together. And by the age of thirty I started to kind of feel it again: to feel like I used to feel, being home, and having my integrity.

The tall ships came into the New York harbor for the bicentennial and you wrote Platoon.

Yeah, around there. I wanted to go back to where I was when I was sixteen. And be straight again, be disciplined again, don't let this madness, this adolescent madness, this raging war—these experiences of life were like combat, spitting in my face—don't let

this blow your mind out. Because I saw a lot of that in 'Nam.
People came back wrecks, carcasses, human burning wreckages of
people. And I was almost one. But it took me time. I wrote. I
wrote, it seems, for therapy. Between twenty-two and thirty, I wrote
eleven screenplays. I never stopped writing. It was my only home.
Every day to write. No matter how dissolute I got—and I took a
lot of fucking drugs, booze, and all that, *bad.* I would get up each
day. Like my dad said, you do something every day you don't want
to do. I felt an obligation, to hold up my sanity, to write.

*After your first period in Vietnam as an English teacher, you wrote
a 1400-page novel,* A Child's Night Dream. *What was it really
about? It began as a suicide note, no?*

Yes, it did. It was a wild sort of Hindu time story, where everything goes back and forth. It started in the present, with a suicide
note, and then it went through Asia, the merchant marine, Custer's
Last Stand, James Joycean poems without any punctuation, trip-
ping on the tongue. I was very influenced by Joyce and Donleavy,
The Ginger Man. Just writing to a beat, to a rhythm.

*Why was the rejection of it by the New York publishing houses so
significant to you? You felt again like a complete bum.*

Well, the thesis, after 1400 pages, is that the person saves himself
from suicide by the act of writing. But then I played it two ways:
I had him also extinguishing himself through the act of writing.
He basically self-destructs at the end of the manuscript. And then
there was another chapter where he saves himself through the
manuscript. So I couldn't decide which way to go. Except at the
end I threw away my manuscript, destroyed it. I thought it was
over for me. I was so depressed. One guy at Simon & Schuster I
owe this to—probably threw it out and said it was a piece of shit.
He gave me a horrible letter, said something horrible about it. Just
remember that when you're up there at the top you can break a
writer's heart. And I thought, I'll never get anything done, with
my life, with my writing. I'm sick of being special; I'm sick of
the act of writing about "self," and therefore I'm going to be anonymous. I'm going to the bottom of the barrel—what the Charlie
Sheen character says in *Platoon,* "I'm going to be anonymous."

I'm going to go into the army, and I'm going to be totally anonymous.

How much of that was self-punishment?

A lot. I was ready for death. A lot of my book was about suicide. *River's Edge* has made it popular now, but teenage suicide was not that talked about in the sixties. Nobody dealt with it, except in *Catcher in the Rye* Salinger deals with it at one point. It was like people would scoff at your pain. It was just before the hippie revolution. It was just before *Time* magazine decided people under twenty-five matter. I remember a world where we were never consulted. It was sort of like: "What pain can you have?" My dad was responsible for a lot of that. He'd say, "What experience do you have? How can you write? What pain do you really feel?"

Is that where your antipsychological bias comes from?

What do you mean?

What you've called your "animus to psychology."

In what connection?

I could go back to The Hand. . . .

Yes, *The Hand.*

Jon Lansdale [Michael Caine] says the new illustrator has "weakened" the cartoon character he draws "by making him look too deeply inside himself."

[Laughs.] Yes, that's right. That's right. That's funny. Oh, God!

So your dad was minimizing your pain, what you felt inside.

Yes, Dad was very antipsychological. Oh, I see! That you're not supposed to talk about your inner feelings, or show them, or be, quote, "an artist." Showing the public—what is art but prostitution, as what's-his-name said, who's that great French author? The fellow who wrote *Madame Bovary,* Flaubert. Flaubert said, "Art is public prostitution," and he's right. Because the prostitute—prostituere—makes public the private. That's what Dad was saying: art is prostitution, because you're making public your private fantasies.

How did your dad take the rejection of your book?

Oh, he was vindicated, you see. Fuck him! I wanted to get out. I hated him.

So going to 'Nam was an actively suicidal choice in many ways.

Oh yeah. I was ready to die, but I didn't want to pull my own trigger. Many a time I stood in the bathroom and looked in the mirror and had the razor out—part of my book was about the eighteen ways the kid tries to kill himself. I went through all the computations of death in my head. I don't know how close I came. I certainly thought about it, and I emotionally identified with it, but I stopped myself. I said, "Look, I'm not going to die this way. If I'm going to die, I'm going to die in combat. I'm either going to make it through or I'm not going to make it through."

Norman Mailer was very important to me at that point. I read all his stuff. I loved *An American Dream*. God, that was a great book. I remember the whole discussion of death and suicide in that. And he'd been in a war, Mailer had. And Hemingway. And I felt like I had to go out there and make it through. And if I don't make it through, it wasn't meant to be.

Would your death have been a way of punishing your parents?

[Pause.] In part. But not wholly. More of punishing myself. I wanted to prove to my father that I was as tough as he was, because he'd been through World War II. And also I wanted to prove that I didn't need him, that I could make my own way in life by being in the army and going to war. And being in combat, which he never was. He was always a lieutenant colonel, on the financial side of it—he was on Eisenhower's staff, actually. He was very important.

You've said you knew it was a mistake, your being there—like Charlie Sheen's character in Platoon—*from the very beginning, yet after you were wounded and were put back into the rear echelon, you fought to get back to the battle. So there's a contradiction there?*

Yes, there is. When I first got there, I got scared right away. My experience was very similar to *Platoon*. I cut point my first day, and I got shot in my first major firefight. I got wounded in the neck, then I got shot again. So I took two hits and got out of it; they had a policy that they evacuated you to the rear. At that point, I was a veteran in a sense. I knew my way around the jungle better than when I had just got there. And I was in the rear, with a bullshit job guarding barracks, and hating it 'cause I had to spit-polish my boots. I had a fight with the sergeant, and he wanted to court-martial me—Article 15—and I said, "Let's make a deal." They might have extended my time in 'Nam and I wanted to get out, so I said, "Let me go back to the combat zone, and you drop the charges."

Because death might be better than a court-martial?

No. No. [Pause.] I missed combat. The truth was I missed it.

The adrenalin?

Yeah, there was something happening. It got me excited. I was bored shitless in the rear. I don't know, it was weird . . . you really hit on something. I just wanted to see if I could do a better job of it than I had done the first two times. I wasn't too proud of my first stint. You live through a lot of shit, and I was scared out of my pants and was shot twice. And I guess I wanted to prove to myself that I was a better soldier.

I went back into the First Cav, and I *was* better. I wasn't great, but I was a better soldier. And I got a bronze medal for some combat action. I was more attuned to the jungle, and I got into the jungle, heavy. The smell, the look, the feel. I remember one thing I did, toward the end. I walked up to a deer, on point. Carrying sixty pounds, with a machete. In other words, I was part of the jungle—to come right up on a deer. That's pretty good.

The other thing that happened was I got into grass, heavy. And then I got into music. It was a good tour, the First Cav. Blacks were my best friends, and they brought me in—believe it or not—as a sort of adopted brother. A blood. Like the scenes in *Platoon*, getting high, high, high, down in the hooches. At the base camp, not in the field—we didn't fuck up in the field. And I listened to that music and it really got to me: Smokey Robinson, Marvin Gaye, the Supremes, the Temptations were the hottest.

I'm struck by how, when you failed so badly at creating—creating your book—you turned so fiercely to destroying, going to war. If you couldn't succeed at creation, maybe you could succeed at destruction?

Yeah, a lot of that, that Lee Harvey Oswald thing. I saw that in this country, that's where I learned it. Going to the dark side, you really see the underside of life. Lee Harvey Oswald. I was in that world. I know that world. I know those people. All those guys, such sad cases, going back to small towns, guys that knew weaponry, hanging out in bus stations.

The worst years of our lives . . .

Yeah! I took the bus all the way down through Oregon, California, talking to guys in bus stations and cheap hotels. And trying to get laid, with hookers in Oakland. I met a lot of Lee Harveys. I met a lot of guys who were really screwed up. The drifter mentality in American society is very interesting. But Lee Harvey Oswald is a lot deeper than everybody thinks he is. He wasn't just a drifter; he was something else too.

How much of your drug use was—

[Upset, frustrated.] I'm trying, I'm trying to get to a point. It came out of a thing about destructiveness. Yeah, so when I got back to New York, I got a cheap apartment on Ninth Street, and I painted the whole thing red. I was doing acid and stuff. I'd really get angry and I'd have rages that were uncontrollable. Like, the Black Panthers were talking their talk and I'd say, "Come on man, stop talking it, *do it!*" So I went to NYU film school, and there was the big minirevolt of 1970, and the construction workers on Wall Street beat up some kids, and I thought, let's go all the way. Let's get some guns and let's do Nixon and let's take over Washington. Let's not talk revolution; let's go do it. Because guys like me, we knew how to shoot. So let's organize some stuff and go do it.

It was pure destruction, not creation. A revolution has to create something, but you didn't have a better thing to put in place of what you wanted to destroy. You weren't even very politicized at that point. You were only anti. You were contra.

I was *contra*. I was contra. I knew something was off in Vietnam, and I knew subconsciously that the government was really shitting us, but I didn't know exactly how. My rage was such that I knew something was wrong. And I thought, let's do the government, let's take it down. What's the big deal? Let's go to Washington with some rockets and some mortars and fucking fight. And we can win it. I just didn't like all the talk, all that hippie bullshit. It made me sick. There was too much talk and not enough do.

I felt a bit like an assassin. I was alone. Like Oswald. A drifter in my own culture. I didn't know where the fuck to go. I couldn't go back to school; I couldn't deal with those people. And the hippies were kind of screwed up—they were into all that [sarcastically] L-O-V-E, love-and-peace. And I was more into Morrison: "Five to one, one in five, baby, no one here gets out alive."

Eight, nine days after coming back from 'Nam I'm in the county jail in San Diego for federal smuggling charges, coming back from Mexico with grass, my Vietnamese grass. I'm walking back stoned out of my head. It was really stupid. I'm facing five to twenty years for smuggling. They throw me in this shit hole where they're supposed to have three to five thousand inmates. They had like fifteen thousand *kids* there. And they were all poor, from the underclass—Mexican, black, some Anglos. All in there sleeping on the floor. And I had this vision in the slammer. People were saying, "Where you been, man, this is the war at home. Wake up! This is happening right here in America." I had come back with this image of Best Years of Our Lives, some shit like that, that I'd be some kind of hero, you know. It wasn't to be. Here was my reception. Welcome back to the USA, Amerika with a capital K! The war at home, revolution, anger! Well, that freaked me out.

I got out after about three weeks and went home to the East Village, and I got robbed. Fucking guy came up to me, stuck a knife right on my fucking stomach, said, "Gimme your money." I got freaked out, very frightened, because I knew either he'd die or I'd die—'cause I knew the meaning of death and he didn't. I was so stunned. I'll never forget it: I looked at him, and he saw my eyes, and I walked away. Just like that, walked away. And he never followed me. He left me alone. But then I got robbed about six times up in that fucking dump. Guys were breaking into my windows and stuff.

America is—what I'm trying to say is, I saw the underside. Never forgot it. Made a severe impression on me, for the rest of my life. I live relatively well now, and I'd like to stay away from it. I have no illusions about it. I'm not in love with it, as a liberal. But I see it and I feel sorry for the root causes of it.

How much of your drug use was self-medicating?

What's "self-medicating"?

A lot of people in a great deal of pain "medicate" themselves with drugs, rather than go to a doctor. A lot of people don't take drugs to "expand their consciousness" so much as to numb themselves out.

I think that's a very good question. That's a tough one, because you cross that line, back and forth, through the years. Because half the time it's expansion of the mind and the other half of the time it sort of creeps into numbing yourself. And I certainly am guilty of both. I was doing grass on a daily basis, getting high, really high; doing great acid, in the Village. I would do acid anywhere, in the subway, in restaurants, I didn't stand on religious grounds about it at all. I never picked environments that were particularly soothing. I'd do it for a rush. I had some heavy bad trips. Volatile trips. And I had some great trips. Looking for a woman, man. I was looking for a woman. Peripatetic affairs. Wild affairs. Crazy women, crazy nutty women loose across the city. One-night stands, here, there. I was just burned out—and no love in the world. I had a few friends that would do some drugs, but I didn't have any vets around New York. My vet friends went back to small southern towns and they would write me about unemployment and drug use and alcohol. It was depressing. I didn't have anybody. There was no network to fall back on. I was alone. I lived in a shit hole on Houston Street. I had a broken window, with the snow drifting in the winter. I'd wake up in the morning and there'd be a pile of snow in my room. [Laughs.] I was writing, though.

Were the drugs fueling your anger or muting your anger?

Both. The alternate expansion and contraction. I'd say acid to expand and grass, eventually, to numb. And music was so important. You can't underestimate that, in the sixties. Listening to Motown, hour after hour, on grass, getting into that mood. And the Doors, Jefferson Airplane, Bob Dylan, the Grateful Dead, Sly and the Family Stone. The Fillmore East.

And then I met this incredible woman named Najwa, who was four years older than me and really psychologically balanced, really strong. She was Lebanese and working for the Moroccans. I married her, and she did a lot to integrate me into a more orthodox kind of life. It was too orthodox eventually, and I left again.

So this woman domesticated you, in a way?

Yeah. Returned me to the fold. But ultimately I rebelled again.

Did you have a need to rebel, no matter what it was you were rebelling against?

At that time, yes. I needed to get my freedom back. I felt like my freedom had been terminated, tamed, put in a cage.

Don't you still have to rebel? Isn't it just "in the soup" with you?

I think it is. How do you know?

I don't know—it just seems like that's part of you. If you're not rebelling against a woman, you're going to rebel against how videocassette rights are sold or how Hollywood is structured or how critics "misinterpret" your work. You get angry about everything, but I'd also like to know, what gives you joy?

Optimism. A good feeling around you. Family. Love. Eros. A feeling that the world is a healthy place. I think that optimism is really necessary. I like to be surrounded by gaiety, by friends who laugh, who have a positive attitude towards life. I like to be surrounded by a lot of light bulbs, turn on a lot of lights. I like to have a TV on once in a while. I like to see movies that are good, that make me appreciate the possibilities of life, that engage the mysteries of life. I like good books, fine wine, beautiful women, intelligent men. *Daring* men. I like ships that sail. I like children. I like toys. Material things. Spiritual things. What do you want, a catalogue? An index?

No.

The book of joy? Joy is a mental state. You have to be healthy to have joy. The doctors are right: life seems to me to be a cycle of pain and of pleasure. It can't all be joy. There is that pain that comes. Aeschylus said, "Suffering that falls, drop by drop, upon the human heart, until it comes to know the infinite wisdom of God." Aeschylus! You ever hear of it? You know the line?

Yeah, Francis [Ford Coppola] quoted it to me.

[Surprised, his thunder stolen.] Did he, really?

Yes, he was talking about his boy, Gio, being killed.

Well then, Aeschylus got it right, so why not quote him.

You've talked about failure and humiliation as a stimulus to learning. I'm interested in this vis-à-vis control. The horse's mouth words are: "It's wrong always to be in control. You'd never learn anything, and learning is more important than being in control. Most of the stuff I've learned in my life has come from humiliation, defeat, or stretching myself and making a fool of myself."

You mean the "Who am I?" scene in *Wall Street?* [Laughs.]

That's the only line the audience actually hooted on—it was a tough New York audience. I'm interested in how you've, as the Buddhists say, taken the poison and made it medicine.

Good question. I think I've told you. Didn't I talk about coming back from 'Nam in that sense, restructuring the personality? Isn't that taking poison? How can I elaborate more?

Well, I'm interested in how it relates to control. Okay? The value,

as you stated, of not being in control. Because now you are at a
point in your life where you are very much in control.

Oh, I see.

You're sober, you're comfortable, you've got a certain amount of
power, and you've matured—

So you're saying, how can I learn anymore? Is that what you're
saying?

How are you going to find it if you're in control all the time?

By not being in control all the time.

How do you do that?

You have to pick your spots. You have to be in a position as a
writer. As a writer, I go to the field and I meet a whole new set of
people, and I listen, and I don't *judge.* I don't prejudge. And I try
to be humble, because that's the only way to approach a new subject. As a writer, as a research journalist (not as a controlling director), that's where you learn. So I'm out there a lot, I travel a
lot. A lot of my time is spent writing and researching. Also in my
home. One can have many fights with a wife, a child, where the
child is the king and you're the slave. The child reverses the roles
on you.

But I think it is more difficult. I think you're right. It's essential to be honest with yourself as a writer. When you're alone with
the page, you can't bullshit yourself that much. If it's no good, it's
no good. It doesn't matter who you are, Woody Allen or Francis
Coppola. The gods of paper, the gods of movies, are ruthless.

Is it okay to fail now, though, when the stakes are so much high-
er? It's one thing to fail in that room painted red, taking acid and
writing the tenth of eleven screenplays, and to go out on the limb
that you're living on; but now with the structure of the deals you're
in, and who you are, and what people's expectations are, doesn't
that get in the way, a little bit?

[Long pause.] Failure is more severe, harsher, but I like to gamble. I'm quite willing to gamble. Knowing that failure is noble, knowing that I've been there before with failure several times in my life, and I've reconstructed myself from failures, most notably, recently, with *The Hand*, I guess.

That was ten years ago, man.

Talk Radio wasn't received particularly well by the audience. It was ignored. It was a good lesson. That was three years ago. *Wall Street* was hooted at by snobby people, but that was fine. I learned from that experience, a lot. *Born on the Fourth of July* was castigated by a lot of people, I think for unfair reasons, but so be it. Each time there's a humiliating thing that goes on.

I don't think being at the Academy Awards and seeing all of my team on *Born* fail in winning awards in all categories was a particularly great night. It was kind of difficult for me to accept that. Because I wanted them to win in their categories. When the sound people lost, it really broke me up, because I thought we had a really great soundtrack. When John Williams lost for music, I just thought there was a lot of politicking going on. And a lot of the people that hated the movie—the intellectual circles—took what they needed from Pat Buchanan and the right-wingers to slam the film. And that hurt!

Come on, so I mean, what are you saying that I don't learn from . . . there's no, the control thing, I mean I get calls every fucking week from the press, with some new scandal or other. I have no control over what they're going to say. What the hell control? What control?

Clive James, the Australian-born writer, says, "It is our failures that civilise us. Triumph confirms us in our habits."

[Long pause.] "Corruption is more ruthless than war." Juvenal. Yes? Yes or no?

Corruption is more ruthless than war?

Yeah. No, excuse me, "Luxury is more ruthless than war."

Yes, because we go to war for it, as we're about to in the [Persian] Gulf for the luxury of cheap gasoline and big cars.

[Defensively.] Did my answer about success and failure, did it convince you? Or are you questioning it still? Do you think I'm complaining about success? I'm being too, uh . . . did you buy what I said? Did you understand what I was trying to say about control?

I think I do understand.

You had no counterargument.

I'm not arguing with you.

No, but I mean, there's no further point you wanted to make on that.

I felt I did understand what you were saying.

[Relieved.] Okay. Success is good. It nourishes, it replenishes the soul. It makes you feel good about yourself, and there are times when you need to do that. And humility keeps you going. Humility is what makes great films. You mustn't believe too much in yourself; you must believe that you're the vessel for an idea. You must believe that your team is with you. That you're working with great people, on all fronts. I think a film is like a football team going to the Super Bowl. You got to play as a team through the whole thing, through all three acts of the movie: the writing, production, editing, and distribution. That's actually four acts. Let's say three creative acts, and then there's the distribution. You're a football team and you really have to be in sync. You can feel the energy. If one actress isn't in sync, it really screws up the flow of the whole movie.

You write from pain, quite personally, but eventually you're going to run out of it. What happens then? Or will you have a replenishing supply to write from?

We'll see. How can I project that?

A lot of people end up making the same movie again and again.

Nothing wrong with that. If you can make it interesting and dress it up in new clothes in a new way, what the hell? Madonna recycles herself every six months.

Yeah, but are you seeking to achieve the level of Madonna with your films?

No, but if you can dress up the old story in a new way that interests you and makes it interesting to the public, what's wrong with that?

Nothing's wrong with it, but you seem, to me, to be a guy who wants a new story.

I think I do. I might be disillusioned, I might not be the best judge. I try to write 'em and make 'em. I admire the prolificness of Balzac and John Ford—they just kept doing it. And Hitchcock. They didn't get too much into regret or remorse, looking back. If they missed 'em, they moved on. Don't get tripped up in your self, your own psyche, or in analysis. I do think there's something to be said about getting out there and doing it.

Are you keeping a diary?

Yeah.

Every day?

For years. I've done a massive tome. Either I throw it away at the end of the course, or otherwise I might do something else with it.

Have you saved them, year by year?

Yes, but now it's getting dangerous.

Why?

[Incredulous.] Why? 'Cause it's a written document.

What are you scared of?

Revelations.

Why?

[More incredulous.] Why? Because it's my most private self.

Why do you write it?

To keep a record with myself of what I felt at such and such a time.

You're afraid that if you didn't write it . . .

I'd lose track, yes. When I was doing most of the drugs, I stopped writing it for several years, and I noticed when I went back to writing it that I felt that I was doing better work. It's like a balancing act, and I'm evaluating day by day. I was taking the time to evaluate the day before, each day. So that it would not be an unexamined life, in a non-Socratic sense.

What did you write about yesterday?

[Long pause.] Yesterday was mainly about the *Doors* cutting. We made some significant cuts, roughly fifteen minutes from the film in the last few days, so it's been a massive intellectual journey into the bowels of the movie, for me. But I've been doing some work on the side involving the writing of *JFK*. Actually, I'm making some big breakthroughs mentally there, in trimming that script. So I'm trimming a script and trimming a film at the same time. Mostly idea work in the last few days. And it's been about that. And also who I met. I met a bunch of actors and actresses, and I wrote what I thought of them.

As a coda for today, I'd like you to enter a scenario. You're a rebel held hostage by a regressive, right-wing government, and you know where the rebel leader is. You're his right-hand man; you're close to him. But they have you, not him. Now, the government men holding you know that you know where the leader is— the hero of the revolution—and they tell you that they are going to round up local villagers, and take them in front of you and shoot them, one a day, until you tell them where your leader is. What do you do?

I wouldn't hesitate at first. I would sacrifice one villager a day up to a certain point. The leader, of course, would know that the villagers are being killed. He would have to show his hand. The situation would have to change in a matter of, let's say, thirty days to sixty days. But I would make a modest sacrifice in that direction. Because if Leader X is important on a larger scale than Villager Y—I'm assuming the revolution will be good for the villagers, I'm not assuming the leader is Bob Kerry of Nebraska, I'm assuming he's going to do something significant—then it's worth sacrificing the villagers. And I assume they are going to catch the leader if I tell them. I would wait.

You'd be strong enough to watch people being killed under your nose?

Yes, I would.

What if you had the option of suicide?

The "option" of suicide?

Yes, let's say your captors in some way couldn't keep you from killing yourself. Now, if you're dead, your captors have no leverage, and there's no need for them to kill the villagers. They're only killing them in front of you to try to get you to break down and give them the information they need—to make you talk. So if you die, they live. Would you kill yourself?

I'd have to. I'd have to. If I had that option, I'd kill myself. You must be ready to die for those stakes.

Session Two

Let's go right to the films. The dominant criticism of your work is that it's too loud in some way, that it tries too hard. I know you're aware of it, and I want to know where you think that criticism comes from.

Probably my hearing. I think that in 'Nam I went to the ear doctor [laughs] and I thought that my hearing had been impaired over there from all the artillery and the bombs. So maybe my mixes are too loud.

You know I'm not speaking literally.

Well, I am. [Laughs.] I think your question has to be dealt with on levels. Anyway, physically, at one point I had my ears checked and the doctor said I had very good hearing. But I feel sometimes that I can't hear people, and he says it's probably a lack of concentration, that I'm not listening.

Obviously, I'm aware of that criticism. And obviously, it's in my interest to practice on myself, refine my thinking, refine my heart, refine all the aspects of myself as I get older. So I try to listen. But one thing I always felt I had, when I was doing all the writing, was a good ear. As a screenplay writer I would go down to Miami and I would listen to people talk, and I feel like after a little time with you I could probably do your rhythm in dialogue. I try to pay attention to details, I try to be a realist, dealing with real things, real people, real events. I think that that sometimes plays loud because it's real.

I think you have to be specific. *Born on the Fourth of July* to me is about a very real thing: certain families that live like this, a blue-collar existence in America. And it came from observations of Massapequa, Long Island, and hanging out with Ron [Kovic], and being in his circle of friends and family. And these people say what's on their mind: they sometimes speak loudly, crudely, wrongly, but I'm putting it down as I hear it. There's nothing wrong with that, because that's part of the vitality of life, it's part of the contrast. But as I get older I want to do more, I'm more and more aware of contrast. Because the older you get, the more and more contrast you get in your life. When you get older, old versus young becomes a lesson. Loud versus soft.

Is that what you asked me, loud? What was the question again?

Not the volume, but that the films in some way try too hard, that you are too much in the audience's face, that you always use the sledgehammer instead of the stiletto. Instead of your response just to that, I'm interested in where you feel this criticism comes from.

Do you agree with it?
Sometimes I do sympathize with the criticism.

Specifically, give me an example.

At the end of Born, *bringing the mother's dream back in, her dream about Ron speaking to a large audience like Kennedy. I feel, and I know other people who felt similarly, that it was hitting us over the head with something that was already in our reading of the film.*

Not everybody is so perceptive. I could argue that it was two-and-a-half hours before, screen time. It was a long film. You'd gone through so many changes. I could argue that people—maybe the majority of the audience—didn't remember. Possibly I go sometimes for the lowest common denominator, in terms of getting the message across, in terms of getting what I want to say across. I think sometimes it's better to be wrong on the side of clarification than of obscurity.

That's the thing my father used to always beat on me for. Because about all my earlier writing, he'd say, "That's too obscure." And all my English teachers would drive me nuts: "This is too obscure. What do you mean?" Something you've broken your heart writing, that's so clear to you, and nobody understands. And I wrote a lot of obscure stuff. The novel was mostly obscure; it was symbolist poetry, it was Rimbaud-like. It's part of that Vietnam thing too—maybe my hearing—and that I just want to be *clear*. It's like you have to be a commander to be a director. You have to be clear, you have to really project yourself, make an effort of projection. Because I come from obscurity and confusion, essentially, and shyness. I was terribly shy in school, always an outsider. Sort of avoided groups and cliques, didn't want to run with any gang. Always wanted to be alone. Reconciled myself to being alone. So I think that maybe part of going the other way is trying to fight all of those earlier tendencies, where I felt like I was totally irrelevant to the human race and that I was totally obscure and confused. 'Cause my childhood was very confused.

Do you ever feel that you compromise subtlety in pursuit of clarity?

Possibly. But subtlety is a technique; I admire subtlety as I would a dance step. And there are some subtle things in my movies that I know are there and have sort of not been seen, *yet,* but they will be seen eventually through time. And I think the movies will last because there are subtleties that few recognize. But as I say, what is subtlety? It's a technique. You're essentially communicating something, but you're doing it another way; it's less "in your face." It's pulled back. But it's essentially the same form of communication.

And I'm all for learning more technique as I go on. But the technique should never overcome the heart of the matter, and a lot of films I see that are always getting praised for subtlety have nothing to say to me and have nothing to do with the life I know around me. They become abstractions. A lot of their subtleties become abstractions, and abstractions, to me, are difficult to respond to, as an audience.

When Born *was screened in Berlin, you were reported to have said you had never seen the audience move so much in their seats at any of your films.*

Yeah, we screened it in East Germany, and it was a very emotional crowd. And they would sigh and gasp and you'd hear them physically moan and suffer along with the protagonist of the movie.

That's what you want?

They shared, they completely crossed the barrier, they were empathetic in the Greek sense of the word. Totally involved! We were affecting them. It was a wonderful thing to experience, for me. I like that. I like the internationalness of film. It's great just to get into Albania, to Greece, Japan, China. When they see me on the street, I'm a friend of theirs, you know. They come up to me and shake my hand, like they know me. I don't know them, but they know me.

Are you ever afraid that it doesn't happen enough, that film is "just a show"—to quote from the end of Talk Radio? *All these horrible, sad, frightening, deep things are discussed on Barry Champlain's [Eric Bogosian's] radio program, and the kid who's invited to the*

*studio interprets it all in a way that completely surprises and ulti-
mately depresses the host, Barry Champlain/Oliver Stone: that it is
"just a show."*

[Laughs.] That's a very—you've been waiting to say that.

*So that people walk out—after this catharsis—and they're back to
square one again.*

[Pause.] I think you got to the heart of it. I have an ambiguous
response to it, definitely. There are times I cross the barrier and I
meet a total stranger and he knows my world. He's shared my
world. And there are other times I feel that everything we do,
all our efforts, are for naught. That we're mere abstractions, that
we're mere reflections of life. We're like a mirror that passes up
to life for two-and-a-half hours and goes into their subconscious,
but often it's forgotten. And there are so many other reflections
going on right now—music, video, television, all kinds of leisure
forms are booming, so movies are even a smaller part of it.

And I see the day where one of two things will happen. Either
movies as a form will disappear. They'll become like antique wood-
working, like cabinets, seen by a few people and brought into a
few homes: very nice but expensive and difficult to come by, a
rarefied art form, like opera. Or, I could see it going another way:
the movie that gets released in one night on a billion screens, all
across the world, and speaks a universal tongue. And will come
into our living rooms on a wide screen. I'd like to have the screens
curved, with a tremendous new Lucas sound system. Digital picture, digital sound. A great home experience. And more people
would see it. That would be great. The future of communication.
Then movies would play a central role.

I would go either way. I would still make movies. I think if
tomorrow I had a series of failures and people didn't want to see
my movies anymore, I would retreat back to a form where I could
do as cheap a movie as I could, like *Salvador,* like my NYU films.

*To go back to the essence of the question, about the function of
film. Rousseau wrote a letter to d'Alembert, about the theater in
which he argues against the theater. For example, you go to watch
a play, let's say its theme is about some social problem, and it's an
effective play, and you weep over the tragedy of this problem as it*

is displayed for you by these characters. And you feel like you've experienced it, and there's a catharsis. But it's a false one. So the man in New York City attending a play about homelessness weeps in the theater, but then steps over a homeless person on his way into the cab that takes him home.

Well, I don't agree with Rousseau at all. If you never had that experience in the theater you'd run the risk of becoming a senseless human being, without any empathy or sympathy or feeling for others. And through the act of empathy you have in the theater, you are able to remember some of the roots of your consciousness. So when you step out in the street and you see that homeless person, you may not do anything, you may step over, but you're thinking about it, and you're seeing life from where he is, for that moment in time. So you've made one small step. So it works for me, the theater.

It also works in a negative way, I suppose, with a horror movie. You step out and you see everything in shadows, in darkness. You see vampires and you see werewolves, like my little kid does. Like I used to, and I still do actually. [Laughs.] The act of imagination, the act of seeing beyond yourself, stepping outside your ordinary, small, mundane life, living a larger life through theater—that can only help you in your everyday life. No matter how mundane your life is, if you can preserve the imagination, it's a wonderful thing. It will make your life so much more joyous, less painful. When I was in my worst periods, driving cabs, horrible times in the army, horrible times in the merchant marine, life was really getting to me and I was starting to feel that I was losing it, it was the retreat to a walled world, an imaginative world, that allowed me escape and freedom.

How would you assess your strengths and weaknesses as a film-maker?

[Pause.] I don't know. Help me on that. If you want an answer to that . . . that's a real leading question. Say anything. [Joking, with Eastern European accent.] Well, I can press six hundred pounds. You see this bicep, here. God, I hate that. Do I have to answer that? Can we just come around to that some other time?

Okay, we'll try to double back to it.

You're very noncommittal. You listen. You're like the *Citizen Kane* character, in the back of your head. You don't agree, disagree. You don't interrupt. You don't lead it, you're just sort of like a Rorschach test.

Is that bad?

Well, sometimes, when you ask cold questions like that. It throws me.

Let's talk about how you feel you've "redefined heroism." That was one of your repeated refrains after Born: *that it had taken you a long time, but what you wanted that movie to do was to redefine heroism.*

[Chuckles.] I said that? I never said that.

Many times.

No. A redefinition of heroism? It's not a verb.

"It took us a long time to redefine heroism." That's a direct quote.

Is that what I said? In what context? See, that's the thing, you're taking it out of context.

No, I'm not. Let's talk about it within context.

I don't remember quite the context. Go ahead.

This is another context: "We wanted to show America and Tom [Cruise] and through Tom, Ron [Kovic] being put in a wheelchair, losing their potency. We wanted to show America being forced to redefine its concept of heroism." Here's the other quote, vis-à-vis vets: "It took us years sometimes. We didn't join the protest movement. It took us a long time to redefine heroism."

I suppose we lived—to put it in a black-and-white era—we grew up believing that to go to war, to be courageous in a war situation, was heroic, in a John Wayne sense. And when *we* went over there, it was more like Marlon Brando goes to war. [Laughs.] You started questioning everything. Nothing was what it seemed to be. Ron went to the end of the road on that matter: he lost his body in what he thought was a courageous action but which he now admits was a foolish action. He came to a reversal of appreciation for what he'd done. He'd charged the enemy blindly, without any reason.

But did he think it was foolish only because he ended up in a wheelchair as a result, or because—

Well, at first he did. He cursed himself for his stupidity in the hospital. He cursed the day he did it. He rued it. He went through a heavy period of self-loathing and self-abnegation. Many times he wanted to be dead. He went through hell. Now he's sort of reached a point where he's accepted his destiny, and he's said to me many times, "I would never have learned the things I did if I hadn't been in this chair. And now I'm a wiser person. What would I have become if I had stayed in Massapequa and never gone to Vietnam? Would I have been like my father?"

Didn't the political conversion come from the personal impotence? It was as if the country had promised you something out of war, out of being a man in a war—the John Wayne idea—and it didn't deliver it, and now you're angry as hell at the country for not giving you what had been promised?

[Pause.] I think in Ron's case there was a lot of that. Because I think Ron was extremely patriotic in the conventional sense of the word, with a love of Motherland. And he felt he had a special bond to Motherland and that Motherland did not pay him back. I think that was a very strong consideration. The film was criticized in intellectual quarters for not dealing with the cerebral basis of his emotional shift, but I have difficulty believing in that basis. I believe that the emotional shift, as you say, was the result of the physical condition. And also of reading books. It's not that he didn't read. He was conditioned by books by Ghandi and Martin Luther King, which were very strong influences.

There's a line of thought which argues that heroism is not changed at all by the end of that movie, that the focus of it may have changed, but the act remains the same. He's now in a wheelchair, and he's telling his comrades to fall out, to "take" the convention hall—he's barking orders again. He's very much in the same place, it's just that there's a different enemy to attack; it's not the Viet Cong, it's the prowar conservatives.

Is that real life, or is that drama? Is that real life, to you? Do you believe it?

Do I believe it? Yeah, very much so.

Once a leader, it's hard not to always be a leader?

I agree with that, yes, but that doesn't redefine heroism in any way. The concept of individual heroic action—the male animal attempting to change the world in a traditionally heroic way—is preserved at the end of the film every bit as much as it's offered in the beginning, with Ron in the diner with his buddies, talking about going to Vietnam to stop the spread of Communism.

Well, maybe what I meant by redefinition was taking loss and making it into victory. Most people would regard loss, as in Vietnam, or as in body, as a negative, and it's not. Pancho Villa had a great line: "The defeats are also battles." And my life, too, has been a series of many defeats, many defeats. [Laughs.] From an early age. Divorce. Institutionalization. Insecurities, fears, failures, the army, Vietnam. Huge amount of rejections in scriptwriting, where I developed a strong rejection virus, immunity. Defeats. But I felt I was able to transcend the defeats by learning from them.

Both heroism and cowardice are reactions to fear, are they not, in your eyes?

Yes. What are you trying to get to? There's a quote.

"Cowardice and heroism are the same emotion—fear—expressed differently."

Hmm. Interesting.

It would be interesting to go through all your protagonists to see how you would interpret their heroic actions in terms of what they feared.

Umm.

You don't sound like you want to do that.

[Pause.] It's a lot of work. You'd have to help me.

Instead, let's talk about the position of women in your films. [Stone sighs.] It's like going to the dentist, Oliver! The world of your films is a boys' club, really. True?

No. I'd say the boys have been the protagonists of those movies, yes, but look at the movies. They were about ideas which primarily concerned men: Vietnam, the world of cocaine smuggling, a prison in Turkey, Wall Street, which is a men's club. But in each film there have been more women, you know. I'm not trying to deny their existence.

No, but due to their marginality, it's interesting to see what position they have. Since your films are not exactly overrun by women, the women that do show up are going to "stand for" more, in sort of inverse proportion to their dominance in the film.

Because less is more?

Not necessarily. Look, if you have seven major women characters in a film, each one does not carry as much weight—representationally—as if you have only one.

I see.

So now. The women in your work tend to be prostitutes, bimbos, housewives, stick figures. And if they're developed at all, they tend to be either emotionally cold or sort of along for the ride, as appendages to the male characters.

Well, Kyra Sedgewick in *Born on the Fourth of July* is a girl who marches to her own beat. She leaves Massapequa, Long Island, and goes to college, and she starts to think for herself. She becomes a terribly influencial figure in Ron's life. She was the girl he never had a date with, but that he loved, that he wanted to love. He was the yearning romantic and went back to see her after the war with the illusion that it could all still be good together. He listens to her, he hears what she has to say. From his generation, from his town, she questions the war. When he first hears it, it's strong coming out.

I think you're picking an exception to the corpus.

Well, it's an important exception.

Even she, though, has an edge of coldness, doesn't she? She just leaves Ron at the foot of the steps to the building she is going into on campus. Of course he can't follow. He's just left there, in his wheelchair.

That's right. And the next day she holds the hand of her boyfriend at the demonstration, which drives him nuts. She had another life, and she knows it.

I'm not going to be noncommittal now, and I want you to address the general issue I brought up. You pointed to a female character who goes the other way—and I think we could find a few others— but the dominant feeling one gets from the work when one sits down and screens all your screenplay and movies is—

Ellen Greene. Ellen Greene in *Talk Radio* has an emotional attachment to Barry Champlain, comes back for him, abandons her boyfriend in Chicago, flies down to Dallas to be with him, extends her heart once more, against all her better judgment—and he breaks it again.

Yeah, she's ready to take more of his abuse.

And, number three, Elpedia Carrillo in *Salvador*—she has enough of James Woods, she tells him to go fuck off, she doesn't want him anymore, she screams at him; he's a drunk, he's a louse, he's no good. He realizes he wants her, and he begins to behave in another way. He expresses his devotion, he goes to church with her, he makes a confession with her, for her, and ultimately he risks all to take her out of the country, back to America, because she in some way has graced him, has transcended him, has given him grace. And he knows it. He knows she's the best thing in his life.

Yes, he says, "She and the kids are the only decent thing I've ever fucked and had in my whole life."

Well, that's his mode of expression, but that doesn't change his feeling toward her. His heart has been transformed in some way. He risks taking her out. And then he has his heart broken, doesn't he? At the end, on the bus. And she does too. He risked it and he lost. He'll never be the same person again. Elpedia was the driving force that changed his heart. These are three examples of women reaching out. And in *The Doors*, Meg Ryan, in a sense, makes Jim more human.

Okay, let's look at the way she's presented in The Doors. *My understanding is that Pam Courson, Morrison's girlfriend, was a lot more independent—less traditional, less monogamous—and displayed a lot more freedom than in the movie, where she is presented almost as the jealous "wife" who's horrified when she sees him with others and who only sleeps with someone else as the "spurned woman," to get back at him.*

Well, that's not what I heard. I heard that she may have had affairs before, but that she really was enamored of the image of a domestic life with Jim. And wanted to make a real home. And prided herself on cooking certain things for him and giving him a warm domestic environment to his previously solitary life. He continued to live in the motel and could not stand, ultimately, domesticity. She was not screwing everything that came along. She had a crush on certain people, often in response to the way Jim was screwing anything he cared to. It was more of a reaction to that than her being that way from the beginning. That's the impression I got from the witnesses. [Pause.] I'm sorry, but I'm trying to defend my position.

Do you feel you've done a good job with the way you've presented women in your films?

Not in *Wall Street.*

They're really commodities in Wall Street.

Yes, I think that was a failure in the writing. But I admire—I adore
women. I've lived with many women in my life. I think women
dispense grace.

I tried to make *Evita*, which would have been interesting. That
would have been my first woman protagonist. The most hated and
loved woman of her time. Meryl Streep would have been great. It
would have been a wonderful movie, but it didn't happen for various reasons. And I have another project that I'm working on that
has a woman for the main character [*Heaven and Earth*, the third
film in Stone's Vietnam trilogy]. I would very much like to make
that kind of movie, because it's nice to work with women. I had
more women working on *The Doors* than on any other film I've
ever done, and I really enjoyed being around them.

You know, beauty is important on the screen. I don't want to
belittle it. I realize that. When you see a beautiful face, you respond. We like to see models of our best-looking sides. It's as old
as the world. It behooves me to use beautiful faces. I could watch
Garbo for many minutes. She just fascinates me. Just her face.

*When I asked you what gave you joy, and you gave me a shopping
list, at one point you said, "Beautiful women. Intelligent men."
There's a dichotomy here. And even now, when you're talking about
having more women, the locus is physical beauty, rapture, and not
intelligence or action.*

Oh, I have the appetite of an African chief! [Laughs.] No, I—of
course there's the other side. But let's say, to a man, a woman
who is intelligent and beautiful is very sexy, and he gets excited
by her, not only physically, but in all ways—talking to her, dealing with her in business, playing sports with her, every aspect of
life becomes a playing field.

At the same time, you know as well as I do that a beautiful
woman without a brain in her head can still be exciting to you. I
don't know if Marilyn Monroe was smart or dumb; my impression
is that she didn't have much of an education. But she turned many
men on. Carole Lombard had intelligence and beauty, and I find
her ravishing, as I do Katharine Hepburn. Greta Garbo is *primal.*

Garbo never showed her intelligence; she never had to: you imput-
ed it. I loved Irene Dunne, because her spunkiness was great. I
always loved her. She was smart, she was fresh. She talked back.
I liked Myrna Loy, because she was bright, more on the refined
side, more sophisticated. A little coldish, not animalistic, but that
was certainly an East Coast woman to me. I loved Ursula Andress
too, because of her animalistic qualities when she was young.

Now, today, actors are like new breeds of flowers: they come
up each season. There are many I would like to work with. From
Meryl to Glenn Close, Julia Roberts is wonderful, I can't even
name them all. Debra Winger is great. She's intelligent, she's fiery; she has both sides. I always had a thing for Jane Fonda, when
I was in Vietnam. I still do. I think she's an incredibly vital woman. Working with Meryl was so exciting because she's so bright.
She's got a mind like a rapier.

And women think differently than men. All the signals that are
given, you have to be a railroad man in this life to figure out all
the signals.

*Anthropologists have actually studied pickup behavior in bars, and
they've been able to catalog a series of gestures that a woman will
perform if she's interested in the man. There's a whole ritualistic
physicalization of desire, I guess, the semiotics of attraction.*

I think Carole Lombard was about as perfect as they came.

That'll be the last word on this subject.

Do you feel I was trying to answer it, or do you think I was . . . ?

Yeah, I think you—I think you tried.

I think there are some unresolved things with my mom, that I always had. Because of the divorce. She was a bit of a foreign—
how do you say?—a foreign queen. She was like a queen to me
when I was a kid. She was sort of living in a fairyland. She'd
come and go. She was sometimes distant and sometimes very close.
It was like ECUs [extreme close-ups] and long shots. It was consistent, or steady, my relationship with her, and it turned into a
messy thing later on in my adolescence, and I think there are still
many unresolved problems with my mom, uh, as there were with

my dad. [Pause.] I always married, I married my opposite, I mean, the opposite of my mom, which is interesting, too.

Showing maybe a kind of contrary dependence?

Yeah. A contrary dependence? How do you define that?

If you reject a certain model—and by doing that need to seek the opposite of the model—you are actually just as dependent on the model as if you were slavishly seeking to duplicate it, as in, let's say, the man who seeks to marry his mother. You still may be equally dependent on the mother, only it's a contrary dependence.

I see. Well, I think I have that. [Laughs.]

Speaking of parents, do you think your career would have gone in a different direction if your father had still been alive?

[Long pause.] No. I think it would have been the same. Because he died right before *Salvador* came out. I'm sorry he missed it, because he would have enjoyed being surprised. [Laughs.]

He's certainly the only man in history who's had both a movie about leftist rebel and a movie about Wall Street *made for him. Both sides of the dialectic . . .*

[Big laugh.] And now I've got to do some things for my mom. She always wants me to do *Gone with the Wind.* "Oliver, why don't you do something romantic? Clark Gable, Claudette Colbert, two people in love!"

Well, you've threatened to do a great love story.

That's something to look forward to. That's something to try. When I'm ready. Well, *Born* is a love story: it's about a boy's heart and his feelings for his country. It's sort of a love affair. The best love stories are—how do you say?—unrequited. Ron's unrequited love for America. [Laughs.]

Richard Boyle in Salvador *has some of that too, no? He's hurt by the deceptions of America when he sees her behaving badly. He* says, *"I believe in America. I believe we stand for something. For a constitution, for human rights, not just for a few people, but for everybody on this planet."* *Are you at one with Richard Boyle on this?*

It's a nice thought. Without becoming an "ism" I would agree with it.

You really think America has betrayed a kind of grand benevolence?

I don't think benevolence was ever the motivating factor in American political history. I think it was already a tough place. I think there were alway neo-, nascent fascists in America. I think half the people during the American Revolution were pro-British.

It was an economic revolution.

Was it?

The Stamp Act, man. It was about autonomy, but not about universal freedom or human rights.

I haven't studied it, but I think that we all as filmmakers and literati and politicians refer to an idealistic America as we do to an idealistic Greece. [Stone's wife, Elizabeth, walks out of the house, towards the garage, and tells him she's going skating. Then she kicks a huge blue ball across the lawn at us.] That's a David Lynch image: blue ball coming at you, blonde wife, retriever by a car.

Where's the garden hose?

[Laughs.] Then a gardener walks out behind her with one eye and a scythe in his left hand and starts to fuck my wife right in front of me!

[Returning to the subject.] It's an idealization, but I do believe in those concepts. I do believe in democracy. I believe the people know better. That people have a cognitive function, that they're able to understand. I don't believe in the secrets of governments. My greatest fear in the twentieth century is totalitarianism. Totalitarianism feeds off of war. War gives the state the authority to control its citizens. It becomes the organizing principle of society, the war-making power.

I fear that governments have too much power and are getting stronger. I resent the liberalism that casts the responsibility onto the government, because it always sets up a new set of problems. I think that governments generally do badly with money and with human functions, though there are examples of their doing well. And the Constitution has been usurped. It was usurped in Vietnam when they declared war, when they declared war.

We never declared war!

Excuse me, when Johnson declared unilaterally without Congress. I think the Constitution—I think there was a coup d'état when John Kennedy was killed. So, the ideals of democracy and freedom are ideals we return to like a Frank Capra movie, because we *have* to believe. It's this battle between hope and despair. The end of the world versus the birth of the world.

So you would favor continually remythologizing American history because we need a better "good" to believe in than the one that we have?

Yes. That's a good point. But at the same time, a balance: you show the truth but you try to show a goodness in the truth, too. It's an argument you have with yourself. It's an argument with yourself, a movie, a screenplay.

[It has gotten cold, and Stone asks that we go inside. We sit in his living room, flanked by two large Julian Schnabel paintings. Stone picks up a little sculpture on the coffee table in front of us.] Sleeping Buddha from Cambodia. It's a national treasure. I took it out.

Bad, bad boy.

Bad.

Let's talk about another major theme in your work: the dominance of death. In all of your films, save Wall Street, *the protagonist kills, or is killed, or barely, barely escapes death. Clearly, in some very*

fundamental way, it's a moving force in what you do—both obses-
sion and wellspring.

"Death shall have no dominion." [More dramatically.] "And death shall have no dominion." Who said that?

Beats me, dad.

You don't know? You don't know? God, it was a great poem by Dylan Thomas. You should hear him do the audios of it. He does his own poetry. He was a man wracked with death, as was Jim Morrison. I admire both of them as giant men who lived in the shadow of death. I feel much less enamored of death than they did; or else I'm running from it and not admitting it. I think it's a strong force in my life. I've used it. It's there. I've thought of death, often. At the age of eighteen I went to Vietnam as a form of death. I was ready to accept death. I saw much of it in Vietnam.

I think the Mexicans are so damn right, I have that thing in my office—a corpse, a skeleton. It grins at me: keep death around as a reminder, make it part of your life. Not to mystify it, or make it something horrific, but to live with it on a daily basis is, I suppose, to prepare for it, to get ready for it. And probably when it comes, the ideal position is to want it, to be tired of life, to have exhausted the variations you intended to play as a human being. And then to go back to the womb. You want to be nascent again. You want to be quiet. You've had enough. You've seen enough people, you ve seen enough colors, you've lived through enough lights and . . . [Sighs] Death is a framing experience of life and birth. Everything is seen in that light to me. I'm very aware of it, on a daily basis, driving around. Looking out the windshield, I see violent accidents in my head. 'Cause I saw a lot of that in Vietnam, and I see death around me—quickly, obscenely being cut off. Every time I get on a plane I have to deal with the concept of death; I have to redefine it for myself, for everyone, for my child, in terms of him being hurt.

So I guess what I'm telling you is: it is a steady and mundane presence in my life, and no, I haven't come to deal with it completely. But I like Dylan Thomas's line, "And death shall have no dominion." So that when it comes, it will come as a friend and

not as a dominant master. It will come as my equal. My spirit will
be equal to my death. I will be wanting and willing to die. That
would be nice.

You've said you feel it coming on.

What do you mean?

Even on "60 Minutes," you said you feel the approach of death.

Yeah. I was talking in terms of the feeling of it, yes. I didn't mean
that it was going to be on Tuesday. The older you become, the
more measured your days. You understand . . . you *see* the length-
ening shadow.

Is your work against death in some way?

All work is. William Butler Yeats said, "Raise your raiments to
the sky, raise your colors, raise your raiments to the sky." Parade
yourself, parade what you know, parade your human beingness,
have fun, stir some shit up, rattle some cages. "The Soft Parade."

*In Jim Morrison, you finally found a protagonist who's as death-
obsessed as you are.*

No, more obsessed. I think more so. Jim lived it. He loved to walk
with it.

The appeal of cinema lies in the fear of death.

[Laughs.] Is that Jim?

Something he wrote while at UCLA.

The appeal of cinema lies in the fear of death? God, what's the
context of that? Is it from his *Lords and New Creatures* poems?

No, I think it was in a paper for a film class.

Well, everything with Jim is death. A bottle of whiskey is death, a woman is death. Death is in every poem. Cinema of course has death in it. So do snakes, fires. [Laughs.]

Well, Roland Barthes argues in *Camera Lucida* that the very act of photographing is tied to the idea of mortality—you preserve the image past.

Yeah, you're aware that the image will never return again.

So that by making the image move, and not be a static impression, you suspend mortality all the more. A denial of, and a pushing past, death in some kind of way.

Well, when each film comes to an end, it always feels like a form of dying. Making that one stamp through time. We all come together as a collective, all these people agreeing to do something, and we share this life experience, and we know we will never do this the same way again. So it's a memory—the moment you shoot it.

Let's focus on you and your protagonists. You very closely identify with your protagonists, I would say as much as any director now working, and I'd like to go through them and have you tell me what's you in them.
   There's a soft parade of assholes you've presented us with: Tony Montana in Scarface, *Stanley White in* Year of the Dragon, *Jon Lansdale in* The Hand, *Matt Scudder in* 8 Million Ways to Die, *Richard Boyle in* Salvador, *Barry Champlain in* Talk Radio, *not to mention Gekko in* Wall Street *and Barnes in* Platoon, *who are not protagonists but leading men. And then there are the innocents: Billy Hayes in* Midnight Express, *Conan in* Conan the Barbarian, *Chris Taylor in* Platoon, *Ron Kovic in* Born on the Fourth of July. *And now you've finally come to the innocent asshole: Jim Morrison in* The Doors.

The Holy Fool.

Let's look at these guys, one by one.

[Long pause.] David, help me.

Tony Montana, let's start with him.

Okay, use some adjectives. What are you looking for?

No, I want to know where you identify.

How I identify myself with Tony?

There's a lot of you in these characters, no?

Yes.

Come on, yes.

Tony Montana. Tony Montana. [Pause.] Well, he was an outsider
to the system. He came from abroad. He jumped tracks. He was
unorthodox. He was a rebel. A nonconformist who at the end of
the day wanted to be a conformist. [Laughs.] And bought into the
dream of the wife with the blonde hair and the mansion [laughs,
looks around at his house] and then started putting security cameras outside his gates to watch the cops watching him. And then he
starts to freak out on drugs.

Me I want what's coming to me, the world. Ambition too, yes?

[Laughs.] Well, there's a little bit of a gangster in me, there's no
question. I like that grandiosity of style. I like the excess. The
concept of excess works in a lot of these characters, in Gordon
Gekko and Jim Morrison. Jim says, "I believe in excess." In the
power of excess. Because through excess I live, I live a larger life.
I inflate my life, and by inflating my life I live *more of* my life;
therefore, I know the world more. I have more experience of the
world. I die a more experienced man.

Stanley White.

Stanley White is based on a character I know called Stanley White,
an LAPD homicide cop. Stanley's a colorful ex-Vietnam veteran
marine, and I spent a lot of time with him in the streets, going
around. His view of the world is not like Tony's at all. It's much
more narrow and in some degree, vicious. Dog-eat-dog world, very

tough, very street oriented. You would not like to meet Stanley White in a fight. A real scrapper, willing to step outside the law to get the job done.

Are you?

I'm talking about him.

I want to know about you. I don't want glosses on these characters. I want to know particularly what you feel is your connection to the character.

Oh, I see.

What of you lives in that character?

Well, not much. Michael Cimino wanted him to be Polish, so he was more of an ethnic blue-collar than I was. I think I identified with the sense, the *Dirty Harry* sense in the film, of wanting to clean things up, of cops not really doing their job. The Chinese were pouring huge amounts of heroin in—which has been proven, by the way!—but at the time the film got a lot of flak for supposedly making up these stories about the Chinese. He was a wounded animal, Stanley, who didn't have that much understanding for himself. He was looking desperately for love with a woman, but I don't see that much closeness to me.

Okay, Jon Lansdale in The Hand.

Boy, that was a strange movie. At the time I thought he was the farthest thing from me, and I still do, I guess. Of course, you could say that that's me, too. If it is, it's certainly my darker side. Intense jealousy, paranoia about his wife, which I've never felt in my personal life, but maybe I'm denying . . .
    See, what's interesting about Lansdale is that everything he denied was true. He was an interesting psychological man, because he repressed everything, as we all do. We all repress something. And everything that he repressed was coming out.

It's all about control, and what you can't control. Very tellingly, the first panel of his cartoon strip that the camera lingers over in

*the beginning of the film says, "For now that I control you, I must
consider how you can best serve me. "*

[Laughs.] That's right!

*Which kind of serves as a metaphor for your relationship with the
camera, too.*

I never want it to be static, to watch the other. That the self and
the other are moving at the same time—that's the way I see the
camera moving.

As a participant and not an observer?

Yeah, I always respected the camera as another actor. I hate the
type of direction that makes the camera a slave. I always respect
the camera. I walk on the set and I see the actor, I see the camera,
and I see myself: I see a triangle. So that the camera, although
inanimate, is as much a human participant to me as I am. It's an
interesting relationship. So often the camera will speak to me on
the day, and say, "Not this, that." And it will become clear to me.
So I might sit here and for days make notes on what I want to do,
as I would with an actor. But when I have the actor and the camera there, they start to talk, and sing, a different kind of song. The
camera is different in each scene. The camera has an eerie kind of
power. It will often suggest to me a better way of doing it.

So you grant it a kind of autonomy.

Yes. Exactly. Thank you for understanding me. Whereas, I've noticed, some directors will treat their cameras like slaves, like fascists. And I think that's so wrong! The camera becomes an *object
of power,* like they're wielding a gun. I've noticed that attitude on
a lot of sets. But I haven't thought about it until you raised this
question today. It's interesting. Because obviously all our politics,
our emotions, our sex lives are all there, aren't they, in our relationship to our cameras.

*So you're looking for what might be described as an "unrepres-
sive" camera style.*

Yes! Totally free. I never saw this before. And I've tried a lot, if you look at the pictures, an enormous number of different moves. It's very complicated stuff, too, that we've tried. On *Born,* Bob [Robert Richardson, Stone's cinematographer] and I were really out there. On *The Doors,* too. It's gotten wilder! Bernardo Bertolucci came up to me after *Wall Street* and gave me a wonderful compliment I'll never forget. He just said, "I love what you do with your camera in *Wall Street.*" And he's an expert of the technique, he has a love of camera, you feel it.

Some people react differently. Instead of being elated by so much movement, they find it—

[Strongly.] It's not about movement. He was saying, "I love the camera, what it did." It's not about a move, it's about what it did even when it's standing still; you pick that moment to stand still.

Some people feel that your camera is pushy, that they almost need to wear a seatbelt watching your films.

That's their problem. The world is spinning much faster than my camera and myself. Some people probably find it too slow. I think movies have to break through the three dimensions, as close as you can get. I think you go for every fucking thing you can to make it *live.* You can't shoot Bunuel-style anymore. You can, if you have very little money, you can do that; I'd do it if I didn't have the money. But it's not enough. We're into new technology. Use everything you can. Make it breathe, make it coil, make it live.

On the other hand, I just want to say that if the movement is wrong, it's bad movement. If it's still and it's wrong, it's wrong. It's not about movement, it's about the camera doing the right thing. And there's a right thing for every scene, for every shot, for every moment. And if you're a good director you might hit it more than 60 percent of the time. But sometimes you can make a film and your camera is in the wrong place 25 percent of the time. And you know it. Maybe it's not that interesting unless you're a real buff, but I know where it's in the wrong spot. I can see a movie for three minutes and if the camera is always in the wrong spot, I know it, and I know I'm not going to like the movie. I think filmmakers have a thing—they can tell a bad movie from shot number three or shot number five. It's that precise.

Louis Kahn, the great American architect, talked about trying to make each building "what it wants to be."

Yes. And each film, each character dictates its own specificity to me. I have a kind of blank-slate approach to it. I walk out of the editing room, I say a bunch of things to the editors. I walk back the next day, and I've forgotten what I said. I want to rediscover the same thing with the camera. I've forgotten the last way I shot a film. And that's what makes it so interesting and fresh to me, because the next time every camera movement is discovered for the first time. Not knowing how I'm going to do it is so much a part of the pleasure of making a film. In my earlier days, I would often rush to get all the shots the way I wanted and to get everything defined, and I think I lost a lot of the magic and feeling.

You're learning more about jazz, then?

Yeah. The nature of improvisation. Definitely.

Let's take another protagonist, Barry Champlain.

He's a . . . I would say—I feel very stupid talking like this because sometimes I'm repressing things that are there, that I don't see—but I would think that he's the furthest away from me. [Big laugh.] I could never get on the air and do that, that blatant confessionalism.

But it's a show for him.

Yeah, that's what's interesting.

In his big speech, he says, "I'm a hypocrite. I ask for sincerity as I lie. I denounce the system as I embrace it. I want money, power, and prestige. I want ratings and success."

Yeah, that's a very bald speech. That's an embarrassing speech. You'd think after that confession he'd get fired, but they love it. They love it. That's the new media age. You can go further and further until you hang yourself on the air. I should have had him shot in the studio, you see; that was stupid.

He also says his greatest fear is being boring. That's a fear of yours, no?

I think my greatest fear is being *bored*. [Laughs.] Marianne Moore had a great line, "The best solution for loneliness is solitude." So boredom is something you fight, and it's important you fight it by finding some other aspect, some other level that you're not paying attention to. One of the most recent boring things I've done—going to a cocktail party. I find it so boring. The conversation is never very interesting; it's always about surface things. And I always get asked the same questions, what am I doing, what have I done? People know more about me, through my films, than I know about them. I prefer to do most of the talking. I prefer to inquire about other people than to have to answer questions about myself. Gore Vidal said that to be interesting, you have to be interested.

But Barry is too much on the nose. He's too out there. Anybody who has to do a talk show has got to be suspect. What do you think Johnny Carson's mind is like at this stage?

Let's not even hazard to guess. Why did you pick that project? It was so clearly someone else's vision—Eric Bogosian's—maybe there was a kind of freedom for you in doing it.

Maybe there was. It was an alien vision, and yet I loved the mood and the atmosphere, and I loved the concept of being able to say anything I wanted to say politically about the state of the country. I loved the concept of not seeing the calls, of playing off audio. I loved the concept of making a movie in a claustrophobic space. Like *Das Boot* or an elevator movie, *Lifeboat*. I saw it at the time as a film noir, very much a film noir of the late forties. No hope. Claustrophobia. Despair. Protagonist being killed. Destructive affairs with women in his life.

And yet, he's offered a rope, speaking of Lifeboat, *by the Ellen Greene character.*

Yeah, she's sort of like a B-character from the forties, a Veronica Lake type. The woman in the dark who comes in, the ex-wife, who

offers you a lifeline and you don't take it, because you're Edmund
O'Brien in *D.O.A.*

*And why not? Because as a woman caller suggests, Barry doesn't
love himself. That the reason he creates so much misery for other
people, and is so mean to them, is because he doesn't love himself.
That's not in Bogosian's original play.*

No, that's not in the play. I think I realized that through the years.
I suppose I was like Barry—you're right, I'm hiding it. When I
was younger, I was very dark, I was a B-film character, driven by
a lot of self-loathing. And I think Elizabeth, my wife, has made
me more aware of that, and made me a happier person, too. And
my son, Sean, has. I'm getting sentimental, I don't want to get
that. [Laughs. Stone calls Rosa, the housekeeper, and says,
"Agua."]

I want to ask you about the videocassette of Platoon.

Jesus, here you go again. This is exhausting!

Now, in The Doors *you are rightly horrified at the notion of the
band selling "Light My Fire" for a car commercial, and yet there's
a Chrysler commercial at the beginning of the* Platoon *cassette.
Lee Iacocca comes on and says,* Platoon *is a memorial, not to war,
but to all the men and women in a time and in a place nobody
really understood, who knew only one thing: they were called, and
they went. It was the same from the first musket fired at Concord
to the rice paddies of the Mekong Delta. They were called, and
they went. That, in the truest sense, is the spirit of America."*

[Stone laughs.] Is that so dishonest?

Fuck that!

Is that so dishonest? Isn't it true?

*That's the spirit of America for you, Oliver? That citizens are just
the mindless body attached to a head telling them to do something
that may or may not be just, right? I was staggered at the notion
of picking up a copy of* Platoon *and seeing this guy doing a fuck-*

ing commercial—first of all, just that fact, but then for him to politicize the commercial by saying the "true spirit of America" is to be called and to go. To me, that's not the spirit of America. The spirit of America's questioning, skeptical. If it weren't, we would never have broken away from the British, we wouldn't even be a country.

We went around on that, you know. The first copy [for the ad] was unacceptable. The first copy dealt with Americans only. I think the opening line is about . . . what is the first line?

This Jeep is a museum piece, a relic of war. Normandy, Anzio, Guadalcanal, Korea, Vietnam. I hope we will never have to build another Jeep for war. This film, Platoon, *is a memorial, not to war, but to all the men and women in a time and in a place nobody really understood," etcetera.*

I think you're right. I think I shouldn't have done that.

What was it doing there? The film made $180 million!

It was a small English company, and it had a lot to do with the video release of the film. It was a good guarantee for Hemdale. And I wasn't that involved. I didn't take a stand on it. I just changed the copy. I said, "This copy is unacceptable," and they came back three or four times with different copy, and I finally signed off on it. I was probably wrong. The copy should have been better. I learned a lesson.

What about the actual act itself of selling a product, or in this more sophisticated case the image of a company, and attaching that to a work of art?

[Long pause.] Yeah. In America, we've been so packaged. You go to a theater and you see the distributing company logo, and you see Universal's logo. You accept labeling, you accept being packaged. The videocassette comes in a wrapper, and it's being advertised like Kellogg's cereal. They're patrons for artists; it's like working for the pope.

But you seem to be embracing it, not merely accepting it.

No, they came to us.

But the whole idea of attaching a corporate identity to a work that was so personal, and so political; and it seems like in The Doors *you really come down on Morrison's side about this song, to the point where you—*

Well, it happened that way. He was very sensitive about that issue.

I know, but Oliver, there are all sorts of ways you could have presented that material. And if you hadn't thought that Jim was correct, I don't think you would have made a special point of it, to the point of showing a commercial in the movie that never was actually made!

Well, it was trivialized, see: they took the music that he had written. [Robby Krieger actually wrote the music.] They didn't do that in this case. They didn't take *Platoon* and turn it into a commercial. They separated the two.

I understand the difference.

I'd rather have *Born on the Fourth of July* on television with schlock commercials in between than not have it on at all. We've grown up with such a corporate culture that one doesn't think twice about it.

What about posing for the Gap ad? Did you think twice about that?

The Gap ad I enjoyed doing, in terms of just a vanity/ego thing, I suppose. I got paid $700. I didn't do it for money. I was at a certain age. I thought those photographs were incredible, and I'd like to have a decent photograph of myself at the age of forty-three in my life. Just as a marker. I like the clothes. They're cheap. It's not like working for Armani. They gave off an image of playfulness, an egalitarian image. What did I do wrong? [Laughs.]

I just wonder if you consider how you "commodify" yourself?
I agree. Yeah. But there's some interest in doing it. I have an Andy

Warhol attitude—we're postmodernists. Look at Andy, he sold everything. He sold his toilet paper, probably.

But he didn't win all the "Man-with-Most-Integrity of the Year" awards that you do, Mr. International Integrity!

[Laughs.] Does that means that I have to have integrity?

Do you?

[Laughs.] Give me a break! Somebody gives me an award, so now I have to have integrity?

You get a lot of awards, man.

I don't solicit them.

Do they mean anything to you?

I can't remember which one it is. Some of them do.

Do you feel the same way about your work that Warhol felt? You're selling one idea today, another tomorrow. No need for consistency, integrity? Are you interested in the Warhol ethic?

I don't want integrity to block my creative growth. Each time I've worked on a film I've put my whole being into it, and hopefully there will be some kind of consistency at the end of the day.

But I know how strongly you identify with Morrison, and I can't see him posing for a Gap ad.

That was the sixties and they were very anti. The war was on, too. There was a different feeling. Look at the way movies are made. Who makes them? Chryslers, Jeeps, whatever? It's the same thing. What does a filmmaker do? He goes to the highest bidder and he whores out his services. He gives his private fantasies public being. He prostitutes. So I don't have a very high self-esteem, maybe that's what you're saying. Maybe because I see myself as . . . an artist basically begging for a patron. I think there's a lot of that in me, that I feel very lucky each time I get the money to make a picture.

When you read me those lines now, they certainly sound like they're in bad taste—that Americans should just go and serve. I think the text is wrong. But is the act of having done it for Chrysler any different that the act of having done it for Matsushita?

Does the irony of your being at Carolco impress you, since they were the people who brought us Rambo?

That's the nature of the business. In the thirties and the forties they would make the potboilers, the formula fare, and then occasionally they'd take a shot at something else. I'd rather be allied with a successful company that can get it out in the marketplace. The irony of it? Yeah. I think Mario Kassar [the head of Carolco] was certainly aware of it, because he made his fortune with Stallone. [Laughs.]

The very thing that you despise and oppose.

[Long Pause.] Listen, I can't say I despise it. I said *Rambo* is a comic book, I never took it beyond that. I did not do *Platoon* as an antidote to *Rambo*; I wrote *Platoon* way before *Rambo* ever fucking existed.

*You said, I quote, "*Platoon *is an antidote to* Top Gun *and* Rambo. *It will make them think twice before they go marching off to another war." And then you called* Top Gun *fascist, and I assume you thought* Rambo *was equally fascist.*

It was. It was a fascist comic book.

As you know, Oliver, people are always most interesting in their contradictions. As you are probing some of Morrison's, it only seems fair that we probe some of yours.

I like Carolco because they put up the money quickly, and they gambled. And there's not much interference. There's one man, that's Mario. He's like an old-time filmmaker. He's the boss. And it's great to deal with him instead of a bureaucracy; that's why I'm there. He likes directors. He likes movies. He really enjoys watching them. He watches his own movies, the ones he produces, six, seven, eight, nine times. He sits there, and he gets a lot of the details.

A question about verismilitude: the demands and responsibilities of doing historical fiction. You've been criticized for taking too many liberties with certain things.

Such as?

The death squad burial site in Salvador, *which I don't think works in the context of the film, because if you had that image, hundreds and hundreds of bodies spread out at a burial site, it would be on every front page of the world. That's not what those burial sites looked like, so I thought the inaccuracy compromised the integrity of the film. And people also complained about your putting the rebels on horseback, as a shameless romanticization of the rebels. I know you're going to get criticism for the* Doors *film over the commercial, which you show on TV, but which Morrison stopped before it ever became a commercial. So I'm curious as to the process of justification: how you justify—or don't justify— altering reality so it will play differently in the film.*

I justify it . . . I suppose [pause] with *Born*, for instance, I justified it at the time as being true to the spirit of the times. Ron was not actually wounded in Miami—gassed and beaten in the street—but he was gassed and beaten other places. But there were riots in Miami and many people were arrested, vets. There was fighting. I think I did the right thing. There was no riot at Syracuse, and the Syracuse police department got all upset, but there were riots that week at many colleges all over the country because of Kent State and the Cambodia invasion. He never went to Georgia to confess his crime, but he wrote about it in his book, didn't he? Which was a confession to him, a very strong confession. So I took the liberty of taking that confession—which was the most important thing in the book, the theme of the book—and externalizing it, having him go to Georgia and telling these people that he killed their son.

Why are we never aware that Ron Kovic/Tom Cruise is conscious of the selfishness of that action?

I think he is aware of it. I think he knows he's hurting those people. I think he's so desperate that he has to; he has to either save
himself or hurt them. But it's more important that he save himself.
And they're not going to die from it. I think those people would
get over it. I think anybody knows that you go to war, *you goes to
war*; if you're killed by friendly fire, or enemy fire, does it really
make a difference?

*In their minds it probably did. They had a certain kind of illusion
about what happened to him.*

Maybe we should shatter their illusion. War shouldn't be illusion.
They should see the corpses. Therefore it was the greater good
versus the greater horror. Ron had to save himself; he did it. He
subordinated the harm done to them to the greater good it did him.

*I'm more interested in how you grapple with subjects that are very
rooted in history, and how you make decisions on when to stray in
service of your fictionalized narrative.*

I would probably do the two *Salvador* things differently now. I
think at that time, being an unknown filmmaker, I wanted to have
maximum impact right away for a subject that would not interest
most Americans. I probably got carried away. I put the rebels on
horseback because I loved the imagery of the tank versus the horse.
I used the maximum number of people in the death field because
it would have visual impact. I would probably do those scenes
differently.

In The Doors, *Morrison's line "I'm not mad—I'm interested in freedom" is like an epitaph for this film. He's not mad as in "crazy,"
but he is mad in the sense of angry," isn't he? My question is, if
you* need *to rebel, to shock authority, to piss on people's carpets—
and it seems like Morrison had that emotional or pyschological
need—are you really free at all? Aren't you just a slave to something else, your own rebellion perhaps, just as much as people who
are slaves to conformity?*

Contrary dependence? The role of the rebel as essentially a slave?

Maybe. I don't doubt that Morrison was interested in freedom, but he was most certainly quite mad, at least in the sense of angry. There's all sorts of hostility radiating out of this guy; that's one of the things that makes him so interesting.

He was interested in freedom from his own madness.

Maybe that's the resolution. He was very conscious of his own will to self-destruction. After Joplin and Hendrix died, he'd tell his friends, "You're drinking with number three."

Yeah. Yeah. I would like to believe that he went out smiling, he liked it, he enjoyed it as it happened, because he was in love with the death experience. He wanted to experience it, and he did. He had busted the limits on sex, for himself; on drugs, he'd taken every kind of drug; on the law, he busted the law, which I think hurt him the most, the trial really beat him down and tired him out, made him more aware of orthodoxy and the inevitable triumph of orthodoxy; and I think he busted through on the concept of success. He had success, he was God on earth for a while, he had everything he wanted, and he got bored with it. I think he became enamored of failure. He went on a failure trip, too, and I think he enjoyed busting through on the failure trip, by making a fool of himself in public, many times. He wanted to be an asshole, he wanted to be hated.

Because maybe then other people's opinion of him would confirm his opinion of himself?

Partly. And when he was a young lion he had a higher opinion of himself.

Where did all his meanness come from, his abusiveness?

Meanness? Abusiveness? The only abusiveness I know of—from all the witnesses—was when he was drinking. The Irish asshole side, the Dylan Thomas side, would come out, and he'd rant and rave and get into fake fights. And he got his ass busted a couple of times by guys who took him seriously. He would make an asshole of himself in public to go through all forms of experience. He wasn't about reserve and dignity, which his father had represented to him.

It seems, though, that when he was sober, or was on other drugs, that he would be one of the gentlest souls. Everyone would refer to how gentle he was, how sensitive, how well spoken, how shy. He certainly had two sides: he'd go from being the most sensitive, loving, caring person, who talked to everybody—he was very democratic in his approach to life, which I love—and then when he performed, he would go into a shamanistic, devil thing, and then when he was drinking, he would be a monster at times. I also heard that when he was drunk sometimes he would behave very sweetly. So everybody attests to Jim's kindness. He gave away everything, you know. There was a Jesus quality about Jim. He gave of himself: his body, his life, his possessions. Nothing was his. He was a sharing person. It's the Irish dichotomy, I suppose.

Were you trying to dramatize that dichotomy in the film?

We tried, you know. That's the hardest stuff to do. To show the holy and the fool at the same time. I tried. Probably, people might say I didn't get enough holy.

Do you view your task as an artist as more demythologizing him or remythologizing him?

That's a good question. Aren't they the same thing?

Oh, no.

Give me some help here.

Demythologizing is stripping away the myths that have been built up around him, either by the person himself or by the forces of the day, media, friends, some of which he may have been trapped by himself; stripping those away to show the real human underneath them, in all his spectacular peculiarity—the person. Remythologizing is taking the corpus of Morrison, twenty years later, with the Doors selling more records than ever, and glorifying and glamorizing the artist as victim, as hero—the myths which Morrison himself was conscious of. He says, "We got to make the myths, we got to make the myths." Well, you're a mythmaker too, you're a filmmaker.

I suppose my answer to that is that we were remythologizing, keeping the myth. Keeping the myth. But to me it includes demythologizing at the same time. I don't know why, it just does. It's not like he's any less a person for being demythologized. We show, certainly, the asshole part of him, but to me it only makes him more mythological. So they perform the same function for me, I don't know why. If you try to strip away from a person, you end up making him greater. By the fact that you're trying to strip. Why? You think you're taking layers away, you may be adding layers. [Laughs.] You understand what I'm saying?

"The road to excess leads to the palace of wisdom." How can we be so sure?

Go. Go.

Maybe it leads to the palace of disintegration, of psychic fracturing, of death.

You need strong *cojones* to take that medicine. You risk becoming larger than life. I guess you could become grotesque. It's a road to travel warily, no question.

Are you at the palace? You've certainly lived through a lot of excess.

I don't know I'm at midlife in my journey, that's for sure. [Laughs.] I'm in a dark wood, babe. I feel often like a neophyte on the road, I really do. I don't say that immodestly. I still feel very innocent, in many ways.

Do you feel like a great artist?

[Long pause.] God, if I told you my true feelings about that, they'd never let go of me. I'd just be setting myself up.

You're thinking about what "they" are going to think. I want to know what you think. I want your true feelings.

My true feelings? [Pause.] I never doubted it, from day one. When I was eighteen, I just felt like I had a call. Like I had a call. And living up to that call has been the hardest part. I've got a lot of work to do on myself, on what I'm doing, on my craft, but I never had a doubt.

That confidence must be a gift.

Yeah, I'm sure it is. Oh, I've had periods of doubt and lack of confidence. I wasn't prepared for all the shit that's thrown on people by others. I always thought it would be just a celebration of joy to do good work. I didn't realize that doing good work is often not enough, that there's a fashion to the times. And there's such a thing as luck. We get buffeted by the storms of temperament— they send us astray for months, sometimes years, at a time. But we all must naturally return to our natural temperament. And when we do, we find ourselves again. Our life is the working out of our destiny, our character. I believe you have a certain character.

Chapter 2

Seizure and
The Hand

The Hysterical Imagination: The Horror Films of Oliver Stone

David Sanjek

We're through the looking glass here. White is black and black is white.

> —Jim Garrison (Kevin Costner) in *JFK* (1991)

I've come to feel that God is both good and evil. Sometimes he speaks to us with terror.

> —Serge (Roger DeKoven) in *Seizure* (1973)

We are, I know not how, double in ourselves, so that what we believe we disbelieve and cannot rid ourselves of what we condemn.

> — Montaigne, epigraph to Marc Brandel's *The Lizard's Tail,* source material of *The Hand* (1981)

While the body of film theorists largely have abandoned use of the auteur principle, the culture industry, on the other hand, continues not only to elevate film directors as sui generis creators but also to use their names, bodies of work, and in some cases their very personalities as marketing tools. Few if any motion pictures currently are released without the requisite "A film by *(fill in the name)*." Timothy Corrigan writes of this matter that "the auteur-star is meaningful primarily as a promotion or recovery of the movie or group of movies, frequently regardless of the filmic text itself."[1] What began as an aesthetic/theoretic proposition has become little more than a marketing strategy, and chief amongst the current objects of the full weight of the culture industry's promotional blitzkrieg is Oliver Stone, the producer/director/writer of nine features since 1974.

Few are aware that Oliver Stone's directorial career dates back, in fact, to the second term of Richard Nixon. There are reasons for that ignorance. It results not from sloppy documentation but the nature and substance of Stone's first two films: *Seizure* (1974) and *The Hand* (1981). Film directors frequently ignore, if not bury, their initial releases, particularly when those films are low budget, not released by a major studio, and examples of what many still consider disreputable genres. One does not find, say, Alan Rudolph waxing nostalgic about *Barn of the Naked Dead* aka *Terror Circus (1973)* or Francis Ford Coppola pointing our attention to the softcore pornographic *Tonight For Sure* (1961). To my knowledge, Oliver Stone has never mentioned *Seizure* in any major interview, and the only direct comment he has made about *The Hand,* other than defaming it as a cynical career move made during a period in Hollywood when he felt, "nobody was making any serious movies," is to complain of his on-set fighting with Michael Caine, the film's star.[2] It would seem that, as Stone has spoken of *JFK* as a "countermyth" in opposition to the dominant narrative of the Warren Commission, he has, whether intentionally or inadvertently, constructed a "counterfilmography" that asserts the origin of his directorial career to be *Salvador* (1986).

If Stone defames *Seizure* and *The Hand,* the former by silence and the latter as a mistaken artistic compromise, both films do exist and are readily available on videotape.[3] Much more important, although both films are far from artistically successful, they nonetheless incorporate narrative practices, thematic materials, and a body of unresolved ideological assumptions that have marked Stone's work from 1974 to the present day. It is my purpose to examine *Seizure* and *The Hand* and indicate how they prefigure salient elements of Stone's subsequent career. Specifically, both films feature masculine patriarchal protagonists. Each is an artist, one a writer and the other a cartoonist, as in one form or another has been the case with all of Stone's protagonists.[4] Each, too, is at the head of a dysfunctional family in which a woman is made to lead a subordinate role, much as she may protest against it. They are both set in pastoral locations perceived, more by the women than the men, as means of escape from an urban environment felt to be inhibiting and treacherous. Both films end violently, the protagonists having immersed themselves in a destructive course of action that lays waste any number of the subsidiary characters.

Even more than these narrative concerns, it is Stone's treatment of them that strikes most vividly viewers familiar with his later work. Then as now, the visual dynamics are offsetting, displaying his characteristic hyperactive camera and jagged editing. That style underscores the irregularity, even incomprehensibility of the protagonists' behavior. Those individuals are weakly dramatized, many if not most of them little more than essentialized embodiments of absolute states of being. Furthermore, their behavior and its outcome displays a thematic dimension only a few critics have commented upon at length: the inchoate but omnipresent religious thrust to Stone's material.[5] It should come as no surprise that a director who has a character in *JFK* refer to the president's assassination as an action "old as the crucifixion" would begin his career with a narrative that features a female embodiment of absolute evil. Finally, Stone's films throughout have been profoundly unresolved, both aesthetically and ideologically. They comprise a body of "incoherent texts," in the sense with which Robin Wood uses that terms: works whose intelligence betray accumulated strains, tensions, and contradictions that reflect not only the creator's ambiguities but also cultural assumptions that remain beyond his or her conscious control. It is, perhaps, most interesting of all that in Stone we have a director who began his career with the horror genre, creating narratives in which the protagonists are terrified by entities that appear to be emanations of their repressed subconscious, and then redirected his attention to the horrors without, those social and political aberrations that result from a collective, institutional malevolence.

However, before examining these early contradictory and ambiguous narratives, it is necessary first to synopsize the omissions from Stone's counterfilmography, *Seizure* and *The Hand*. Then I need to briefly place the two films in the context of the generic dynamics of the horror narrative as well as the melodrama, arguably, in the words of Michael Walker, "the most important generic root of the American cinema."[6]

Seizure, an original script by Edward Mann and Oliver Stone from a source story by Stone, was filmed in Canada and released by the Cinerama Company as the lower-half of a double bill in 1974. It depicts a weekend gathering at the rural home of Edmund

Blackstone, "the Edgar Allan Poe of modern American fiction" (Jonathan Frid). The author has been plagued by nightmares in which his wife (Christina Pickles), son (Timothy Ousey), and friends are attacked and, in most cases, executed by three demonic figures: an imperious woman, a malevolent dwarf, and a silent, powerful black man (Martine Beswick, Herve Villechaize, and Henry Baker). Soon the guests arrive (variously played by Joe Sirola, Roger DeKoven, Mary Woronov, Troy Donahue, and Anne Meachum). The figures from Edmund's nightmares appear in the flesh, although, as a radio broadcast indicates, they could just as well be escapees from a psychiatric institute for the criminally insane. Whatever the case, the trio takes control of the house. The "Queen of Evil" announces that their mission is to torment and kill all but one of the characters in a trial of the fittest. Each of the adults perishes at the hands of one another or the three invaders. In the end, Edmund alone remains and is given the choice of his own survival or the sacrifice of his son. He chooses the latter, only to discover his wife, who earlier had committed suicide to escape a worse fate, has returned from the dead, ready to sacrifice her mate for her child. As he is about to die, Edmund awakes. However, he once again finds his wife's suicide note and, returning to their bed, in her place the "Queen of Evil." As she bears down upon him, the narrative recapitulates its opening sequence, only this time Edmund's son unsuccessfully attempts to awaken his father, dead of a heart attack: a victim of his weak heart or the "Queen of Evil"?

The Hand is adapted by Stone from Marc Brandel's novel *The Lizard's Tail* (New York: Simon and Schuster, 1979.[7] Its protagonist, cartoonist Jon Lansdale (Michael Caine), creator of the Conan-like comic strip "Mandor," resides in Vermont much to the annoyance of his wife (Andrea Marcovicci), who misses the social and cultural opportunities of New York City. They argue over their contradictory desires as Lansdale's wife drives him to deliver his most recent drawings. An accident ensues as, attempting to avoid a tailgating female driver, the car passes too close to an oncoming truck and the cartoonist's drawing hand is severed and then lost in the underbrush of the countryside. In the accident's aftermath, the marriage, already tenuous, collapses as Lansdale, his wife, and young daughter return to Manhattan. Unable to draw, he abandons "Mandor" and accepts a teaching position at a rural college. Meanwhile, seemingly unbeknownst to Lansdale, his severed hand has reanimated and begun malevolently to attack his enemies. It appears to kill a young coed (Annie McEnroe), with whom Lansdale has an affair, as well as a fellow faculty member (Bruce McGill), who Lansdale perceives as a sexual adversary. When his wife and daughter visit Lansdale, his weak grip on reality dissolves altogether as the hand appears to attack his wife. Police are summoned, discover the bodies of the young woman and teacher, and arrest the cartoonist. The final sequence finds Lansdale in a psychiatric hospital with a therapist (Viveca Lindfors) who attempts to cure him of his delusions. However, the disembodied limb once again appears and kills the therapist, leaving Lansdale alone, in psychotic laughter.

Stone's first two films historically can be assigned as manifestations of the modern era of the horror genre, whose point of origin, as Gregory Waller argues, lies with the 1968 release of George Romero's *Night of the Living Dead* and Roman Polanski's *Rosemary's Baby*. These films situated horror in everyday life and the milieu of contemporary America. They respond too to the breakdown of the family and the continuing debate over women's role in society and the "crisis of bourgeois patriarchy" of which Vivian Sobchack has written.[8] Stone also evokes the genre's collective memory by flaunting the horror form's generic inheritance. To an astute observer, *The Hand* clearly borrows the homicidal limbs of the German *Orlac's Haende* aka *The Hands of Orlac* (1924), its American remake *Mad Love* (1935) as well as the 1946 *The Beast With Five Fingers* in which a disattached hand appears to survive its amputation.[9] Stone's casting further indicates his acquaintance with the horror genre: Jonathan Frid, *Seizure*'s lead, is best known for his portrayal of the sympathetic vampire Barnabas Collins in the ABC-television Gothic soap opera *Dark Shadows;* Martine Beswick, the "Queen of Evil," was featured in several British Hammer films, most memorably *Doctor Jeckyll and Sister Hyde* (1971); and Michael Caine in 1980 portrayed the homicidal transsexual psychiatrist in Brian Da Palma's *Dressed To Kill*.

However, if the true subject, as Robin Wood has asserted, of the horror film is "the struggle for recognition of all that our civilization *re*presses and *op*presses," then Stone fails to satisfy this definition.[10] His narratives instead transform an ideological conflict into trivial exercises in perceptual sleight of hand that avoid any substantial consideration of what distinguishes normality from the "other." *Seizure* and *The Hand,* to borrow James Twitchells' distinctions, are works of terror rather than horror; their frissons are external and short-lived, not internal and long-lasting.[11] Their artificiality temporarily subverts little more than our state of well-being. The mere presentation of seemingly impossible activities is not by itself a radical endeavor. As Rosemary Jackson writes, fantastic texts subvert only if their dislocations truly disturb an audience.[12] When they do not, they produce only "phantom feelings" no more genuine than the vestigial sensations Jon Lansdale is told by his physician he will perceive emanating from his severed limb.

Oliver Stone is reported to have asserted that to be a successful horror director one must be a "visual sadist," something one could not accuse him of being in either of the films under examination. Although as the creator of the VA hospital sequences in *Born on the Fourth of July* (1990) and the reenactment of the assassinated president's autopsy in *JFK* (1991), he might well merit this attribution.[13] One might alternately then effectively assess *Seizure* and *The Hand* as instances of melodrama. For all the evidence of social criticism in Stone's work, the most consistent element of his narratives is their schematic characterization and neat division of mankind into distinct moral categories. Wherever you look in his films, as Pauline Kael writes of *Born On The Fourth of July,* you find "representative figures rather than people."[14] Divisions appear to be all too clear-cut in his thinking. "In melodrama," Michael Walker writes, "it is the world that is divided into good and evil, weak and strong, oppressed and oppressors. The hero of melodrama is himself undivided, 'whole,' free from tensions of choosing between conflicting loyalties, imperatives, and desires. The forces with which such a hero must fight are external: oppression, corruption, villainy in general, natural disasters." Furthermore, the characters in Stone's later explicitly social and political narratives are "whole" in the manner Walker describes—as, for example, the angelic warrior Elias and the death-worshipping Barnes in *Platoon* or the tantalizingly venal Gordon Gekko in *Wall Street.* The protagonists in *Seizure* and *The Hand*, however, typify yet another character type Walker sees as typical of melodrama: the "divided character"—individuals who are "trapped within ideologies which oblige them to behave in certain ways whilst denying them the possibility of either understanding why or freeing themselves."[15] Both Edmund Blackstone and Jon Lansdale are victims of narcissistic self-obsessions that in the former case allows him to choose his child's death over his own and in the latter leads him to exterminate any human obstacles in his path, either through his own hand (no pun intended) or by supernatural forces, depending upon one's reading of the narrative. If Edmund Blackstone has, in fact, willed the three demonic figures in *Seizure* into existence, then he appears unprepared to question what portion of his personality they express. Instead, he preoccupies himself with his own survival and that of the "intellectual fantasies," as his wife refers to them, that have been the substance of his writing career. Jon Lansdale, like Edmund, cannot balance his devotion to his wife with the love of his family. Rather than determine appropriate expressions of his rage, he sublimates it (or at least seems to do so) in the form of a homicidal limb.

Both protagonists are clearly victims of patriarchy. Their flimsy marriages reflect the disintegration of the once homogeneous family unit. In turn, the wives perceive their mates as possessive and manipulative, ready to place their existence and that of their work above all else. Gender relations in all of Stone's films are problematic. A number of the marriages are dysfunctional, like that of Barry and Ellen Champlain (Eric Bogosian and Ellen Greene) in *Talk Radio* (1989). In other cases women are idealized unrealistically, as in the case most egregiously of Maria (Elpidia Carrillo), Richard Boyle's (James Woods') madonna-like *anamorata* in *Salvador* (1986).[16] Stone admitted to interviewer Marc Cooper that his female characters are weak. However, his explanation of why this is so reeks of disingenuousness: "I have not done movies about women. I have always picked areas that involve extremist ideas that to date have involved men mostly . . . Though I do have women in my films and I happen to like the portrayals—Cindy Gibb as the nun in *Salvador*; Michelle Pfeiffer as the basic bimbo hanging around this Cuban gangster in Scarface. I know they're small roles, but I don't think any of them are inauthentic."[17] That Stone can consider both performances indistinguishably "authentic" leads one to wonder how distant his own thinking is from his flawed protagonists.

Stone's inability to comprehend how his female characters might lack authenticity is but one of many examples that support the relevance of Robin Wood's theory of the "incoherent text" to his work. Contradiction runs rampant in Stone's narratives, particularly as regards his use of the traditional figure of the charismatic, individualist hero. Wood argues that endemic to the contemporary American cinema is a lack of belief in this figure, coupled with an inability to relinquish it, because nothing exists to take its place.[18] Stone for his part wishes at one and the same time to privilege and pillage such figures. Richard Boyle in *Salvador* is both scumbag and social activist. In *JFK* Stone salvages the "one man-one gun" narrative of the Warren Commission but sanctifies the single investigatory conscience of Jim Garrison (Kevin Costner). Such patterns begin with *Seizure* and *The Hand,* particularly in regards to the protagonists' point of view. Edmund Blackstone and Jon Lansdale exist on the thin edge of sanity. While they both dominate and direct their stories, neither provides the audience with a dependable handle on the perplexing events that follow. In the case of *Seizure,* the three malevolent invaders may or may not be emanations of the writer's tormented consciousness. As Tim Lucas commented in one of the few perceptive reviews of *Seizure,* Stone offers us a "grab bag of reasons" for the invaders' behavior, thereby imposing an "overwhelming, consuming mystery over the entire picture."[19] *The Hand* is an even more egregious culprit because the indeterminacy of Jon Lansdale's point of view extends even to the use of contrasting film stocks.[20] Stone employs both black-and-white and color footage, the former during those sequences in which the appendage attacks and kills other characters. However, as the film progresses and grows even more out of control, this neat distinction collapses, most notably and annoyingly in the final sequence. The attack upon the psychiatrist, during which we, and Jon, observe the hand in full view and in *color,* abandons any resolution of the question of its agency. It is little more than a piece of cheap, last-minute fright show claptrap that has nothing to do with the preceding events. Jon's hysterical laughter in the final frame comes across as a cynical comment on the audiences' gullibility.

If the actions of Stone's films are terribly problematic, so, too, are their settings. To a considerable degree, Stone employs the melodramatic paradigm of the threatening urban and liberating pastoral environment. Both Edmund Blackstone and Jon Lansdale explicitly have abandoned the urban metropolis for a pastoral retreat in order better to support their artistic productivity. Their wives perceive those choices as inhibiting their behavior and abandoning them to perform the role of supportive helpmate and little else. The city, in turn, is portrayed as alienating and corrupting in most of Stone's films, an environment in which men lose their power and their function. These patterns appear later in Stone's

work as one associates the predominantly urban environments of
Wall Street, Talk Radio, the suburban and hospital sequences of
Born on the Fourth of July, and the governmental and legal locations *of JFK* with the nightmare of incipient fascism or the oppression of hegemonic control. However, there is an odd and
unsettling conflict that disrupts the familiar environmental paradigm in *Seizure* and *The Hand.* In both films, the horror is identified with, even emerges from, the pastoral surroundings. The three
invaders that attack Edmund's house seem literally to emerge from
the woods as they at first appear merely as swift flashes of movement glimpsed through the trees. Jon Lansdale's murderous limb
initially is severed in a pastoral location and emerges from it to
begin its homicidal trajectory. Whether this makes urban and pastoral environments equally threatening is an open question, but it
is clear that Stone both uses and subverts the melodramatic environmental paradigm.

Perhaps the chief cause of the incoherence of Stone's narratives
is his penchant for allegory, his separation of the world into a virtually Manichean dualism. To employ Jim Garrison's discourse,
when we enter Stone's universe, we are indeed through the looking glass, trapped in a realm where blacks and whites alone exist
and collide. Any time Stone addresses complex social and political
issues, he reduces the material to a war of conflicting moral points
of view that obfuscates much of their ideological content. As
Pauline Kael writes of *Platoon,* while Stone depicts modern warfare without flinching from all its physical and technological carnage, he nonetheless makes the struggle a personal, not a political
matter: "The film is about victimizing ourselves as well as others;
it doesn't deal with what the war is about—it's conceived strictly
in terms of what these American infantrymen go through."[21] Stone
himself corroborates Kael's critique; as he stated in a 1987 address
before the National Press Club: "We were destined to lose (Vietnam) because the war had no moral purpose, and it was fought
without any moral integrity. And we did lose because basically, as
a character in *Platoon* says, 'We were not the good guys anymore.'"[22] Stone's predilection for such simplification began with
his first two films. How striking that in *Seizure* the antagonists
should be an imperious woman accompanied by a foreign-accent-
ed dwarf and a silent, physically threatening black man. Each of
them is an "other" to the individuals they threaten and yet, as the
dwarf explains, the trio might in fact be emanations of the charac-

ters' venality; he speaks of his wrath having been "born inside your belly." However, just as soon as this notion is raised, it passes out of the narrative. The three antagonists deliver upon their promise of "darkness, damnation, and meaningless death," but their actions have no more rationale than those of the hand Jon Lansdale has lost. These narratives seem to exist alone for the purpose of recording the victimization of a set of unpleasant but by no means contemptible characters.

If coherence can be found in Stone's films, a considerable portion can be attributed to their religious discourse, an element often referred to by critics and scholars but rarely examined in any depth. Religious language and imagery would seem to be almost second nature to an artist who engages in moral allegory to the degree that Stone does. His works to date show a consistent pattern of martyrology (the deaths of Elias in *Platoon,* Barry Chaplain in *Talk Radio*, Jim Morrison in *The Doors*, and the President in *JFK*). It comes as no surprise that an individual who speaks of having served in Vietnam as a means of atonement; who considers the title of his first major film to refer at once to the country and the act of salvation, *Salvador*; who makes his protagonist, Richard Boyle, in that film the age of Christ (thirty-three years having been his life span) has an obsession with theology.

The ur-scene for that obsession is in *Seizure* and argues for this flawed film's centrality to Stone's work. What it may lack in cohesion, it makes up for in its profusion of undeveloped but potent imagery and ideas, a phenomenon few critics, with the exception of Tim Lucas, managed to notice at the time. In the scene Edmund Blackstone and his aged friend Serge (Roger DeKoven) attempt to understand who their oppressors are and why their intentions are so malign. Edmund refuses to accept that the trio might be supernatural in origin, especially the leader who he calls the "Queen of Evil." Serge, on the other hand, not only possesses an equanimity about their situation and their eventual fate but also an inquiring attitude regarding the nature and origin of their oppressors. He says to Edmund, "Maniacs, as you call them, have a reputation for telling the truth." He draws upon analogies from myth, both of Western and Third World origin, to explain why they, and in turn all evil, exist. Most interesting to him is the queen, who he associates with the Hindu goddess Kali, though he realizes it is difficult for westerners, like Edmund, to imagine "a mother contaminated by the dark principle." He also hypothesizes that she and her companions might be emanations of Edmund's subconscious, a proposition he rejects as much as that of their mythic substance. For Edmund, his oppressors are just that, intrusions upon his well-ordered, prosperous life of mysterious but natural origin. For Serge, they might not only be other than human but also act as triggers for an examination of the substance of human existence in all its forms. Later, when the time comes for Serge's death—he is decapitated by the silent black figure at the queen's command—he goes to his demise willingly and with a stoic acceptance. "I think death, true death is a companion, not an enemy, to life," he says. When the queen asks him if he believes in God, Serge replies, "I believe in myself and therefore I believe in him."

Serge is an unusual character in that Stone deliberately and unhysterically examines the nature and substance of human existence. His meditations on the profound duality of life, the conjunction of beauty and terror, birth and mortality possess a balance that one seeks in vain in the films that follow *Seizure*. Serge states early in the film, "We must learn that nature holds no account of our disasters." If nature is not at fault, then who or what is? Admittedly, there is a danger in essentializing nature and searching for resolutions to life's dilemmas in abstract, not social or political terms. Stone has variously attributed life's fatality and brutality to the United States government, the financial community, the military industrial complex, and the neo-Nazi underground, but the questions Serge raises speak to profound considerations, not the lapses of a fallible human order. Also, in that Stone is such a masculine-centered director, it is interesting that he expresses his fear of women in such a raw form throughout *Seizure*. He appears to worry so over women's empowerment that in later films he virtually dispenses with them altogether by treating them as Madonnas, bimbos, or valorized matriarchs of the nuclear family. Clearly, such issues of nature, gender, and power engage Stone's imagination, but the plaster saints and devils he has too often provided offer no coherent answers to the propositions raised at the start of his career in *Seizure*.

What then accounts for the power and popularity of Oliver Stone's films? One could cynically assert that the wheels of the culture industry have ground exceedingly well on his behalf. Or that he has often been at one with the *zeitgeist* of the Reagan and post-Reagan eras. Perhaps he is instead an exemplary manifestation of the paradoxical postmodernism which, as Linda Hutcheon

writes, engages in postures of "complicity and critique, of reflex-
ivity and historicity, that at once inscribes and subverts the conventions and ideologies of the dominant social forces of the
twentieth-century world." One could easily apply to him Anne Frieberg's clever parody of Dickens which Hutcheon quotes: "It was
conservative politics, it was subversive politics, it was the return
of tradition, it was the unmasking of patriarchy, it was the reasser-
tion of patriarchy."[23] Stone may not undo what Hutcheon, Frieberg,
and others feel needs to be undone, but he does know what needs
undoing. We are left with the unfortunate prospect that in answer
to the question of who is America's foremost director of socially
and politically conscious films, we must reply, as André Gide did
of Victor Hugo, "Oliver Stone, alas." And yet, perhaps Stone, like
many of us, is the victim of the politics of "false choices" which
E. J. Dionne Jr. argues in *Why Americans Hate Politics* is the cause
of the fragmentation of the American political system. Stone's work
is symptomatic of "the nation's split identity, which emphasizes
individual liberty and the importance of community."[24] He clearly
has a selective and overly romantic view of American history. As
Alexander Cockburn has written of the speech in *JFK* that equates
the American public with Hamlet and the slain president with a
"father leader," such rhetoric trades fact for fantasy: "The 'Hamlet' speech is an important one, for in its truly fascist yearning for
the 'father-leader' taken from the children-people by conspiracy, it
accurately catches the crippling nuttiness of what passes in many
radical circles for mature analysis: that virtue in government died
in Dallas and that a 'secret agenda' has perverted the national destiny ever since."[25] Adam Barker amplifies Cockburn's point from a
cinematic perspective by comparing Stone's film with three major
conspiracy thrillers of the 1970's: *The Parallax View* (1974), *The
Conversation* (1974), and *All The President's Men* (1976). While
the Woodward-Bernstein adaptation shares much with Stone, particularly the use of the "heroic quest" paradigm and visual opposi-
tions to highlight moral conflict, the other two films refuse to
engage in the kind of moral certainties that lead Stone to possess,
as Baker writes, "a remarkable naiveté about cinema's ability to
present 'the truth.'"[26] Conspiracy theories may just as easily obscure the already hazy events they purport to explicate.

This split identity or fissure within Stone brings to mind the
first of the few cameo appearances he has made in his own films.
It occurs in *The Hand.* The director briefly portrays a one-armed

street person who bumps into Jon Lansdale on his return from being equipped with a prosthetic limb. The two struggle momentarily, and when Landsdale leaves, a black-and-white point-of-view shot establishes the perspective of the severed limb that proceeds to attack the vagrant. The rest of the film leaves to the viewer whether the appendage acts independently or on Lansdale's behalf. One might then ask, to paraphrase Marianne Moore, is this an imaginary limb in a real alley or vice versa or neither? Perhaps that quandary represents the incoherence not only of Stone's horror films but of his whole career as well.

Notes

1. Timothy Corrigan, *A Cinema without Walls, Movies and Culture after Vietnam* (New Brunswick, N.J.: Rutgers Univ. Press, 1991), 105.

2. Marc Cooper, "Playboy Interview: Oliver Stone." *Playboy*, February 1988, 63. This comment seems more self-serving than accurate, for one would be hard put not to consider any of the following American films made between 1980–86, roughly the period of the production of *The Hand* and the release of *Salvador*, devoid of seriousness: *Raging Bull* (1980), *Ms. 45* (1980), *Blow Out* (1981), *Cutter's Way* (1981), *Reds* (1981), *Blade Runner* (1982), *Videodrome* (1982), *Dead Zone* (1983), *Zelig* (1983), *Under Fire* (1983), and *King of Comedy* (1983) to name a few.

3. *Seizure* is on Starmaker and *The Hand* on Warner Video.

4. This pattern may not be immediately clear. Certainly Jim Morrison of *The Doors* is a poet/songwriter and Barry Champlain of *Talk Radio* a free-form radio performer. However, one should not dismiss the arbitrage of *Wall Street* as uncreative activity (even if it can be accurately argued that it creates only profits for the few) or the voice-over narrative of *Platoon* as a fictionalized manifestation of Stone's own adolescent voice (Stone having admitted to the autobiographical thrust of the film), or the speechmaking and self-history–creating of Ron Kovic a creative aspect of *Born on the Fourth of July*, or the construction of an alternative conspiratorial narrative by Jim Garrison in *JFK*.

5. For discussion of this thematic dimension of Stone's films see Richard Combs, "Beating God to the Draw," *Sight and Sound* 56, no. 2 (Spring 1987): 136–38; J. Hoberman, "Freedom Now?", *Village Voice*, 20 December 1988, 83; Gary Indiana, "Being and Nothingness American Style," *Village Voice Film Special,* 31 December 1991, 17–18, 20.

6. Michael Walker, "Melodrama and the American Cinema," *Movie* 29/30 (1982): 2.

7. While one must grant the old saw about adaptation and the crucial

distinctions between fictional and cinematic modes of presentation, the differences between Brandel's novel and Stone's film are considerable and significant. First, the name of the central character in Brandel is Martin Trask, not Jon Lansdale. Also, his comic strip is not an imitation of the Robert E. Howard character, Conan, as was Mandro, perhaps a reflection of Stone's work at the time on the script of John Milius's film of the character (released in 1982). Instead he is a Third World male named Miguel and is published in the more or less countercultural weekly newspaper *The Village Voice*. Miguel is, Trask says, "an expression of my indignation and protest" with the "follies and contradictions of American life" (10). Second, the depiction of Trask's wife, Ruth, is far less misogynistic. Trask realizes how he has allowed her to sublimate her own life to his: "She had lived through me for too long, sharing my life, eager to learn from me and share my convictions, too, half of my 'we,' but never completely 'I,' until the demands of her own individuality had overwhelmed her" (19). He realized too the effect of their isolation in Vermont and sympathizes with his wife's desire for a move. Also, their daughter, Sophie, is more crucial to the novel than the film. In the latter she seems a mere appendage whereas for Trask being with her allows for "a feeling of companionship . . . that was easier than any other relationship in my life" (15). The accident in the film seems the expression of female rage against Lansdale, for the other driver is a woman and his own wife seems almost vengefully to veer to the opposite side of the road, only to be hit by a moving truck. There is no other woman in the novel's depiction of the accident and, in fact, the reason that his wife cannot properly signal is that prior to their leaving the house, Trask accidentally breaks the left indicator. The novel doesn't play such games as the film about the agency of the hand. Its existence is still in doubt, both Stone and Brandel making it, for the most part, an expression of the protagonist's rage. In fact, the conclusion of the novel is far more chilling than the film as it dispenses altogether with the psychiatrist and the sudden attack upon her. Instead, it reveals that Trask believes the hand to be "an instrument through which my submerged self could express itself" (282). He realizes that he may not have committed the crimes he is charged with (in particular, the murder of Stella because fellow teacher Brian Mellor is injured and not killed in the novel), but he is guilty of them nonetheless. By not making the character of Trask a raging misogynist and allowing the dramatic arc of the novel to proceed more methodically than Stone's screenplay, *The Lizard's Tail* is a subtle, chilling first-person narrative of a mind slowly losing touch with reality.

   8. Gregory Waller, "Introduction," in *American Horror: Essays in the Modern American Horror Film*, ed. Gregory Waller (Urbana: Univ. of Illinois Press, 1987), 2, 12.
   9. Other films that have included an ambulatory, murderous limb in-

clude two further remakes of *The Hands of Orlac*, one using the same title (1960) and the other called *Hands of a Stranger* (1967). Further examples are *Tormented* (1960), *Dr. Terror's House of Horrors* (1964), *Blood from the Mummy's Tomb* (1970), and *And Now the Screaming Starts* (1973).

10. Robin Wood, *Hollywood from Vietnam to Reagan* (New York: Columbia Univ. Press, 1986), 75.

11. Joseph Twitchell, *Dreadful Pleasures: An Anatomy of Modern Horror* (New York: Oxford Univ. Press, 1985), 10.

12. Rosemary Jackson, *Fantasy: The Literature of Subversion* (London: Methuen, 1981), 23.

13. Stanley Wiater, *Dark Visions: Conversations with the Masters of the Horror Film* (New York: Avon, 1991), 78.

14. Pauline Kael, *Movie Love* (New York: William Abrams, 1991), 250.

15. Walker, "Melodrama," 2, 23.

16. Another film that features the same actress, Elpidia Carrillo, in the role of Third-World Madonna who comes to the moral rescue of a confused masculine protagonist (Jack Nicholson) is Tony Richardson's *The Border* (1982). It too idealizes the Mexican woman while demeaning the protagonist's wife (Valerie Perrine) as an avaricious social-climbing virago.

17. Cooper, "Playboy Interview," 112.

18. Wood, *Hollywood*, 53.

19. Tim Lucas, *"Seizure," Cinefantastique* 4, no. 2 (1975): 33.

20. The use of contrasting film stocks occurs to an extreme in *JFK*. There, Stone employs fifteen different forms of film, everything from 35 millimeter Panavision stock to Super 8, 16 millimeter, and various television transmissions. The narrative also blends documentary footage with expertly rendered reconstructions, thereby blurring the line between fictional and nonfictional modes. For a staunch defense of the film and an astute reading of Stone's use of Eisensteinian montage techniques see Armond White, "JFK Blasts '90s Denial—And Stone Triumphs," *New York Sun,* 29 January–4 February 1992, 22.

21. Pauline Kael, *Hooked* (New York: E. P. Dutton, 1989), 252.

22. Oliver Stone, "We Were Not the Good Guys Anymore," *Massachusetts Review* 28, no. 3 (1988): 424.

23. Linda Hutcheon, *The Politics of Postmodernism* (London: Routledge, 1985), 11, 13.

24. E. J. Dionne Jr., *Why Americans Hate Politics* (New York: Simon & Schuster, 1991), 314.

25. Alexander Cockburn, "John and Oliver's Bogus Adventure," *Sight and Sound* 1, no. 10 (February 1992): 22–23.

26. Adam Baker, "Cries and Whispers," *Sight and Sound* 1, no. 10 (February 1992): 25.

Chapter 3

Salvador

Manifestations of Foreign Culture through Paradox in *Salvador*

John F. Stone

It has long been an axiom of assorted theorists that film has a special capacity for furnishing people with knowledge about how to perceive something new that was otherwise unknown.[1] The importance of this didactic function should not be misprized. In an age when a significant portion of the American public is vexed when asked to locate Mexico on a world map, it should be little wonder that many Americans claim they attend feature films with the intent to find out information about other people and places.[2]

At no time might this phenomenon be more significant than when a film offers information about a foreign land to an American film audience whose appetite has been whet by a series of recurrent headlines. Many foreign names and places make their way to the forefront of the American "current events psyche" propped up by little more than their recognition value. Lacking an understanding of the more significant historical forces that operate to make such names and places newsworthy, many Americans may view or understand these people and places as little more than the basis for an annoying cognitive itch. A tidy film narrative—providing a rich mosaic of a foreign culture and its operative forces—may serve as a most convenient and appreciable scratch. Hence, feature films of the last decade such as *Cry Freedom* (1987) or, more particularly, those that have dealt with U.S. complicity in Third World repressions such as *The Year of Living Dangerously* (1983), *The Killing Fields* (1984), or *Under Fire* (1983) function not only as vehicles for sociopolitical commentary but also as canvases for expositions of foreign culture.

Such is not to suggest that the on-screen manifestations of a particular land or its people are necessarily anything more than incidental by-products of a larger filmmaking agenda. *Salvador* (1986) would seem, for instance, at one level, to be primarily a chronicle of the adventures of real-life photojournalist Richard Boyle (James Woods)—depicted as a whore-chasing, booze-swilling, pill-popping, foulmouthed swindler—on his "last chance" mission to salvage his career on the margins of respectable journalism. At another level, the film seeks to establish the bane of American involvement in foreign affairs as Boyle leads the viewer through a series of re-creations of such well-publicized events as the atrocities of the right-wing death squads, the assassination of Archbishop Romero, and the brutal rape and murder of four American Catholic layworkers in civil-war-stricken El Salvador circa 1980–1981.[3] Nonetheless, springing from Boyle's manic adventures generally and the historical re-creations, specifically, is a distinct portrait of the Salvadoran people—a portrait that results from the centrifugal forces of a significant paradox.

Alienation and Anglocentrism

At one point, Boyle's equally odious sidekick Dr. Rock (James Belushi) remarks about the Salvadoran surroundings: "Everywhere I turn there are dogs screwing other dogs, pigs in the street, it's like Baltimore or something. . . ." More than just an illustration of the film's comedic undertones, this remark is a poignant tongue-in-cheek reminder of a litany of significant differences that separate life in the United States from El Salvador. For although they may be naive about the essence of a given foreign society, American filmgoers are themselves members of a culture earmarked by its ubiquitous information. As such, it is inevitable that they possess criterion assumptions about what elements are essential to and, in turn, most appropriately signify a particular foreign culture.

Gratifying such expectations with images of an uncivilized, agrestic world conjured up by Dr. Rock's remarks is a primitive but vital first step in reorienting viewers to the presence of on-screen culture that is different from his/her own. Rich floral backdrops and a soundtrack littered with the simple, major key rhythms of marimbas or a cascade of Spanish phonemes that roll off the tongues of native characters as easily as they elude the viewer are significant because they are the typical connections made with a

Central American locale. These are relatively innocuous signs that adhere to stereotypical associations likely derived from sources ranging from *National Geographic* to ads for tortilla chips and are credible because of their prevalence.

Beyond these stereotypical sops to the setting is a constellation of more deeply seeded assumptions about the Latin character that originated with what Charles Gibson has deemed the Black Legend.[4] The pejorative characterizations that are part and parcel of this legend—a legend that holds badness is inherent in the Spanish and their essential heirs—are reified in *Salvador* with varying degrees of both intensity and complexity. The languid shots of peasant women lazily washing clothes under the shade of the tree in a river, or the view of a voodoo pharmacist working on a concoction to cure Dr. Rock's diarrhea in this land of nondigestable ingestibles, romanticize the purity of this agrestic world but also pander to prepotent legends regarding this culture's perpetual rejection of progress. Similarly, the gaggle of "Tic-tac Monsters" [natives intoxicated on a cheap local drink] spend their days weaving in and out of oncoming traffic and begging for spare change. They drool as readily as they drink and seem out of control even to the debaucherous Boyle, who observes, "If you give them anything, you can't get rid of them." They are at once disgusting and manifestations of Anglocentric assumptions about the indolent, unhygienic, and intemperate nature of the Latin soul.[5]

These simple caricatures, while consonant with the themes of the Black Legend, are ancillary to a more dominant personality trait: a penchant for barbarous violence. This quality, long having been assumed to be part of the Latin character,[6] is reaffirmed throughout the film. In a shot framed by the confines of an armored car's gun slit, a young army lieutenant casually shoots a student in the forehead, stepping away quickly so as not to stain his neatly ironed pants. In masking this single two-second shot, the camera concentrates attention on the notably nonchalant nature of the assassination, signifying much about the routine nature of such an act. Minutes later another scene opens with a slow crane shot revealing hundreds of partially clothed corpses as a gruesome subtitle appears. To a viewer whose culture's obsession has been with where best to dispose of diapers and newspapers, "'El Playon' Dump Site for Death Squad Victims" borders on the tragically unfathomable.

If the single shot is the filmmaker's most distinctive unit for making a claim,[7] these shots are among the film's most crucial in synecdochically underscoring the operative brutality of this country. For while Boyle might be able to look over and casually dismiss the visage of charred and still-smoldering remains of a corpse as "just some guy," the viewer cannot. Such horrifying images not only transcend viewer experiences but are exponentially more traumatic because of what they suggest. These are a different people who are part of a culture well removed from the United States. This is a different universe because it is largely void of laws that are constitutional, criminal, or moral.

This most disturbing quality, initially, appeals to Boyle. He admiringly describes it as a place where "you can drive drunk and can get anyone killed for fifty bucks" and admiringly deems it "pig heaven." Yet, after standing at the shallow graves of four nuns and a Catholic layworker who were raped and then mercilessly shot in the face, even the indurate Boyle comes to recognize this is not merely a playground for his baser motivations. Laws that govern a culture are the baseline for still more significant cultural values—values that provide parameters for life by indicating what is right/ wrong, good/bad, normal/abnormal. These are crucial prescriptions that not only aid individuals in interpreting the world around them but guide individual behaviors essential to the larger process of living together.

In that vein, El Salvador seems to be void of the simple but vital conventions that bind traditional Western civilizations together. A land where an archbishop is openly assassinated while consecrating the host or suspected revolutionaries are grabbed off the street and beheaded is one where there appears no baseline for human decency. When Boyle bails a soon-to-be-executed Dr. Rock out of jail with an old television and bottle of Johnny Walker, or when he barters his way out of life-threatening confrontations by dipping into his cache of wrist watches, his actions suggest a world of selfish corruption, an interest in personal wealth not public service. More than that, these actions are symptomatic of a world where the value of human life has become wildly and catostrophically skewed. Are the essential pacts for a reasonable civilization even possible when life can be purchased for such a material pittance, when the price that separates life and death is so miniscule?

What is one left to conclude about an outwardly laconic and passive people prone to wild swings of heinous violence? Can these people be trusted? The death squad leader that invites Boyle to go for a midnight stroll is certainly operating with ulterior motives. But what about the duplicity of a cleric who uses a pulpit affiliated with peace and forgiveness to preach of war and revenge? For inasmuch as Archbishop Romero (Jose Carlos Ruiz) functions as the film's romantic icon of humanity in the battle against the repressive military/government, a papal figure who declares that "Christians are not afraid of combat" or speaks of the "legitimate right to insurrectional violence" he would seem more prepared to identify an enemy a heretic than offer him salvation. Such irony is lost on the throngs of Salvadoran peasants who flock to the church with an allegiance an Anglo mind assumes was reserved only for a seventeen-cent bottle of tequila. Fervent Catholicism here isn't a sign of an increased spirituality but rather of a lack of rationality and theological maturity.[8] Boyle hints at the incipience of this fealty to Catholic doctrine when he closes his confession flippantly observing, "Twelve 'Our Fathers' and ten 'Hail Marys'? That's it!? If I'd known this, I'd come, ya know, earlier, before thirty-two years."

Collectively, these cultural personifications are the by-products of a century-old social Darwinism that has undergirded Euro-American justifications of foreign expansion and intervention. This is a rational racism as this litany of attributes is quite dissonant with Anglo-American honesty, industriousness, temperance, frugality, and progress—ideals culled from the Puritan ethic. In a sense, this chauvinism is symptomatic of a severe form of ethnocentrism that results in a sort of "cultural evisceration"—separating those parts of the secondary culture that need reform. Americanization of these people and the effective transplant of our cultural traits are necessary and understood to be part of a leader of civilization on a mission.

Ultimately, this evisceration promotes fissures between the viewers' perceptions of the world in which they reside and the milieu chronicled on screen. The culture sketched here will be recognized as foreign. But beyond that, a deeper cognitive appreciation is developed by the series of events within the film narrative, events that fall well outside the viewer's expectations or experiences. In that vein, the remorseless acts of the death squads in *Salvador* not only propel the evolution in Boyle's character from, in the words of one film critic, "a sleazy operator to a sleazy operator with a conscience"[9] but also construct a vivid mosaic of a savage habitat that is unfamiliar to viewers. Indeed, the more macabre the on-screen actions, the more probable the cognitive separation between the civilized world of the viewer and the world chronicled on screen.

The Assimilation of Hegemonic Myth

"I think if Shakespeare had been alive today," observed *Salvador's* director/cowriter Oliver Stone, "he'd be writing about El Salvador because it's the stuff of history, the stuff of drama."[10] Such a remark is primarily promotional hyperbole. Likening the activities in El Salvador to the interests of, arguably, Western civilization's most acclaimed dramatist demands both a leap of faith and a disregard of many discrepancies. The remark, however, is instructive in that it suggests that a very important creative force in the film was prone to comprehend the events in El Salvador through a lens that was ground from western European traditions.

That Stone would, in turn, rely so readily on mythic constructs common to American culture in re-creating the historic events in El Salvador is hardly surprising. If a film's meaning must be constructed by the viewer,[11] playing to the subconscious, collective perceptions of an American audience specifically would seem to facilitate that process, much like employing a white narrator (even one as invidious as Boyle). And the decision to establish Boyle's romantic involvement with a beautiful Salvadoran peasant are as much concessions for enhancing the likelihood of the film's commercial success as they are bids to capture the facts of this "true story."[12]

Beyond that the mythic allusions function to form a collective understanding of the Salvadoran people in a dimension not yet hampered by other stereotypes. Vassiliou, Triandis, Vassiliou, and McGuire refer to "non-normative stereotypes" as those based not on the information derived from other sources (normative stereotypes) but as those that are purely projective in nature.[13] It is not uncommon, they theorize, for us to project stereotypes we have ourselves on foreign people with whom we have had no previous contact. Hence, to the extent that an American film audience shares a mythic understanding of themselves, these myths may be fodder for forming an interpretation of the Salvadoran people.

Major Max (Tony Plana), leader of the right-wing military, first appears in a scene that opens with a shot of a life-sized figure of

Christ on the crucifix. In working its way around the large candle-lit banquet room, the camera allows the viewer the presence of only wine, bread, and the twelve men who rise to volunteer when Max queries, "Who among you will rid me of this Romero?" In ceremoniously kissing the chosen assassin on the cheek, he signals the end of a confluence of mythic symbols, allegorically linking himself to Henry II and Judas and casting Archbishop Romero into a pool with other noteworthy Western martyrs. Soldiers salute Major Max by snapping their heels together and quickly putting their clenched fists across their chests, looking momentarily as though all they omitted was the "Heil Hitler"—actions quite consonant with the view of the Salvadoran Army goose-stepping into position to break up a public demonstration. This army may not inspire the same fear as the other historically unconscionable villains, but they do deserve the same moral indignation. While such metaphoric references make but fleeting appearances on screen, they are recurrent significations cued to emotions that are sunk deep within the viewer, significations that couple the disdain for a truly mythic enemy with a yet undefined villain operating in a different place and time.

But if, on the whole, the right wing is best understood in macrocultural manifestations of evil common to the myths of Western civilization generally, the laudable peasant/rebel faction is registered in more microcultural symbols, symbols more richly reminiscent of American populism. Interestingly, most of the narrative and filmic manifestations of the populist myth in American feature films have been typically associated with the genre of American film comedy.[14] *Salvador* doesn't owe much to the ideograms emergent from this genre. It is as far removed from these films as Boyle's persona is from the cracker-barrel Yankee philosophers that were the protagonists of the genre. Nonetheless, *Salvador's* obedience to a doctrine that harkens back to the original foundations of democracy and celebrates such concepts as rural small-town life, honest labor, a nostalgic taste for traditional values, the importance of the individual, and antielitism, is as vivid as the loud floral patterns on Boyle's shirt. Edward Shils' claim that populism is the belief that "the will of the people as such is supreme over every other standard"[15] is parroted nearly verbatim by the commander of the rebel forces, Captain Marti (Miguel Ehrenberg), when he declares that "the will of the people or the march of history cannot be changed, not even by the Norteamericanos."

At best, Marti's remarks are loosely veiled references to a historic creed. When the camera turns to the rebel camp or their push for liberation, *Salvador* becomes awash in a more definitive populism-based, metaphorically induced nostalgia. From children intently studying a blackboard to an old woman cooking on an open fire, from children playing in a pile of straw to a pair of young rebels passionately engaged in a kiss, the images meld as a large, sonorous chorus passionately sings the refrains of a Salvadoran folk song. Five of the final shots in the sequence, focusing on men, women, and mother and father with children are taken from a perspective such that they are understood to be still photographs. As such, they function as portraits, samplings of everyday life that affirm the significance of the family unit in this subculture.[16]

These filmic sequences aren't simply a crude ethnographic sketch, they are part of a panache of sights and sounds that are requisite to a populist nirvana, leaving little room to debate amongst most Anglophiles that such events deserve to be Kodak moments. Similarly, when a pair of rebels struggles to push their flag up against a stiff breeze in a shot so iconicized that Iwo Jima seems as though it were yesterday, or when a fife and drum swells on the soundtrack as the rebel cavalry charges into battle, there is a plucking at heartstrings closely tethered to the American legacy. These are not Salvadoran peasant/rebels; they are spirited colleagues fraternally united with American forefathers in a cruciblic quest for self-determination.

This is not a "debunking" but a "rebunking" of Salvadoran history. The symbolic exposition of the events in El Salvador in terms that are such a significant part of the viewer's conscious and unconscious is syndromic of a cultural hegemony. Latin history isn't denied per se as much as it is made subservient to and then assimilated by another. In that vein, the strident symbols of assorted American myth suggest an inherent affinity between the essential desires and experiences between two cultures that were to heretofore assumed to be none too similar. The suggestion here isn't that life in El Salvador is identical to life fifteen hundred miles due north. The stereotypes indicating otherwise are too virulent for that. Rather, it is that these two apparently very different worlds are linked by certain "cultural universals"—core events and behaviors that are shared by two civilizations that have much in common.

Messages of the Paradox

What results from the radial tugs of a paradox that invites the viewer, on the one hand, to understand the on-screen world and its inhabitants as radically different from his/her own and, on the other hand, to understand the values and aspirations of the Salvadoran citizen as quite similar to those firmly ensconced in the American character?

In one sense, there is simple encouragement to approach El Salvador as a synecdochial sign. For while the promotion of certain normative stereotypes competes with and contradicts other depictions consonant with American myth, both processes—stereotyping and mythification—invite a lack of cognitive discretion. Viewers are not to understand the Salvadoran people as distinct or to appreciate the nuances of their culture. In pandering to the stereotypes gleaned from other sources within the viewer's culture, the actions of the Salvadoran characters become little more than part of a complex of behaviors common to people "south of the border." In much the same way, the reliance on American myth in presenting Salvadoran life, generally, and re-creating recent events, specifically, functionally sequesters Salvadoran history to the unremarkable category. Viewers are issued a carte blanche invitation to understand the events in El Salvador not in terms of that country's unique linear chronology but rather in the same terms and with the same filters and rational processes that guide the interpretations of their own native world.

Ultimately, both cognitive processes encourage a homogenization. Salvadorans simply become manifestations of a more convenient genus known as "Latin Americans." Historian George Shuster writes,

> Of course we will agree that in an important sense there are no such people. Anyone who has spent some time in Rio or São Paulo knows that the breadth of the tropics fills every cranny of men's souls and that there is an entirely different world from Chile stretched out like an eel from one cluster of mountains to another. Nevertheless, one can from another point of view conclude there is a Latin American. He [sic] is aware that his [sic] culture is of European origin and still in significant ways is pre-western.[17]

Shuster's observation is significant because it suggests that current conceptualizations of the Latin world are pinned to assumptions that these cultures are not as civilized as their counterparts in the Western Hemisphere. Such is not to suggest that El Salvador is hopelessly backwater. Quite the contrary. The images that link the Salvadoran struggle for independence with the patriotic endeavors that are part and parcel of this country's early history attest that El Salvador is, potentially, a United States in a nascent stage.

Not that there is an expectation to fulfill such promise. The barbarism that seems to be so much a part of that world is not a function of cultural maturity, a symptom of a culture still developing. Clearly, the beheading of a suspected revolutionary is hardly akin to a shoot-out in the American West. The latter was an indicator of a nation taming itself; the former is an echo of the essential character of a foreign people. When U.S. Ambassador Tom Kelly (Michael Murphy) threatens a subordinate to comply or be prepared to "count fucking spears in Rhodanda," there is the suggestion of a global cultural hierarchy. In so doing, El Salvador is deemed not as primitive as some but, at best, should be prepared to join other cultures near the median. In that vein, the superiority of the United States is defined by its ubiquitous involvement, not only in El Salvador but in civilizations even more primitive.

This point is what would seem to be at the core of the film's indictment of U.S. foreign policy. The romantic populist depictions of the peasant/rebels underscore the purity of a world that essentially has been violated by U.S. presence.[18] Left to their own affairs, would El Salvador be so stricken with civil strife? Stone's enthymeme suggests not.

Such a claim, however, is undermined by the same stereotypes and myths that bring it to life. The film's perpetuation of Latin stereotypes, coupled with the then current headlines about the civil war in Nicaragua, confirm the legacy that the Latin American approach to government is either strongman rule or revolution and discontentment.[19] As such, El Salvador emerges as just another "banana republic" in the midst of ongoing upheaval. The United States' involvement, military and otherwise, can be construed as an effort to actively stop this vicious cycle, ultimately saving the Salvadoran citizen from him/herself. The significance of such intervention is essentially confirmed with a number of narrative sequences chronicling the need for missionary welfare assistance, some with images seemingly less than a generation removed from a UNICEF ad.

Historian Arthur Schlesinger has observed that "the American identity will never be fixed and final, it will always be in the making."[20] Interestingly, the same would not seem to be the case of American manifestation of foreign identities. The propensity to accommodate previous perceptions of foreign people and their rituals, foibles, motivations, aspirations, and tendencies suggests a cognitive immutability. Continuing to play to such perceptions has its inevitable consequences. To the extent that symbol sharing amongst members is key to a culture reinforcing similarity in perceptions, sharing myths promotes a homogeneity in understanding the nature of one's own culture. As such, *Salvador's* reliance on stereotypes of Latin culture and constructs which are common to Western myths generally and American myths specifically affirms the significance of those elements for future interpretations. Hence, it can be of little surprise that our popular manifestations of foreign lands and people may, ultimately, tell us more about our culture than theirs.

Acknowledgment

The research for this project was made possible in part by a grant from the Harold Leonard Memorial Fellowship for Film Study.

Notes

1. Ron Johnson and Jan Bone, *Understanding the Film* (Skokie, Ill: National Textbook, 1990), 19.
2. Phillip Palmgreen, Patsy L. Cook, Jerry G. Harvill, and David M. Helm, "The Motivational Framework of Moviegoing: Uses and Avoidances of Theatrical Films," in *Current Research in Film: Audiences, Economics, and Law*, vol. IV, ed. Bruce A. Austin (Norwood, N.J.: Ablex, 1988), 1–23.
3. Cowriter/director Oliver Stone has remarked that the film was produced by John Daly of Hemdale Studios in England because he "was able to view *Salvador* with a little more irony than the American financiers, who saw it as an attack on America, as opposed to an attack on American foreign policy." See Gerald Percy, "The Ballad of a Haunted Soldier," *Macleans*, 30 March 1987, 61.
4. Charles Gibson, *The Black Legend: Anti-Spanish Attitudes in the Old World and the New* (New York: Knopf, 1971).

5. For a synopsis of the assumptions associated with the Black Legend and Latin Americans, see John J. Johnson, *Latin America in Caricature* (Austin: Univ. of Texas Press, 1980), 10–12.

6. Allen Woll does a very thorough job of developing just this claim in his work, *The Latin Image in American Film,* revised ed. (Los Angeles: UCLA Latin Center Publications, 1980).

7. See David Cook, A *History of Narrative Film* (New York: W. W. Norton, 1981), 17.

8. Johnson and Bone, *Understanding*, 11.

9. Paul Attanasio, "Bold, Vivid, *Salvador*," rev. of *Salvador, Washington Post,* 4 April 1986, sec. D, p. ll.

10. Stone made this remark in an interview with Sally Hibbin, printed in "Blood From Stone," *Films and Filming,* January 1987, 18.

11. The claim that the viewer is the most significant party in constructing the narrative is most thoroughly set forth in David Bordwell, *Narration in the Fiction Film* (Madison: Univ. of Wisconsin Press, 1985), 31–35.

12. Interestingly, when the movie was first screened by North American film audiences, many remarked that they weren't sure whether the film was a comedy or a serious political movie. Interestingly, Stone declared, in an interview with Pat McGilligan, that this was because viewers were "stuck in an Anglo frame of mind." See *Film Comment,* January/February 1987, 19.

13. Vasso Vassiliou, Harry Triandis, George Vassiliou, and Howard McGuire, "Interpersonal Contact and Stereotyping," in *The Analysis of Subjective Culture*, ed. Harry Triandis (New York: Wiley, 1972).

14. See, for instance, Wes D. Gehring, "Populist Comedy," in *Handbook of American Film Genres,* ed. Wes D. Gehring (New York: Greenwood Press, 1988), 124–41.

15. Edward A. Shils, *The Torment of Secrecy* (London: William Heinemann, 1956), 98.

16. Musello argues that family photographs are "samplings of everyday life that give a positive accounting of important and appropriate family subjects." See "Family Photography," in *Images of Information,* ed. James Wagner (Beverly Hills: Sage, 1979), 101–18.

17. George Shuster, "United States Cultures and Its Capacity for Collaboration," in *Cultural Factors in Inter-American Relations,* ed. Samuel Shapiro (Notre Dame: Univ. of Notre Dame Press, 1968), 256.

18. For a discussion of how Latin American cultures are frequently portrayed as virgin females, see Johnson and Bone, *Understanding*, 72–116.

19. Johnson and Bone, *Understanding*, 10.

20. Arthur M. Schlesinger, *The Disuniting of America: Reflections on a Multicultural Society* (Memphis: Whittle Direct Books, 1991), 82.

Salvador: Oliver Stone and the Center of Indifference

Richard Keenan

British philosopher and essayist Thomas Carlyle concludes "The Center of Indifference," a chapter from his masterwork of social criticism, *Sartor Resartus* (1834), with the following: "This . . . was the *Center of Indifference* I had now reached; through which whoso travels from the Negative Pole to the Positive must necessarily pass."[1] Carlyle's pause at the center of indifference is the nadir of his own spiritual journey, one that, if successfully completed, will have taken him from the intense negativism toward a dominant civilization that seemed hopelessly corrupt and materialistic to a profound redemption found in the light of truth that enables salvation. Although published more than a century ago, Carlyle's excursion of the soul offers an appropriate and pertinent parallel to Oliver Stone's *Salvador* (1986), the first of the important political films written and directed by Stone in the '80s and '90s. *Salvador* is a political commentary, a cinematic analysis of a senseless, bloody, protracted war by a director whose anger at the toll of human suffering is clearly evident. The abdication of the United States during the Reagan presidency from its moral/ethical responsibility, its blindness to the ramifications of any issue in which "Communism" is a factor, the refusal and/or halfhearted effort of the major television networks to practice thorough and honest investigative journalism during the Central American crisis, and the resultant public complacency are the combined stimulants of Stone's indignation. Just as Carlyle's masterwork was intended as a clarion call to awaken the public from moral and ethical torpor, *Salvador* was the first in a series of films that would have very much the same intention, films Stone intended to arouse moral indignation and to provoke questions rather than provide answers.

Media critics and political pundits took a different view of Stone's motives, particularly in the wake of *JFK* (1991), and its reawakening of the conspiracy controversy that had quieted considerably in the more than twenty years following the Warren Commission's controversial report on the Kennedy assassination. Although widely celebrated in 1986 for the intense psychological realism of men at war and the truth of jungle combat depicted in the much-praised *Platoon*, the film which brought him Academy Awards for Best Picture and Best Director of 1986, Stone was now widely vilified. *JFK* reopened emotional wounds and brought a reassessment, and with it a media reaction that charged him with irresponsible speculation and willful distortion of history. *Salvador*, which had not been widely distributed when it was initially released, has been subsequently reexamined and offered by the detractors of *JFK* as collateral and supporting evidence of the director's general indifference to truth, particularly when a more creative option beckons. The guerrilla army on horseback charging the military installation at the battle of Santa Ana, for example, is a purely romantic touch on Stone's part; it has no historical foundation.[2] The distinctions regarding responsibilities of implied documentary and the freedom traditionally inherent in fictional treatment are often intentionally (and necessarily) blurred. But Stone is hardly indifferent to truth; in *Salvador* he treats it in a larger context that, although admittedly more nebulous, is paradoxically more substantive, more akin, perhaps, to a Joycean epiphany, or a "moment of grace" such as one finds in the work of Flannery O'Connor. The protagonist discovers it in process, when events and actions suddenly reveal new depths of personal awareness and altered perspective. The film audience, Stone hopes, will follow suit. For Stone the truth in *Salvador* is relative rather than absolute, subsumed within the film's primary theme of salvation,[3] a salvation from the soul-deadening effects of complacency and indifference.

Stone's protagonist in *Salvador* is based on a true character, photojournalist Richard Boyle (James Woods). Boyle also cowrote, with Stone, the script for the film. Like many of Stone's "heroes," he is alternately engaging and repugnant. The Boyle rendered by Woods' stellar performance is, from our first encounter with him on screen, at the aforementioned center of indifference: life at a low ebb. The opening credits are superimposed on newsreel footage of crowds of Salvadorans running and stumbling on the steps of the main cathedral as they are fired on by the military. The drama of the scene is heightened by the machine-gun quality of the percussion in George Delerue's score. The credits completed, the news footage focuses and clarifies to a television screen. The voice-over narration of a network commentator intones statistics of the dead and missing. Cut to Boyle, slowly awakening in a rundown, third-rate San Francisco apartment, indifferent to the plight of the Salvadorans and equally oblivious to the other sounds that surround him: a wailing infant, a landlord pounding on the door and threatening eviction, an Italian wife screaming in anger and hopeless frustration. Life for Boyle is a tiresome burden, hardly worth getting up for. Even from that point, things go rapidly downhill. In short order, he is evicted, his wife leaves him, and he is arrested for speeding, largely because the police officer's routine records check revealed forty-three unpaid traffic violations, four of which had become warrants, and an invalid driving license. But Boyle has the uncanny ability to escape trouble as easily as he evades responsibility. Bailed out by his friend and alter ego Dr. Rock (James Belushi), an equally down-on-his-luck, unemployed disc jockey, he decides to head for El Salvador, enticing Rock with stories of abundant booze, dope, and virgins at a discount. Following an abrupt transition from a San Francisco freeway to mid-Central America, they are shown approaching the border (passports and other such legal niceties apparently matters of negligible concern along the way). Before ten minutes of film time have elapsed, we know that Richard Boyle is a chronic liar, a grifter who borrows money he has no intention of repaying, and a general all-round sleaze. By his own self-definition, he is a "weasel." Although a photojournalist who has written a book about the war in Vietnam and has reported from Beirut and Cambodia, his war experiences have more than wearied him; they have calcified his soul. Unlike his fellow photojournalist John Cassady (John Savage), for whom the experience of documenting on film the destruction of El Salvador is a combination of a war junkie "high" and an all-consuming moral mission, the fourth estate is hardly a noble calling for Boyle; it is simply what he does to continue reflexively his shallow existence. His return to El Salvador, however, initiates his redemption to what he does well and why he does it. It is a journey through a contemporary hell that will shift him from the moral stasis at the center of indifference toward the redeeming of, in Stone's terms, "his identity, his integrity, and his soul."[4]

The real Richard Boyle (who coauthored the script with Stone) had worked as a stringer in Central America, making seven trips to El Salvador between 1979 and 1982, to cover the events following the overthrow of strongman dictator General Oscar Humberto Romero in October 1980 and the establishment of a five-man ruling junta, sustained in power largely by support from the United States government. From the beginning, the junta and the general populace were caught in a political and literal crossfire. Terrorist groups from the leftist FMLN (Farabundo Martí National Liberation Front) fought to establish a Marxist government and to elicit support from Cuba, while right-wing terrorists fought with even greater tenacity to return control of the government and the country at large to the established propertied interests and to the Salvadoran military which supported them.

Boyle kept a diary in which he recorded his first-hand observations of the Salvadoran upheaval in 1980–81, particularly the two most shocking events that brought international recognition of the horror of the Salvadoran civil war: the assassination of the Roman Catholic Archbishop of the capital city of San Salvador, Oscar Arnulfo Romero (no relation to the deposed dictator), and the rape/murder of three Catholic nuns and a social worker.[5] All five murders were presumably the work of right-wing "death squads," extensions of the ARENA (Alianza Republicana Nacionalista) party, led by Roberto D'Aubuisson.

Stone's treatment of this collection of murders offers the most memorable and intensely harrowing scenes of the film. The sequence depicting the murder of Archbishop Romero in particular has significant implications related to its shocking dramatic effect. Religion, the once powerful force for stability, sacrosanct and venerated, has become at best neutralized, at worst, inverted and distorted. An earlier scene depicts the conclusion of an all-male formal dinner, presided over by Major Maximilian Casanova, known as "Major Max" (Tony Plana). Major Max, the character based on right-wing ARENA party leader D'Aubuisson, speaks compellingly to a rapt audience of loyal Myrmidons of the threat of Romero, whom he identifies as a Communist desecrator of true religion. Holding aloft a single bullet destined for the archbishop, Major Max calls for one of his disciples to step forward and accept the

honor of purging this desecration. Instantly the younger men arise
from the table, their faces brightly intent with the seriousness of
the mission. Major Max, clearly (albeit melodramatically) savor-
ing his power and control, points emphatically and selects a young,
uniformed volunteer. The ritual presentation of the bullet is followed by a kiss on both cheeks. "You will," Major Max intones
with barely contained enthusiasm, "become famous!" The scene is,
as Pauline Kael has noted, "a posh, sinister version of "The Last
Supper,"[6] complete with a form of the Judas kiss.

At the end of the room, behind Major Max, is a life-size crucifix suspended before a pleated, red drapery. The figure of Christ is
a cold, metallic, silvered sculpture, more property than piety, and
related, in an implied visual sense, to the ritual assassin's bullet.
Despite the traditional position of abject suffering, the figure has
an adamantine, rigid quality, markedly distant from the suffering
for humankind it is supposed to suggest. Several scenes later, Archbishop Romero officiates at a mass in the main cathedral of the
capital city of San Salvador. In his homily he firmly denounces
the terrorists and calls for the end of the violence that plagues his
country. Moving among the faithful as the archbishop's words echo
through the cathedral, armed soldiers scan the crowd as if anticipating trouble. Behind Romero is another life-size crucifix; this
one, however, with the flesh tones and lifelike qualities so dramatically characteristic of the Catholic churches of Central and South
America. Designed to suggest graphically and vividly the suffering
of Christ for mankind, it serves only as mute witness of the failure
of established religion in El Salvador to exert any real power for
good. As he moves beneath the crucifix along the row of kneeling
communicants, dispensing the communion wafer that celebrates the
participation of the faithful in the body and blood of their "savior," Romero stops before a hesitant communicant, Major Max's
volunteer assassin. Abruptly and defiantly the young assassin spits
on the communion wafer, and with a curse fires his pistol point
blank at Romero. The crowd disperses amid gunfire and pandemo-
nium, as the military make selective arrests.

Stone's juxtaposition of Major Max's communal dinner and the
violation of the communion meal of the faithful that is the core of
the Catholic mass dramatically underscore for the outside world,
which rapidly is settling for limited duration news highlights and
authoritative sound bites, the degree to which El Salvador has become a contemporary hell.

Religion, the mainstay of peace, is helpless and impotent in this moral crisis, and Stone endeavors to make that abundantly clear. God is either dead or indifferent. In addition to his somewhat freely rendered depiction of the Romero murder,[7] and the murder and rape of the social worker and the nuns,[8] events that actually occurred, Stone adds additional scenes to further underscore the loss of this spiritual mainstay. Particularly notable is the scene in which Boyle goes to confession in what he avows to Maria (Elpedia Carrillo), the Salvadoran woman with whom he has fallen in love, is a sincere effort to become a good Catholic, something she stubbornly requires him to do if she is to accept the offer of marriage that will enable her to leave the country as the wife of an American citizen. That he is lying to her about obtaining a divorce from his previous wife notwithstanding, Boyle makes a genuinely honest confession and personal character assessment in one of the best scenes in the picture. Explaining himself and his motivation to the priest, he seemingly discovers, in the process of openly examining who and what he is, that he genuinely loves Maria. "If God gave me this woman," he reasons, "then there must be a God." The reasoning proves both prophetic and ironic; at the conclusion of the film, Maria is taken from him by the U.S. Immigration Service, presumably never to be seen again. Another scene offers an even greater sense of despair. After a frightening encounter with thugs from one of Major Max's death squads, Boyle drives one of the several adolescent boys who have become part of the omnipresent entourage that surrounds Boyle and Maria to the foothills of the mountains, where the boy, clearly no more than fourteen, intends to join the guerrillas. As he moves off into the night, Boyle calls after him the conventional farewell: "Vaya con Dios" ("Go with God"). Momentarily, the boy turns and replies in world-weary tones of quiet conviction, "In my country, Amigo, there is no more God!" It is a brief but surprisingly poignant scene, this child in his American football jersey, the number "15" on the back, moving off into darkness, deprived of both God and childhood. The spiritual darkness which the boy also enters is painfully apparent when Boyle encounters him once more, this time as a young guerrilla, participating in the summary execution (a bullet through the back of the head) of captured government troops immediately following the short-lived victory of FLMN forces over the small military outpost at Santa Ana. Boyle shouts as he is forcibly led away, "You have become just like them!"

At the core of this moral vacuum is the American political cum diplomatic presence, more inept than sinister, and simplistically developed in Stone's depiction. In contrast to the Salvadoran characters, the American military and diplomatic corps is represented by one-dimensional caricatures, personalities who illustrate Stone's annoyance, but reflect little if any balanced political perception or searching commentary. Jack Morgan (Colby Chester), the State Department/CIA presence, is an Ivy League parody of a career diplomat. Colonel Bentley Hyde (Will Macmillan) seems directly derived from the memorable General Jack D. Ripper (complete with phallic cigar) in Stanley Kubrick's *Dr. Strangelove* (1964). Pauline Axelrod (Valerie Wildman), the media glamour puss whose political insight is limited to the incumbency line and "what the networks are gonna want," suggests something of the vapidity of the news personality played by William Hurt in James L. Brooks's *Broadcast News* (1987).

The character of Dr. Rock appears at first a similarly shallow caricature, but he's far more important than the others. Rock is an integral part of the process of Boyle's shift from the center of indifference. He is one of two comrades with whom Boyle has a close relationship, two polar opposites who are Boyle's contending alter egos. This protagonist/alter ego pattern is one that Stone would use in subsequent films: the conflicting influences of Barnes and Elias, for example, on Chris Taylor in *Platoon*, and the similar divided effect of Gordon Gekko and Carl Fox on Bud Fox in *Wall Street* (1987). Rock is that part of Boyle's personality and recent past that is '60s and '70s burnout, having chosen anesthetic over action. Disheveled, dirty, alternately obnoxious and comically engaging, James Belushi's performance as Rock draws heavily on his brother John's in *National Lampoon's Animal House* (1978). As the political situation in *Salvador* gradually worsens, Rock sinks deeper into degradation. Although he ultimately recovers, he is at one point on his way to becoming a "Tic-tac Monster," begging in outdoor cafes, an addict to cheap "white lightning" pot-still alcohol called "tic-tac" in local parlance, and widely available at seventeen cents a bottle.

The opposite pull on Boyle is John Cassady, the dedicated photojournalist whose hero is Robert Capa, known for his dramatic photographs of the Spanish Civil War. Capa's most famous photograph captures a soldier falling backward, seemingly suspended in midair as he is struck by the bullet that takes his life. Cassady's reference to Capa offers an ominous foreshadowing. For Cassady, Capa came closest to capturing the elusive moment of truth, the inexplicable blend of heroism, futility, sorrow, and sacrifice that somehow transcends the political issues that set war's destructive process in motion. Stone based the character of John Cassady on John Hoagland, a *Newsweek* photographer killed in El Salvador.[9] It is Cassady, unremittingly dedicated to his calling, who introduces Boyle to the horrors of El Playon, the expansive human landfill of victims of right-wing death squads. It is Boyle and Cassady together who run through the streets of Santa Ana, photographing the battle as the guerrillas attack, are briefly victorious, but are soon repelled by an eleventh-hour restoration of U.S. military aid to the Salvadoran army. Cassady, strafed by an American plane, dies in battle, as did his hero Robert Capa, killed in 1954 covering the fighting in Indochina. He dies holding his position to get the ultimate photograph, the effort that for him is apparently worth life itself. His last words to Boyle, in whose arms he dies, are spoken with his boyish enthusiasm intact: "I got the shot."

Determined to get Maria and the children safely out of the country and to get Cassady's film to New York, Boyle completes his gradual character transition and now undertakes the first purely unselfish action we have seen. Although unsuccessful, the attempt to save Maria and the children and to see Cassady's film published are actions which validate his existence and effect his redemption. In their exodus from El Salvador, they survive detection of Maria's forged passport and being brutalized by Salvadoran border guards, only to be stopped on a bus in southern Texas by the American Immigration and Naturalization Service (INS). In his juxtaposition of the Salvadoran border guards and the INS, Stone offers an interesting parallel. The INS police are second-generation hispanics, superficially polite and trimly and consistently uniformed. On the surface they are unlike their Salvadoran correlative, who are more suggestive of a biker gang than a governmental law enforcement unit. The burly, unshaven officer in charge at the Salvadoran border, for example, wears dark glases, a boot camp fatigue cap, and an Oakland Raiders T-shirt. But the INS, for all their military professionalism, are no less indifferent to the plight of human suffering. They are separated from their Salvadoran counterparts by little more than a thin veneer of political stability. As Maria is taken away from Boyle to be deported and never seen again, Boyle, in handcuffs, cries out in the vast stretches of

Texas desert, "You don't know what it's like there!" The arresting officers are deaf to his entreaties, but if the film has worked, the audience is not. It, too, will have shifted from the center of indifference. Questions will be asked, facile answers discarded, and Stone will have achieved his purpose.

Notes

1. *English Prose of the Victorian Era,* ed. Charles F. Harrold and William Templeman (New York: Oxford Univ. Press, 1938), 127.

2. Stone: "We knew the horseback scene wasn't accurate, but we went with it because essentially we were romantics and we just wanted a charge on horseback. Also, at that time, in 1981, the feeling was that the guerrillas had no chance against the greater weapons of the government, and, to some extent, that was symbolized by the scene of horses against tanks." Gary Crowdus, "Personal Struggles and Political Issues: An Interview with Oliver Stone," *Cineaste* 16, no. 3 (1988): 18.

3. "When asked in an interview if the title might have been a mistake in selling the film to U.S. audiences, Stone replied: 'Some folks assumed it was a documentary or a purely political film and stayed clear. . . . I did plan to call it *South of the Border* at one point but *Salvador* to me meant both the country and Salvation.'" See Richard Combs, "Beating God to the Draw: *Salvador* and *Platoon,*" *Sight and Sound* 56 (Spring 1987): 137.

4. "In an interview after the release of *Wall Street* (1987), Stone commented on the character of his protagonists. What films such as *Salvador*, *Platoon* and *Wall Street* have in common, according to Stone, is "the story of an individual in a struggle with his identity, his integrity, and his soul. In many of [my] movies, the character's soul is stolen from him, lost, and in some cases he gets it back at the end." Combs, "Beating," 138.

5. Frank Beaver, *Oliver Stone: Wakeup Cinema* (New York: Twayne, 1994), 68–69.

6. Pauline Kael, "Pig Heaven," *the New Yorker,* 28 July 1986, 79.

7. "Salvador Archbishop Assassinated by Sniper While Officiating at Mass," *New York Times*, 25 March 1980, 1.

8. "Bodies of Four American Women Are Found in El Salvador," *New York Times,* 5 December 1980, sec. A, p. 3.

9. Jack Kroll, "Hell at Close Range: El Salvador's Nightmare," *Newsweek*, 17 March 1986, 80.

Chapter 4

Platoon

The Colonialist Subtext in *Platoon*

Clyde Taylor

Platoon manages a few significant ruptures with Hollywood's past portrayal of the Vietnam War, fewer yet with its classical hold on American myth and storytelling practices. It bows, however, to familiar limits of discourse in its deployment of black troops.

True to the revisionary trend in black imagery, the blacks in *Platoon* are shifted from the token status of *Apocalypse Now,* from the background where the Vietnamese are either victims of atrocities or vigorously fight back, but short of the foreground, rather under it, off its center. They occupy a second tier where they are deployed as shadows deepening the moral conflict between Elias and Barnes for Charlie Taylor's soul, an archetypal Western male narrative discourse that reverberates *The Man Who Shot Liberty Valance, Billy Budd* and, most classically, *Paradise Lost.* The precepts of Elias and Barnes are echoed on this lower frequency by the examples of two black foot soldiers, King and Junior.

King eases Charlie into the tent of the smoke-heads, Elias's perch, where the values of communal, antipatriarchal sharing are celebrated, where head-tightened men dance together to "Track of My Tears." Junior lays miserably in the tent of the whiskey-heads where Barnes hangs out, sour with sadistic, macho male self-testing and Junior's jingoistic rants against whites. Like Elias and Barnes, their names signify—"King" matched with nobility (savage?) and generosity, qualities he shares with his namesake, America's most charismatic moral figure of those times. "Junior" signifies a stage of moral minority and immaturity. It also signifies his derivativeness.

These black shadows register with a difference that relates to

109

their unoriginality and dependence, the reduction of their being to appendages of the moral principles. In Lawrence Kohlberg's five-stage schema of moral development, King and Junior rest at stages stepped down from those of Elias and Barnes. King is actually more of a father figure to Charlie than Elias; but deprived of the moral authority that neither the film nor its primary audience will grant him, his characterization tips toward the familiar role of black male mammy to innocent white youth. A Nigger Jim who protectingly advises, "Come back to the foxhole, Chuck, honey." Where Barnes' negativity is an abstract, militaristic dehumanization, Junior's is a reversion to childhood and primitivism. Where Elias's affirmation is an activist, apocalyptic salvationism, King's is a brotherly accommodationism.

These shadow qualities don't come out of nowhere. King is a convention, a soulful, down-home, church-mothered brother. But the genealogy of Junior's persona, once decoded, is even more classical. He is, on top, the black nationalist of Hollywood fabrication, most visible in black exploitation movies, negative, petty, whining, unfair, and dramatically ineffectual. The negative stereotyping in *Platoon* that angers black vets is mostly located in Junior. He sleeps on guard, causing casualties and blaming Charlie. Though he shadows Barnes in negativity, the two are not allies, as shown in the battle scene where he malingers until Barnes shouts, "Get up, Nigger, or I'll shoot you." Minutes later he wheels in fearful flight, smack into a tree, knocking himself out.

These are throwback bits from the golden age of Hollywood, the humorous reflex actions of grotesques like Stepin Fetchit and Willie Best. The origin in old-time coon stereotypes is masked here (nobody laughed in two audiences) by the violent terror of the battle scenes. Their lineage traverses Hollywood Sambo figures to classical Western portraits of the African as otherness, a negation, idolatrous and superstitious in relation to "real knowledge" which grants whites and their perceptions priority.

Under his contemporary trappings, Junior is an infidel from the evergreen colonialist scenario who literally lacks faith, is outside the faith, and displays infidelity or disloyalty to the accepted knowledge and creed that both Barnes and Elias share. His tree-collision is another of those instances in Western cinema where the character-destiny of the infidel, his just reward, is death or defeat by his own self-destructive action, thereby confirming the power and infallibility of the true faith more convincingly than punishment at the hands of the faithful.

A dilemma weakly faced by Stone in dealing with the war's color politics is that actually many more black troops than whites felt they had little real stake in the war, as I discovered while researching *Vietnam and Black America*.[1] They therefore had more complex reasons for taking on less moral responsibility for their conduct than indicated in the portrayals of King and Junior. The film's reference for this complex, anticolonialist rage and anguish, is expressed in a black pride movement, a symbol of racial identity. Black Panther units, mutinies, officer-fragging, and shoot-outs with white units, is the parodistic mask of Junior's antics.

Viewed from the vantage point of this underground black subtext, *Platoon* cannot escape the paradigm of the colonialist warrior narrative. This myth patiently awaits any competitive male drama peopled interracially—cops in the ghetto, basketball—but particularly those texts where white men fight nonwhites with faithful and unfaithful nonwhite helpers. *Platoon*'s unsuccessful confrontations with the limits of this discourse loses ground at two heavily defended positions of its paradigm, the foregrounding of the white hero and the question of political violence.

What kind of rupture would have been made if Charlie had been cast as black, subject to the doubts and questions troubling many black troops? We should recall here that even Charlie has his black alter ego. But instead of occupying the foreground, this new recruit cowers behind him until emboldened by Charlie's courageous actions. While Charlie is medevac helicoptered with honorably earned wounds, his black shadow stabs himself in the leg to get off the front line.

But if Charlie were black, his blowing away of Barnes would have burst the repressive limits of colonialist mythmaking, challenged the nervousness in American movie culture about black political violence, and released the unspeakable text of anticolonialist violence. A revealing double standard in this colonialist discourse is made clear by noting what is allowable in *Platoon*, compared to *A Soldier's Story,* where all the principals are black. When Charlie survives his killing of Barnes, both physically and psychologically—Billy Budd killing Claggart—an intriguing break is made with order-must-be-preserved traditions. But when a black infantryman in *A Soldier's Story* kills a black sergeant as fascist as Barnes, the film's text condemns him—another black militant made an example of. The black lieutenant pronounces the approved moral judgment: Who gave you the right to decide who could be black? When the real question, unless black is other than human,

might be whether Sarge and his lethal self-hate had a right to survive.

The simplest key to the depiction of blacks in *Platoon,* as in
the tradition, is that they are made attractive or repulsive on the
strength of their acceptance of Western preeminence and values—
the good nigger/bad nigger schema of characterization. As Ngugi
points out for colonialist literature, "The reader's sympathies are
guided in such a way as to make him identify with Africans
collaborating with colonialism and to make him distance himself from those offering political and military resistance to colonialism."[2] Significantly, King and Junior never confront each
other, as these types often do in colonialist movies. If they had,
what could they fight about except whether to risk their lives for
white interests?

Because it must deal with the colonial complex and its bottom-
line take on race and power, *Platoon* puts into perspective the current revision of black imagery in American films, reminiscent of
the "Negro interest" phenomenon of 1949–50. Like most of these
revisionist portrayals, it elevates the sympathy and humanity of
blacks to a semicolonial limbo, not so far as to break the limits of
dependency, but far enough to separate them from Third World
people, gaining visibility as terrorist baddies. To make this last
point, *Platoon* pictures Mannings, a black soldier, mutilated by the
Vietnamese.

As an ultimate illumination, "We were at war with ourselves"
is an easy, consumable, almost obligatory thematic sentiment to
sound on Vietnam, no different from a dozen other Hollywood films
or network soliloquies. It sounds an echo as hollow as the suspect moral pronouncement of *A Soldier's Story.* How can Americans find resolution to their war with themselves so long as they
continue to repress, through myth, ideological masks, and atavistic
stereotypes, their much more violent war upon others that is its
projection?

Notes

1. *Vietnam and Black America: An Anthology of Protest and
Resistance,* ed. Clyde Taylor (Garden City, N.Y.: Doubleday/Anchor,
1973).

2. Ngugi wa Thiongo, *Decolonizing the Mind* (Portsmouth, N.H.:
Heinemann, 1986), 92.

Oliver Stone's Journey to Myth-Country: *Platoon* and the Cultural History of Adventure

Donald Whaley

To understand Oliver Stone's *Platoon*, it is necessary to understand that film's relationship to the cultural history of adventure. Paul Zweig has examined that history.[1]

Zweig, in *The Adventurer*, argues that adventure was central to ancient cultures. "The tales of Greek mythology are filled with episodes of high adventure," he writes. "In fact, the raw material of mythologies throughout the world seems largely to be made up of perilous journeys, encounters with inhuman monsters, ordeals of loneliness and hunger, descents into the underworld." According to Zweig, the adventurer in the ancient world took two forms: "human heroes who venture into myth-countries at the risk of their lives" and "the shaman plunging mentally into his trance voyage to the spirit world." What ancient cultures valued, Zweig argues, were the "tales of the world beyond men" adventurers brought back from their journeys, tales considered to enlarge human knowledge.[2]

Zweig chronicles a change in Western culture between the sixteenth and eighteenth centuries. The Enlightenment destroyed belief, crucial for adventure mythology, in "an objectively magical world" and substituted the idea of a world governed by natural law. Knowledge was now to be gained not by the adventurer's journey but by science. The rise of the Protestant ethic meant that work replaced adventure as the central value of Western culture. The Protestant ethic also insisted that human beings engage in "due and regular conduct" enforced by law, morality, and conscience. Adventure came to be seen as at worst "a sinful action to be exorcized by prayer" and at best as frivolous, a subject fit for "a second-rate literature, appropriate for pulp magazines and low-grade movies."[3]

In the nineteenth century, Zweig argues, a group of "rare modern writers" began to reject "our domestically inclined culture" and to create "a new adventure myth." This new myth saw Western culture—with that culture's insistence on "due and regular conduct," on obedience to law and conscience—as a prison from which adventure offered escape. According to Zweig, the new adventure literature—for example, Melville's *Moby Dick* or Conrad's *Heart of Darkness* or *Lord Jim*—dramatized "dark emotions." "Adventure becomes an act of revolt," Zweig writes, and "adventurers of the nineteenth century will be rebels and criminals."[4]

The philosopher of this new adventure myth, Zweig says, was Nietzsche, who despised "the modern ideal of domesticity." Nietzsche saw in the universe no rational order of the kind described by the Enlightenment and no natural moral order of the kind assumed by the Protestant ethic. Instead Nietzsche saw a chaos in which human beings struggled to impose their sense of meaning on one another. Zweig argues that Nietzsche "presents his Overman as an adventurer, questing for an order of experience beyond domestic categories, 'beyond good and evil.'"[5]

Zweig contends that the new adventure myth developed in the nineteenth century was carried forward in the twentieth century by Norman Mailer.[6] It is possible to read Mailer's essay "The White Negro" as a statement of that myth. In his essay Mailer portrays American society as a totalitarian society where "one is jailed in the prison air of other people's habits." Mailer's heroes are white hipsters, "urban adventurers." The urban adventurer is "a rebel," "a frontiersman in the Wild West of American night life" who has set out on that "uncharted journey with the rebellious imperatives of the self."[7]

But Zweig also saw a change in the adventure myth in the twentieth century. Explorers had mapped the world. There existed no more unknown lands to which adventurers could travel. Increasingly, Zweig argued, the adventurer's voyage became "a voyage into the depths of the psyche." Twentieth-century adventurers, in a way similar to the ancient shaman, took "interior voyages" into "interior space." Twentieth-century adventure literature saw drugs as a way of inducing this interior voyage. Zweig cites, for example, Carlos Castaneda's tales of drug experiences that Castaneda had under the guidance of Don Juan, an "Indian sage."[8]

"Adventure stories," Zweig wrote, "transpose our dalliance with risk into a sustained vision." As a freshman at Yale, Oliver Stone became a convert to the "sustained vision" offered by adventure stories. As Stone has written:

> At Yale I saw myself as a product, an East Coast socioeconomic product, and I wanted to break out of the mold. I felt squeezed, suffocated. I remember reading *Lord Jim* by Joseph Conrad and becoming enchanted by it. Conrad's world was exotic and lush. He was a purveyor of the darker side. He understood that there were various layers of human behavior. *Lord Jim* pulled me, the exotic smell of the Orient pulled me.[10]

Stone dropped out of Yale, taught school in Vietnam, sailed the Pacific with the merchant marine, then returned to Vietnam as a combat soldier.[11] He came to view himself as an adventurer and his life as an adventurer's journey. Describing an LSD trip that he experienced shortly after returning home from Vietnam, Stone said, "I had this image that my life would be a series of islands that I would visit. And I thought of Ulysses, the Greek sailor, who goes from island to island and has this series of adventures and challenges."[12] Like Carlos Castaneda, Stone has used drugs in a kind of spiritual quest (the name of Stone's production company, Ixtlan Productions, comes from the title of Castaneda's *Journey to Ixtlan*); Stone has participated in Indian peyote ceremonies and has taken ayahuasca with members of a religious cult in Brazil.[13] Stone has argued that the "director should be a kind of Shaman," and Stone's friend, Richard Rutowski, sees Stone as "a Shamanistic film director" who uses his films as "an exploration of what's going on inside him."[14]

In *Platoon* Stone explores his Vietnam experience. The film, set in Vietnam in 1967, tells the story of Chris Taylor, a character based on Stone. Taylor has dropped out of college, joined the army, and has been assigned to an infantry company operating along the Cambodian border. He experiences a patrol in the jungle, a night ambush in which he is wounded, an interlude in base camp. It becomes clear that Taylor's platoon is split between what Stone described as "on the one hand, the lifers, the juicers, and the moron white element (part Southern, part rural)," and on the other hand, the "heads," "the hippie, dope smoking, black, and progressive white element."[15] Barnes, a cruel, ruthless, tyrannical sergeant who ignores rules of civilized warfare and makes up his own rules, leads the juicers. Elias, a sergeant who deals kindly with his men, tries to teach them everything they need to know to survive and fights within rules of civilized warfare, leads the heads, the group Taylor joins. After the platoon discovers a North Vietnamese Army (NVA) bunker-and-tunnel complex, where three members of the platoon are killed by an unseen enemy, the men move into a nearby village where enemy troops have been sighted. The platoon finds no NVA troops, but discovers a weapons cache. Enraged by the deaths of his men and frustrated because he can't find the enemy, Barnes interrogates the village chief. Unsatisfied with the chief's answers, Barnes murders the chief's wife and threatens to kill the chief's daughter. Elias fights with Barnes, stops the killing, and, back at base camp, brings charges against Barnes. Shortly after, the captain orders the platoon back into the bunker complex. During a resulting firefight between Americans and NVA troops, Barnes deliberately shoots Elias and leaves him for dead. As helicopters evacuate American troops, Elias reappears, running into the landing zone from the jungle. Taylor, Barnes, and the other Americans watch as NVA troops gun down Elias. Taylor suspects Barnes is responsible for Elias's death and tries to incite the other heads to take revenge. The Americans fight a climatic night battle against the NVA in which the American perimeter is overrun and the American commander calls for an air strike on his own position. As the battle rages, Taylor and Barnes confront each other. Barnes is about to kill Taylor when the air strike arrives. Both men are left unconscious. The morning after, Taylor, wounded, regains consciousness and finds Barnes, also wounded. Taylor takes revenge by shooting Barnes. The film ends as a helicopter evacuates Taylor, with other wounded, from the battlefield.

Stone drew on the classic story of the adventurer's journey for the narrative structure of *Platoon*. Joseph Campbell, in *The Hero with a Thousand Faces*, has called the story of the adventurer's journey a "monomyth," a story told in various forms in many different cultures, a story that always follows the same pattern:

A hero ventures forth from the world of common day into a region of supernatural wonder: fabulous forces are there encoun-

tered and a decisive victory is won: the hero comes back from
this mysterious adventure with the power to bestow boons on his
fellow man.[16]

According to Campbell, versions of this monomyth include the story of the crucifixion and resurrection of Christ; various tales involving a knight who sets out on a quest; and the story of the visit
by Aeneas to the underworld, the land of the dead, to consult his
dead father and learn the future. The victory achieved may be the
gaining of wisdom (as in the story of the Buddha's enlightenment),
the killing of a tyrannical father figure (as in the story of Oedipus), or sexual union with a woman (which Campbell also views
as Oedipal: for Campbell, this union represents the hero mastering
life and taking his father's place).

Platoon makes reference to several versions of the adventurer's
journey. Chris's name identifies Chris with Christ, as does a verbal
exchange that occurs when King, a black soldier, introduces Chris
to the heads. Rhah, one of the heads, calls Chris "Taylor." "This
ain't Taylor," King corrects Rhah. "Taylor been shot. This man is
Chris. He been resurrected." King also calls Chris a "crusader,"
bringing to mind the knight's quest. When Chris is on night ambush, we see over his shoulder a giant stone Buddha, calling to
mind the story of the Buddha's enlightenment.

Two versions of the adventurer's journey, the trip to the underworld and the story of Oedipus, play especially important roles in
Platoon. The film opens with a group of soldiers, including Taylor, emerging from a military transport plane that has just landed.
The first thing the soldiers see are body bags filled with corpses.
This scene establishes the metaphor of Vietnam as the land of the
dead into which Taylor has descended ("What are you doing in the
underworld, Taylor?" Rhah asks later in the film). In the film's
final scene, Taylor ascends in a helicopter, leaving the underworld
of Vietnam and beginning his return to the surface, bringing back
the boon to his fellow human beings; he promises to return home
to build and to teach what he knows. The idea of Vietnam as the
underworld was part of Stone's thinking from the earliest conception of *Platoon*. Stone has said, "The basis of *Platoon* was hatched
somewhere in the aftermath of the war, in New York in December
1969."[17] In that month Stone began writing *Break*, a screenplay that
dealt with his Vietnam experience. James Riordan has pointed out

that *Break* "contains the roots of many projects that Stone would create later, especially *Platoon*. The script is filled with the characters who would form the heart of *Platoon*—Rhah, King, Bunny, Lehner, Barnes, and Elias. . . ."[18] In *Break* a Pharaoh god holds the lead character, Anthony Darnell, prisoner in the Egyptian underworld.[19] References to the Egyptian underworld survive in *Platoon*. Rhah's name calls to mind Ra, the Egyptian sun god. Taylor wears an ankh symbol around his neck at the end of the film. Barnes and Rhah wear kerchiefs that resemble ancient Egyptian headdress.

But the underworld in *Platoon* also calls to mind the Greek underworld visited by Aeneas. Edith Hamilton has described the regions of that underworld. One region was where "the wicked" resided, "ruled over by stern Rhadamanthus," a region that corresponds to the lifers' hootch, ruled over by the tyrannical Barnes, in *Platoon*. Another region of the underworld was the Elysian Fields, where "everything was delightful . . . , an abode of peace and happiness. Here dwelt the great and good dead, heroes, poets, priests, and all who had made men remember them by helping others."[20] That region corresponds in the film to the heads' bunker, where Elias, who helps his men, resides, and where the men experience ecstasy, getting high and dancing together.

Stone also had Oedipus in mind from the earliest conception of *Platoon*. Riordan reports that while working on *Break,* Stone was "listening incessantly to Jim Morrison; dropping acid, playing "The End" over and over, thinking about Vietnam."[21] "The End," a song written by Morrison, lead singer for the Doors, is about a son who kills his father and sleeps with his mother. Morrison had been inspired to write it by reading about Oedipus in Nietzsche's *The Birth of Tragedy*.[22] In *Break* Anthony's mother enters a blue bus ("The End" contains the line "meet me in the back of the blue bus"). Anthony peeks into the back window of the bus and sees his mother naked. Later Anthony, as Riordan describes it, "has sex with one of his mother's friends whom the narrative explains could, in her relationship to Anthony, be the same as his mother."[23] *Platoon* keeps the Oedipal theme that Stone developed in *Break* but transforms the Oedipal scenario from sleeping with the mother to killing the father. Chris says at the end of *Platoon* that he is a child of "two fathers," Barnes and Elias. The decisive victory won by Chris is his killing the tyrannical father figure, Barnes.

Stone also drew on adventure literature for the characters in *Platoon*. One source was *The Iliad*. Barnes was Achilles, Stone has written, and Elias was Hector: "Two gods. Two different views of the war. The angry Achilles versus the conscience-stricken Hector fighting for a lost cause on the dusty plains of Troy."[24] Stone has also acknowledged *Moby Dick* as a source. Barnes, he wrote, was "the Captain Ahab of the platoon"[25] (a point made in a voice-over in the film when Chris says, "Barnes was the eye of our rage, our Captain Ahab"). Like Ahab, Barnes is a man pursuing an elusive quarry, a man intent on revenge.

Stone has cited Jim Morrison as a source for Elias.[26] Morrison is a figure connected with the new adventure myth developed in the nineteenth and twentieth centuries. Morrison's favorite philosopher was Nietzsche.[27] Morrison regarded himself as a shaman whose performances were "an attempt to communicate, to involve many people in a private world of thought," and, as Morrison's biographer has written, "Aware of a shaman's relationship to his inner world via peyote, and Castaneda's experience with Don Juan, Jim ingested psychedelics."[28] Morrison's biographer has also written that "Jim wanted to be like a shooting star; now you see him, now you don't, but for that brief moment he burns as the brightest star in the galaxy."[29] As Elias watches the night sky in *Platoon* a shooting star appears, a symbol that associates Elias with Morrison.

Stone has said that Morrison "was a god for me, a Dionysian figure."[30] Elias is also a Dionysian figure. Edith Hamilton has written of Dionysus, "The God of Wine could be kind and beneficent. He could also be cruel. . . ." She continued, "The worship of Dionysus was centered in these two ideas so far apart—of freedom and ecstatic joy and of savage brutality." Elias displays both sides of Dionysus's character. He is kind to his men and brings Chris joy by introducing Chris to marijuana. But Elias is also a brutal warrior. At one point he runs through the jungle, gunning down NVA soldiers as he goes, an action that calls to mind the Bacchantes, followers of Dionysus, who, according to Hamilton, were said to run through the forest and rip to pieces wild beasts they encountered.[31]

In one scene in *Platoon*, Elias and Chris are looking at the night sky. Elias says, "I love this place at night. The stars. There's no right or wrong in 'em. They're just there." Elias is articulating Nietzsche's view of the universe, a view in which there is no natural moral order, a universe in which human beings with differing views of the world struggle to impose their sense of meaning on

others, as Barnes and Elias struggle to impose their differing views
of the war on each other. It is appropriate for Elias to articulate
that view since Jim Morrison was a follower of Nietzsche and
Nietzsche considered himself a disciple of Dionysus.[32]

Dionysus is also the Greek god of resurrection. That fact accounts both for the seeming resurrection of Elias—he is apparently
killed by Barnes but reappears to be killed again by the NVA—
and for the association of Elias with Christ. Barnes calls Elias "a
water walker" and Sergeant O'Neill says that Elias "thinks he's
Jesus fucking Christ." In Elias's death scene, as Elias is hit by
NVA bullets he throws his arms apart in a crucifixion posture. Even
that scene seems to have been inspired by adventure literature. In
Conrad's *Lord Jim,* a novel that Stone says he closely associates
with his Vietnam experience, a brave warrior, Dain Waris, was shot
to death by a gang led by the evil Brown, a character who, like
Barnes in *Platoon,* was motivated by desire for revenge. As Dain
Waris was hit by the fatal bullet, a witness "saw him fling his arms
wide open before he fell."[33]

The vision found in *Platoon* is the vision offered by the new
adventure myth developed in the nineteenth and twentieth centuries. In the new adventure myth the adventurer was a rebel or criminal. *Platoon* begins with an act of rebellion. Chris has dropped
out of college, refusing to play the role expected of him. In Vietnam he is attracted to the dark side of life. He admires Barnes in
the beginning. Chris shares Barnes's rage at the deaths of members of the platoon in the NVA bunker complex. When the platoon
moves into the Vietnamese village, Chris in his anger fires his M-
16 at a one-legged Vietnamese man, forcing the man to dance. But
Chris pulls back from his anger and stops other members of the
platoon from raping village girls. Chris is still bound by traditional morality, symbolized in the film by his siding with Elias in the
civil war within the platoon. In the end, however, Chris becomes
not only a rebel, but a criminal, refusing to let the law deal with
Barnes and murdering Barnes in an act of vengeance.

Like other twentieth-century adventure stories, Chris's journey
to Vietnam is a journey into his own psyche, a voyage of self-
discovery. If Chris is Oedipus, what Chris discovers about himself
as he takes revenge on Barnes is the same thing Oedipus discovered when Oedipus sought the murderer of King Laius. As the
prophet Teiresias told Oedipus, "You are yourself the murderer you
seek."[34] Chris is Barnes, a point the film makes when Rhah says,

"The only thing that can kill Barnes is Barnes." Chris discovers the evil within himself.

Campbell argues that whatever the version of the adventure story, the hero undergoes a spiritual rebirth. Stone has described the spiritual rebirth that Chris goes through in the film and that Stone himself went through in Vietnam. Chris, Stone's alter ego, is

> forced to act—to take responsibility and a moral stand. And in the process grow to a manhood I'd never dreamed I'd have to go to. To a place where in order to go on existing I'd have to shed the innocence and accept the evil the Homeric gods had thrown into the world. To be both good and evil. To move from this East Coast social product to a more visceral manhood, where I finally felt the war not in my head, but in my gut and soul.[35]

At the end of *Platoon*, Chris has escaped from the prison of law and conscience and transcended into Nietzche's "order of experience beyond domestic categories, 'beyond good and evil.'" Norman Mailer, in "The White Negro," has described such an order of experience. Mailer explained the philosophy of Hip, which he said had no interest "in judging human nature, from a set of standards conceived a priori to the experience, standards inherited from the past." From "the view of character implicit in Hip," he continued,

> men are not seen as good or bad (that they are good and bad is taken for granted) but rather each man is glimpsed as a collection of possibilities, some more possible than others . . . and some humans are considered more capable than others of reaching more possibilities within themselves in less time, provided, and this is the dynamic, provided the particular character can swing at the right time. . . .
>
> Character being thus seen as perpetually ambivalent and dynamic enters into an absolute relativity where there are no truths other than the isolated truths of what each observer feels at each instance of his existence.[36]

Stone had Mailer's philosophy in mind at the end of *Platoon*. In a voice-over in the final scene, Chris says, "The war is over for me now. But it will always be there for the rest of my days, as I'm sure Elias will be, fighting with Barnes for what Rhah called possession of my soul." At the end of *Platoon* Chris is both good and bad, his character "perpetually ambivalent and dynamic" in the way Mailer described. Chris's internal struggle is not only between good and evil, it is between idealism and real life. Barnes says in the film, "I am reality. There's what oughta be, and there's what is. Elias was full of shit. Elias was a crusader." Stone has described that internal struggle in words that echo Mailer's: "Idealism versus real life, the absolutist strain versus the relativist strain. And the absolute man generally goes nuts, as Nietzsche said. You have to learn to swing."[37]

Commentators on *Platoon* have dealt with that film either in the context of Vietnam War movies or in the context of Oliver Stone's other films. But *Platoon* should be dealt with in another context as well—the cultural history of adventure. *Platoon* stands—with the writings of Norman Mailer, the performances of the Doors, and the drug narratives of Carlos Castaneda—as an important expression of the adventure myth in the late twentieth century.

Notes

1. Paul Zweig, *The Adventurer* (New York: Basic Books, 1974).

2. Zweig, *Adventurer*, 6, vii.

3. Zweig, *Adventurer*, 114, 101, 16, 9.

4. Zweig, *Adventurer*, viii, 15, 17, 187.

5. Zweig, *Adventurer*, 209, 17.

6. Zweig calls Mailer's *The Naked and the Dead* "probably our last nineteenth-century novel," *Adventurer*, 249.

7. Norman Mailer, "The White Negro," in *The Sixties Papers: Documents of a Rebellious Decade*, ed. Judith Clavir Albert and Stewart Edward Albert (New York: Praeger, 1984), 95–97.

8. Zweig, *Adventurer*, 227, 247.

9. Zweig, *Adventurer*, 4.

10. Quoted in James Riordan, *Stone: The Controversies, Excesses, and Exploits of a Radical Filmmaker* (New York: Hyperion, 1995), 32–33.

11. Riordan, *Stone*, 33–41.

12. Quoted in Riordan, *Stone*, 92.

13. Riordan, *Stone*, 107, 321, 429–30.

14. Riordan, *Stone*, 321, 416, 514.

15. Oliver Stone, "One from the Heart," *American Film*, January–February 1987, 19.

16. Joseph Campbell, *The Hero with a Thousand Faces*, 52nd ed., Bollingen Ser. 17 (Princeton, N.J.: Princeton Univ. Press, 1968), 30.

17. Stone, "Heart," 17.

18. Riordan, *Stone*, 68.

19. A summary of *Break* may be found in Riordan, *Stone*, 525–27.

20. Edith Hamilton, *Mythology: Timeless Tales of God and Heroes* (1940; New York: Meridian, 1989), 228.

21. Riordan, *Stone*, 67.

22. Jerry Hopkins and Danny Sugarman, *No One Here Gets Out Alive* (New York: Warner Books, 1995), 98.

23. Riordan, *Stone*, 526.

24. Stone, "Heart," 19.

25. Stone, "Heart," 18.

26. Stone, "Heart," 18; Riordan, *Stone*, 54.

27. Sugarman, foreword to *No One*, xiii.

28. Hopkins and Sugarman, *No One*, 158; Sugarman, foreword to *No One*, xi, xiv.

29. Sugarman, foreword to *No One*, xvii.

30. Quoted in Susan Mackey-Kallis, *Oliver Stone's America: "Dreaming the Myth Outward"* (Boulder, Colo.: Westview Press, 1996), 93.

31. Hamilton, *Mythology*, 56, 57.

32. Zweig, *Adventurer*, 220.

33. Joseph Conrad, *Lord Jim* (1900; New York: Bantam, 1981), 263.

34. Hamilton, *Mythology*, 259.

35. Stone, "Heart," 19.

36. Mailer, "White Negro," 99–100.

37. Quoted in Mackey-Kallis, *Stone's America*, 27. Stone has cited Mailer as an influence on the unpublished novel Stone wrote while in college. See Riordan, *Stone*, 39.

Chapter 5

Wall Street

Wall Street: The Commodification of Perception

Jack Boozer Jr.

> The richest 1 percent of this country owns half our country's wealth—
> five trillion dollars. One-third of that comes from hard work, two-
> thirds comes from inheritance, interest on interest accumulating.
> You've got 90 percent of the American public out there with little
> or no net worth.
>
> —Gordon Gekko, *Wall Street*

On one level, *Wall Street* (1987) is a realistic parody, a dig at
the world of corporate raiders in 1985. But Gordon Gekko (Michael Douglas) is such a magician of speculative deal-making that
he clearly demonstrates the appeal of this high-finance gamesman-
ship. Gekko's attraction, therefore, is both disdained and indulged
in a way that suggests a blank or ironic parody. More than this,
the story of Gekko and his seductive power serves as a metaphor,
a new version of the American dream. The impossible romantic
longing of a Great Gatsby (*G.G.*) in Fitzgerald's time has become
Gordon Gekko's tyrannical lust for financial adventurism and power in the era of Reagan-Bush. Nick Carraway's ironic view of Gatsby's misguided but hopeful vision of the 1920s becomes the
panderism of a Bud Fox (Charlie Sheen) groveling after a master
profit-taker in the 1980s. Unlike Gatsby, who at least dreams of a
future, Gekko sells the future into debt for cash returns *now*. Gatsby's attainment of wealth for a personal idealism becomes Gekko's
worship of the almighty dollar for its own sake. Idealism has been
reduced to the raw omnivore of monetary power.

The movie audience of the late 1980s, which has followed business news such as the spectacular $25.07 billion leveraged buyout of America's nineteenth largest conglomerate, RJR Nabisco,[1] would have to feel that an exaggeration of financial audacity was hardly possible. Reality defies fiction, not to mention the monetary imagination of the average citizen. Just as there is no precedent for America's $2.8 trillion debt in 1988,[2] there is no specific precedent for the fast-track international capitalist speculation represented in Oliver Stone's film. *Wall Street* serves in part to begin to illuminate the interior workings of this new version of power brokering and this new level of spectacle and desire.

The financial markets that are the backdrop to *Wall Street* are the institutional foundations of the capitalist hierarchy; they exist as an equivalent, abstract system intended to be a rough measure of both use and display value. In fact, the expansion of the markets and their formulation of share equivalents for monetary and commodity values have become increasingly tenuous and complex. When Gekko decides to raid a company, or to garner profit from a company's purchase by another investor, he can suddenly buy or sell hundreds of millions in shares and influence others to do the same. In a normative market condition, there tends to be a more direct and fairly stable correlation between a company's balance sheet and the price and number of shares that represent its worth. This is not true in a speculative market condition, as characterized by the 1980s merger and raider mania and by this film. Whereas the stock exchange once served as a resource and measure of real industrial wealth, the American corporate hierarchy has apparently become the plaything of Wall Street and beyond.

Specifically, because the share value of a company is controlled by market demand, this demand can be controlled in selected cases with huge capital outlays and information leaks by influencial speculators. Gekko even has an inside connection with the Wall Street "*Chronicle*" when he wants to motivate other brokers. Most important in this scenario is the availability of immense capital resources that can be secured on credit (usually in the form of high-interest junk bonds).[3] This means that a speculator's ability to package a convincing deal exceeds the importance of his personal or company wealth. Salesmanship and packaging, the creation of the image, thus become a more potent factor than who may initially develop a company or own a majority of its shares. Contemporary examples of such a truism are abundant. The seemingly direct connection between individuals and their pension funds (an important source of floating capital), for example, may be more distant than that between some speculator and those same funds, which he might either profit or bankrupt as a temporary borrower. Financial institutions are equally vulnerable in this abstract realm of speculation as the recent bankruptcy of hundreds of American savings and loan companies makes clear. Therefore, the development of the financial image takes on a radical new level of power where the relationships between people and their productions are removed into the abstract and symbolic.

Gekko simplifies every situation according to his bottom-line but image-conscious philosophy: "It's all about bucks, kid. The rest is conversation. . . . Money itself isn't lost or made, it's simply transferred from one perception to another like magic." Gekko's correlation of wealth with meaning and meaning with the ability to influence perception could not be more revealing. Gekko's statement describes commercialism's illusory power and domination of the processes of perception. Speculators thrive where monetary values have invaded the foundation of every domain of cultural and private awareness.

The frenzy of the speculative marketplace is driven by a war of competing appearances. Gekko wants neither the responsibility of ownership nor the burden of management. He chooses serial exchange over long-term ownership and tries to control the short-term exchange process. Controlling this process is a matter of image based on liquid capital, credit, information, and timing. The real player thrives not only on information about the commodity (quarterly reports, for example) but on information concerning the activities of other corporate investors. He is interested mainly in manipulating the valuation system and not in the things to be valorized.

This is not to say that Gekko is representative of most corporate speculators, since his criminal tactics are clearly delineated in the text. But the spectator might also sit in judgment of Gekko as crook and overlook the fine line that separates him from entirely legal, contemporary speculative practice. Gekko is meant to represent a level of cynical detachment and aggressive self-interest that exists at the pinnacle of the financial empire. What possible ideological rationale, then, can be offered to support it? Gekko answers that question in his most important pep talk to Bud Fox:

I create nothing. I own. We make the rules, pal. The news, war, peace, famine, upheaval, the price of paper clips. We pick that rabbit out of the hat while everybody stands around wondering how the hell we did it. Now, you're not naive enough to think we're living in a democracy, are you, buddy? It's a free market, and you're a part of it.

Gekko doesn't concern himself with hiding behind vague institutional ideals. He obviously doesn't feel it's any longer necessary or useful to do so. Presumably, the private interests of the financial elite should determine *all* social and institutional authority. This was the intent of supply-side Reaganomics and deregulation, and it is part of an insider attitude that pervades the 1980s.[4] Meanwhile, the Keynesian theory and policy that national governmental controls can somehow be made to compensate for the excesses of capitalist trading in the real world come under increasing attack, and for good reason. Susan Strange writes in *Casino Capitalism:*

> Moreover the moment is rapidly approaching when for all financial dealing, there will no longer be "financial centers" in the old sense, but one widespread global market in financial futures, government stocks and shares. Already the financial futures markets have arranged to link up with each other so that dealing can go on around the clock, for 24 hours a day, linked only by satellites and computers. . . . It can only be a matter of time before the operators run so far ahead of the regulations that this global financial casino will be working non-stop—but with rather hazy and indeterminate rules and few prudential controls.[5]

More important even than the more obvious legal and moral issues suggested by Strange, however, is the extent to which the local and transnational marketplaces and new communicational networks have tended, almost imperceptibly, to change the way individuals perceive themselves and their world, tend, that is, to realign patterns of individual associations and identity formations. Distinct categories of personal experience—occupational, political, psychological, and historical—like cultural-economic boundaries, have begun to crumble into one great pastiche of commercial semiotics, one grand free market of consumer language and signs. The old utopianism in the form of political ideologies (and now even communism) is being superseded by promises of immediate fulfillment through variations of capitalism. Democracy, meanwhile, is more than ever encumbered with an insidious economic colonialism.

For while the appeal of consumer culture is unavoidable and almost irresistible, significant participation in the marketplace is restricted and does not come free. Raised expectations and desires do not necessarily result in fulfillment. In his raid on Teldar Paper, Gekko exploits these kinds of consumer-profit expectations to very divisive effect. Loaded with facts and figures, Gekko assures the Teldar stockholders that bad management and inefficiency invite change, and that as a speculator he is a liberator of companies, not a destroyer. His tactics thrive in an atmosphere of competitive mistrust where so few are on the inside with the resources and information,[6] often simply the best theatrics, and so many are marginal and unable to assimilate complex information and rapidly changing circumstances.

Wall Street is directly concerned with this dimension of socioeconomic and cultural change, since it is organized around a story of initiation. Bud Fox struggles between two opposing father figures and two distinct sets of values. The family melodrama developed in the latter half of the film is dwarfed by the spectacular economic seduction of the first half. The stages of Bud's fall from innocence deserve a brief summation.

A steadicam follows Bud around the chaotic open spaces of the brokerage office where he works. Under the pressure of the clock, he gets stuck with the losses of an unethical client. After work, he looks up his dad, Carl (Martin Sheen), in a blue-collar bar and borrows money. The next day, he is admitted to Gekko's office after weeks of effort, and Gekko takes him up on an offer of insider information about Bluestar Airlines. By the end of the first act, Gekko has taken Bud to lunch, given him a million dollar cashier's check for investments, and sent a limousine and prostitute around to entertain him. Bud is unsuccessful in investing Gekko's money, however, and Gekko is ready to drop him after learning that Bud's dad works for Bluestar. Gekko gives him a final chance by asking him to tail Larry Wildman (Terence Stamp), a competitive speculator and archenemy from Britain. Bud responds, "If the SEC found out, I could go to jail. That's inside information, isn't it?" To which Gekko responds:

> You mean like when a father tells a son about a court ruling on an airline? Or someone overhears I'm buying Teldar Paper and decides

to buy some for himself? Or chairman of the board of XYZ decides it's time to blow out XYZ?

And when Bud brings up the hard-work ethic, Gekko shoots back:

> My father worked like an elephant pushing electrical supplies until he dropped dead at 49 with a heart attack and tax bills. . . . I'm talking about liquid. Rich enough to have your own jet. Rich enough not to waste time. Fifty, one hundred million dollars, buddy. A player or nothing.

When Bud doesn't accept Gekko's assignment immediately, he gets dropped off in the cold rain. The camera remains on Gekko and on the plush comfort of his limousine. We hear Bud rap on the closed window before his face appears, distorted by a fish-eye lens. "Okay, Mr. Gekko," he says, "you got me."

From the moment Bud takes this offer, his involvement becomes immensely profitable, socially disorienting, and increasingly illegal. His first acquisition is one of Gordon's ex-lovers, Derian Taylor (Daryl Hannah), an interior designer who, like Bud, is thriving off Gekko's resources. The penthouse Bud pays for and Derian decorates is very similar to the interior of Gekko's house; they both look more like postmodern museums, places devoted to display, than homes to be lived in. Derian insists that her apartment design work be photographed by *Better Homes* before she allows them to move in. In case we don't get the point from the knowing blankness of the ghoulish art and the topless coffee table, Bud also comments on a homemade gourmet dinner, "Let's not even eat it; we'll just watch it, think about it." The height of farce is reserved for Derian, who has lines such as: "I want to produce a line of high-quality antiques at a low price," or "I want a perfect Canary diamond and world peace." This beautiful muse is assigned all the markings of commodity culture. She is upscale, seductive, financially demanding, apparently accommodating, and finally troublesome and expendable. She is also a slightly exaggerated mirror image of Bud. When they eventually separate because of his hostility toward Gekko, they both seem surprised at the depth of their emotional discomfort.

Additional foils provide similar comments on Bud's social disconnection and criminal preoccupation. His young colleague at the brokerage reproaches Bud's new isolationist attitude. And Bud's senior director (Hal Holbrook) continues to warn him that there are no shortcuts and that "the main thing about money, it makes you do things you don't want to do." Gekko offers the most uncompromising advice. To Bud he says, "If you need a friend, get a dog," and to Derian, "We are smart enough not to buy into the oldest myth running—love. A fiction created to keep people from jumping out of windows." Following in Gekko's footsteps, Bud finally demonstrates how well he has learned his lessons. He asks an old college buddy, now a corporate lawyer, to help him hide large profits. Bud promises, "You'll make lots of money, and nobody gets hurt."

Comparable Stories

Bud's aggressive form of ambition in *Wall Street* is also a prominent characteristic among the protagonists of several other coming-of-age-in-business films of the 1980s such as Tess (Melanie Griffith) in *Working Girl* (1988).[7] Calculated ambition is presumed as part of the young person's essential equipment for success. Obsessive drive is accepted at face value; chutzpah is clearly required to move up the ladder. The entire orientation of these contemporary heroes is the attainment of a certain economic status without which, it seems, one simply has no voice! Their respective blue-collar homeplaces of New Jersey and Staten Island are at the mercy of the urban power centers of investment capital where the real decisions are made. Such modest financial origins are assumed to be incapable of providing the knowledge and contacts required for success. Similarly, when these same protagonists form their own urban family units (unmarried couples in this case), they are completely dominated by commercial values. Their heterosexual relationships are a socioeconomic convenience first and only secondarily an emotional bonding. Presumably, these bonds are good so long as the partnerships are financially advantageous. The overwhelming desire to enter even the bottom rung of the commercial power system, therefore, can be viewed in the context of this consciousness of powerlessness. The narrowly focused drive of Bud and Tess results from an apparent absence of alternatives.

In order to place the extremes of these 1980s films into perspective, one need only recall a cycle of comparable business films of the 1950s, including *Executive Suite (1954)* and *Sabrina (1954),* among others.[8] Not surprisingly, the 1950s products seem quaint by comparison, whatever the generic category. In addition to the fact that these earlier celebrations of American individualism tend to be more serious in tone—with neurotic bad guys and square-jawed, well-meaning heroes who express all-American values—they also go out of their way to excuse any suggestion of outright ambition on the part of the protagonist. William Holden plays a dedicated design engineer in *Executive Suite* who must be pressured by unusual circumstances in order to realize his inclination to become company president. He is so busy being creative at what he does (or being in love, as Audrey Hepburn is in *Sabrina*) that he (she) hardly thinks about moving up. Personal qualities of charm and forthright honesty seem to propel these young heroes to the top almost in spite of their intentions. And where a wife or father may not always go along with the notion of upward mobility, they are easily won over by the success of the hero(ine) in the end.

A second major point of contrast with the 1950s cycle of business films concerns ethics. In the recent business films, the young protagonist is not only ambitious but deceitful and dishonest in his/her pursuit of the American dream. Typically, this behavior is indulged in a context of knowing parody, as an entertainingly twisted excess of basically good intentions. Part of this mystique is that the young people must pay their dues up front in order to work their way onto the ground floor. The assumption is that serious compromise and deceit in the beginning stages of one's career can be balanced by more responsible behavior later as one gains prestige. But having already felt compelled by desire and fear to breach certain ethics at the entry level, why is it assumed that a character will not falter under even higher stakes and greater pressures later on?

In *Working Girl* Tess has few qualms posing as her boss or crashing a family wedding in order to get to her CEO, and she is equally aggressive and glib in later scenes. These methods are repeatedly excused on the premise of revenge against the dishonesty of her immediate supervisor. The difference between Tess assuming a false identity and her boss stealing an idea from her would provide an interesting subject for debate on situational ethics. What is important in the *Working Girl* narrative is not so much what one does to gain the advantage but how one goes about it, one's attitude and style. Where Tess is a resourceful and creative underdog, her boss (Sigourney Weaver) is a patronizing snob unwilling to admit her own insecurities and inadequacies, that is, lack of creativity. Weaver's character has learned that image is everything, and she has dedicated herself to that end, presumably losing whatever initiative and originality she may have once possessed. She has been corrupted in her fundamental orientation in a way that Tess has not, at least not yet. It is easy for Tess to give up her neighborhood boyfriend once she has set her sights on a man more appropriate to her ambitions, just as it is easy for her coconspirator (Harrison Ford) to deny the broken-legged Sigourney Weaver his attention after involving himself with Tess. Their too-easy choices and "competitive spirit" (small scams) result not only in job promotions but in the predictable romantic comedy ending in loving embrace. Deceit gets results.

By contrast, in the romance *Sabrina* and the vice-presidential competition of the more realistic *Executive Suite.* the protagonists' main prerequisites seem only to be honesty, energy, and attractiveness. For Sabrina, love, sincerity, and wealth are equally uncomplicated and virtually synonymous. Cinderella Sabrina doesn't have to cheat to be successful; the prince will come to her. The price of being forced to see the blatant shallowness of her initial love interest (Bogart's playboy brother) is a trip to Europe and long hours of sailboating and night life in the Bogart character's company. Sabrina's ultimate romantic connection with this dutiful overseer of his family's fortune is based on a recognition of his solid virtues and in a circumstance where wealth is always assumed. The strong association between financial success and virtue is implicit throughout—the worthy and good rise to the top, however talented. William Holden's character in *Executive Suite,* although far less sentimental than Sabrina, is every bit as sincere and virtuous. His masculine presentation of these traits combined with his idealistic pitch for the production of quality merchandise over cheap, mass-profit items catapults him to the position of company president. But his belief in quality furniture over quick profits is never tested in the context of the film. And the potential conflict between his family and his business commitments is glossed over in his wife's dutiful embrace of his big promotion.

Bud Fox, on the other hand, impatient as he is for monetary success and the fast lane, enslaves himself to Gordon Gekko and quickly finds his personal world badly compromised. He becomes president of Bluestar Airlines but inadvertently betrays this com-

pany where his father has worked his entire adult life. Personal
and economic goals are contradictory for Bud. We follow his
step-by-step absorption into the adversarial netherland of inside
raiders with a clear sense of apprehension. The jargon and tactics
at this level of competition could not be more uncompromisingly
mil-itaristic and aggressive. The desire to "make a killing" spills
over in Gekko's orders to his assistant, called "The Terminator."
"Rip their fucking throats out! Stuff 'em in your garbage com-
pactor," he says gleefully, "I want every orifice in his fucking body
flowing red . . . dilute the son of a bitch!" Gekko's methods also
imitate those of covert warfare, as he explains to Bud how he once
kept a "mole" in Larry Wildman's operation who could supply
inside information. This is free-market profiteering gone berserk,
a complete battle zone at the heart of an economic system that
asserts freedom and opportunity but lives by the warrior code of
Sun Tsu.[9] Bud's financial profits bring with them power and excitement, but he is finally unable to duplicate the ruthlessness of
his dynamic role model.

Gekko is the embodiment of contemporary patriarchy; he represents an extreme form of that particular order of meaning. He is
one with the privileged signifiers of money, power, knowledge,
plenitude, authoritative vision, and so forth. Gekko believes that
significant dollar commitment equals power, that value is defined
by capital rather than the other way around. He proves this by
buying his way onto the board of the Bronx Zoo for one million
dollars. "That's the thing you gotta remember about WASPs," he
tells Bud (and could as easily have been referring to the Buchan-
ans in *The Great Gatsby)* "They love animals; they can't stand
people." So much for philanthropy. Gekko works tirelessly and
thinks that those who quibble over legalities and humane concerns
lack spine. He assumes that everyone would make and break the
rules if one had the guts and know-how to try. Knowledge is for
control. He is fixated on inside information and the credit-lever-
aged monetary gamble. He has even turned his passion for the
power deal into an ideology: "Greed for life, for money, for love,
knowledge, has marked the upward surge of mankind. And greed
will not only save Teldar Paper, but that other malfunctioning corporation called the U.S.A." Gekko's self-justifying social Darwinism enshrines profit as the supreme God and its acquisition as his
religious practice.

And so America becomes commodity, simply another corporation to be bought and sold in some imaginary evolutionary cycle of laissez-faire, of transnational capitalistic speculation.[10] Although he doesn't mention it at the Teldar meeting, Gekko further combines his philosophy of greed with Sun Tsu's philosophy of war and thus differs from more blatantly illegal capitalists (Mafia) only in the use of paramilitary force. Sun Tsu developed the idea in China in the sixth century, B.C., that the essence of warfare is to undermine the central identity—and thus the ability to focus a common will—of the enemy. Actual fighting is only minimally necessary where the main will is already diffused (or bought off). Gekko's global perspective challenges the issues of company allegiance and patriotism versus a world-market economy; it suggests instead the extent to which the nation-state is becoming a staging ground or guardian to international speculators and corporate interests of whatever legitimacy.

Just as the abstraction of capital and shares in the high-speed transnational markets erodes the essence of local and national hegemony, so can Bud lose any vestige of coherent private self separate from his economic standing. The staples of democracies, individual rights, are only useful as their exercise can move the individual toward freedom from unwanted domination. And such a move is predicated on a consciousness of significant alternative. But the integration of consumer values and large, extremely sophisticated communication systems and networks leaves little room for objective contemplation. These communicational systems (particularly television) and their domination by wealthy private interests intrude upon individual consciousness at every phase of its formation. Gekko's high-energy appeal and ability to manipulate Bud, therefore, is analogous to the spectacles delivered over the predominant media systems, the endless images of commanding fulfillment through commerce. Individual sovereignty and social relations are thoroughly tainted. Television, in particular, discourages social interaction and isolates the individual viewer. More traditional identity groupings based on family and community interaction are turned into media market groupings based on product consumption.

Gekko's address to the Teldar stockholders' meeting is a bold example of intrusive marketing style over democratic autonomy. No one seems to suffer from Gekko's overstated speech except for the company managers, who have had their hands spanked for being too greedy with their own perks and salaries. Apparently, greed

is only good when one can get away with it by passing negative
repercussions on to someone else. This is Gekko's art. His style is
so entertaining and uncompromising that the spectacle of his performance obfuscates the end results. The stockholder majority want
to make money, and they want to be entertained with an optimistic
"vision" of profits. Gekko creates a consensus through his appeal
to profit motivation although the company may be sold off or liq-
uidated after his buyout. The perception is worth more than the
actual probability. Gekko's world of speculative capitalism has no
interest in products or people; it battles in the name of control over
perception and desire. It's a gambler's addiction, and it is the con-
glomerates and ultimately the nations and communities of the
world that are the major players blue chips.

The patriarchal alternative to Gekko, Bud's father Carl Fox
(Martin Sheen), represents a very different problematic. He's an
airline machinist, a union manager who enjoys teamwork with other
men committed to good craftsmanship. He believes in the traditional way, an honest day's work, camaraderie, and a moral family
life centered around his wife who stays home and runs the house-
hold. The narrative clearly privileges Carl at the expense of Gekko
on the ethical level. Carl instructs his son to "create, instead of
living off the buying and selling of others." Carl has the advantage of being Bud's natural father, and he stands strongly against
the buyout offer Gekko and Bud pitch to his Bluestar Airline people. When Bud (who is dressed and behaves just like Gekko) becomes too insulting, Carl responds to his son, "At least I don't
measure a man's success by the size of his wallet!" Yet Carl continues to have faith in the formal justice of a system that has almost killed him and nearly destroyed his son. His last words to
Bud as he delivers him to the courthouse are, "Maybe a little time
will do you good." Carl's world is the mythological realm of family values America would like to hold on to, the mythical Midwest
Nick Carraway wants to return to at the end of *The Great Gatsby*.
Wall Street may parody the extremes of Gekko, but he is part of a
new image-consciousness that thrives on spectacle. The world in
which Bud struggles is no longer the world of Nick Carraway or
Bud's father. The old ways are rapidly disintegrating. And although
Gekko may eventually be forced to serve a term in prison because
Bud turns state's witness, the law seems little more than a techni-
cality[11] in an issue that goes to the heart of the pervasive ideology,

an ideology inseparable from the relentlessly projected images of the good life.

Postmodern theorists such as Baudrillard and Jameson have demonstrated how the mediated and increasingly multinational economic code has come to dictate the social and economic realms. Baudrillard speaks of the contemporary mechanism by which cultural meaning is circulated by free-floating signs that have increasingly replaced the initial social relations they purport to represent.[12] Individual experience is obviously becoming more highly mediated than ever before, which both expands and limits the nature of personal interaction. The problem is that this increased mediation is not neutral but contains built-in assumptions and demands that are inseparable from the media forms and the self-serving intent of media owners and advertisers. The particular discourses and signs of the media come to dominate both the actual event reported and the functional value of the commodity advertised.[13] The individual finds it nearly impossible to distinguish direct personal experience from mediated images of similar experience. As Ian Angus explains: "At present, we need to go beyond representation to the recognition that *media constitute reality,* that media are constituents of the social world."[14] This mediated reality is characterized by a conflation of information and commodity signs that amount to a broadly unified sign system or code of consumerism. Angus continues:

> The system of production, exchange, and consumption of signs is the cultural cement of the monopoly capitalist form of life. In this system the role of media, of communication is expanded from its "mediational" function in liberal society to become the major determinant in this cultural cement. The cultural code of monopoly capitalism becomes a unified, closed system. . . .[15]

To what extent then is the *Wall Street* narrative determinant with rather than determined by socioeconomic conditions? To the extent that it creates an increased awareness of how excessive the economic determinant has become. Bud Fox is *not* a parody. He is a realistic example—not primarily because he is caught but because he had more reasons than most to reject Gekko's clear-cut temptation in the first place. He knew precisely what he was doing, but the desire to be on the inside of the knowledge and capital that mean power is shown to be almost irresistible. The contemporary myth that is more than once articulated verbally—"We can make lots of money and nobody gets hurt"—becomes increasingly ironic over the course of the narrative. Though most of the victims or potential victims of Gordon's and Bud's speculative techniques are never shown, the mise-en-scène is nevertheless full of background figures—fishermen, window washers, aging stockbrokers being laid off—who quietly go about their work or stand in shocked silence as the noisy "in" crowd charges past them. Bud's father's suffering seems metonymical for those displaced by quick-fix profiteering. Bud's own attempt to come of age by moving from an older patriarchy into a newer one is a direct confrontation with the fantasy that drives the system. So seductive is Gekko's approach that we almost forget that father Carl's alternative advice, however ethical, doesn't answer to Bud's experience. He has developed expectations and desires over which his parents have little influence.

Bud hungers for an excitement and intensification in his life that he believes can only be satisfied through the leverage of cash, through economic domination. Gekko exemplifies Bud's dream of economic power. This dream is an exaggerated version of the promise of consumerism. And since the mediated reality is already thoroughly complicit with consumerism, we see that meaning hardly exists outside of the consumer code of valuation and exchange. As Baudrillard puts it, "What society seeks through production, and overproduction, is the restoration of the real which escapes it."[16] Where the real is absent, the main pressure in consumer systems is felt at the level of surfaces and images. Because young people like Bud have already been immersed in this kind of extravagant promise of consumer images, the process of coding that occurs in the act of perception is already compromised, is already in effect commodified. Bud does succeed in turning himself into a dealer, a trader in the abstract market system. And, therefore, his perception does literally become commodified. And although his tears during his arrest in the brokerage office may be a legitimate recognition on his part of buying in just a little bit too far, Bud's story nevertheless reaffirms how completely the consumerist mandate asserts its influence. The final shot shows Bud climbing the stairs of the quaint old courthouse. The camera ascends far overhead, replacing him in the bowels of the New York financial district at the very fulcrum of the grand city skyline as the theme "Fly Me to the Moon" is played one last time. It seems obvious that *Wall Street*'s faith in the traditional family and legal system is only token, and that it hardly detracts from the presentation of self-serving excess in this free-market game of power images.

High-finance manipulation, however, is neither new nor necessarily more blameworthy than any other significant evasion of the primary ontological crisis in contemporary culture. But it does serve as a central metaphor of the displacement of meaningful signifieds by the very artistry of signification. On the market exchanges, in particular, appearances rule. There is little sense of a reality behind the image. There is mainly a continuous recirculation and recombining of images. Gekko is the consummate postmodern man. He doesn't confuse means with ends, as Gatsby did, but lives fully in the means, the constant rearrangement of signifiers to gain more signifiers. He remains unbeaten, or in any case as infinitely replaceable as any drug czar.[17]

The strength of this particular text is that it does manage to capture something of the aggressive longing and disappointment, the economic insecurity and fear of the mainstream of American youth, not to mention the large marginal groups at the farthest reaches from what is called opportunity. Bud can't make ends meet on $50,000 a year. And so the dominant economic order is shown to elicit a growing price, inevitably increased by a growing debt against the future.

It is in this way that *Wall Street* serves as a political-economic allegory of America in the 1980s. The characters of the 1950s business films would have understood the monetary attraction but not the pervasive levels of reasoned cynicism, dishonesty, and personal separation demonstrated in *Wall Street.* Where American cultural observers of the 1950s spoke in terms of conformity to and alienation from new roles and socioeconomic groups,[18] postmodern theorists speak of the impossibility of subjectivity much less objectivity in the flood of commercial mediation. The contemporary young business protagonist's disorientation is neither a conformity to nor an alienation from family or social groups (as in *Sabrina* and *Executive Suite).* Rather, it takes the form of a submergence, an implosion, in a totalizing round of mediated reality, a closed system of illusory polarities whose final meaning is only consumption.[19] The rush of high-roller financial competition only highlights the absence of the real.

A memorable image persists of Bud Fox in the middle of a fog-

gy Central Park, wired for information, and getting his face slapped
around by Gekko so that, with him or in spite of him, Bud can
continue to stay tuned to the only major networks playing.

Notes

1. Peter Mantius, "Double the Pleasure: Many Stockholders Have the
Chance to Make 100% Profit," *Atlanta Journal and Constitution,* 2 December 1988, sec. D, p. 6. The RJR Nabisco buyout is referred to here as
"the deal of the century."

2. U.S. Bureau of the Census, *Statistical Abstract of the United States
1996,* 116th edition (Washington, D.C.: U.S. Bureau of the Census, 1996),
329.

3. As an example see Stephen Labaton, "The Trials and Errors of
Boyd Jefferies," *New York Times,* 15 January 1989, sec. 3, p.1.

4. Perhaps a wink that passes among the major players in the RJR
Nabisco deal, where estimates of potential fees run as high as $500 mil-
lion. *New York Times,* 13 November 1988, Business sec., p. 8.

5. Susan Strange, *Casino Capitalism* (New York: Basil Blackwell,
1987), 115–16.

6. According to Susan Strange in *Casino Capitalism,* Chief Financial
Officers (CFOs) have become more important than the managers, engi-
neers, and scientists within the corporate community.

7. Also *Bright Lights, Big City* and *The Secret of My Success,* not to
mention several film projects involving capitalism and prostitution, such
as *Risky Business, Night Shift, Trading Places,* and *Doctor Detroit.*
In addition to his role in *Risky Business* Tom Cruise plays fast-track
entrepreneurs in *Rain Man* and *Cocktail.* Like Bud Fox, the Charlie Babitt
and Brian Flanagan protagonists feel that the world owes them something,
and they are out to collect. And like Bud, what Charlie and Brian discover
is a kind of "family" (brother Raymond or girlfriend Jordan Mooney) they
at first betray but learn to love above any allegiance to money. These films
ultimately express the same sentimentality as in *Working Girl* where the
hero(ine) gets his (her) cake and gets to eat it, too.

8. Also *Man in the Gray Flannel Suit* (1956) and *Woman's World*
(1954). Both of these films strongly demonstrate that honesty is more
important than ambition, which tends to be punished.

9. Sun Tsu's *The Art of War* was recently translated by Samuel B.
Griffith (New York: Oxford Univ. Press, 1972). Sun Tsu is quoted or referred
to by both Gekko and Bud as a kind of insider's philosopher. A brief
summary of his basic philosophy is given later in this article.

10. Reuters, "Japan Ranked No. 1 Last Year in Companies Increasing
Direct Investment in U.S. Assets," *Atlanta Journal and Constitution,* 20

March 1989, sec. C, p. 12. In the year ending 1988, Britain had $88.2 billion in direct investment in the United States, while the Netherlands had $50.8 billion and Japan $48.5 billion.

11. "The securities markets and their laws have become so complex that technical violations are often just millimeters away from criminal conduct. . . . It may be prudent to have at least some control over the free-market system we have sanctioned. But few people can understand—much less control—an industry of unregulated commissions, unbridled competition and sprawling complexity. We have constructed a house of mirrors where foundation is indistinguishable from artifice." Tim Stone, "Forum: Wall Street Ethics," *New York Times,* 19 March 1989, Business sec.

12. Jean Baudrillard, *The Mirror of Production,* trans. Mark Poster (St. Louis: Telos Press, 1975).

13. Frederic Jameson, "Postmodernism, or the Cultural Logic of Late Capitalism," *New Left Review* no. 146 (July–August 1984): 66.

14. Ian Angus, "Media Beyond Representation," eds. Ian Angus and Sut Jholly, *Cultural Politics in Contemporary America* (New York: Routledge, 1989), 339.

15. Angus, "Media," 340.

16. Jean Baudrillard, *Simulations* (New York: Semiotext[e], 1983), 44.

17. In an interview with Alexander Cockburn in *American Film* 13 (December 1987): 22, Oliver Stone comments on the entrepreneurial speculations of the cartel bosses: "Wall Street is the equivalent of the cocaine trade in some ways." Stone, *Wall Street*'s director, also dedicated this film to his father, a broker who died in 1985, who, according to his son, would hardly have recognized the Wall Street of today.

18. David Riesman, N. Glazer, and R. Denney, *The Lonely Crowd* (New York: Doubleday, 1956).

19. Jean Baudrillard, "The Ecstasy of Communication," trans. John Johnston, *The Anti-Aesthetic: Essays on Postmodern Culture,* ed. Hal Foster (Port Townsend, Wash.: Bay Press, 1983).

Chapter 6

Talk Radio

Oliver Stone's *Talk Radio*

Don Kunz

Released just after *Wall Street* (1987) and just before *Born on the Fourth of July* (1989), Oliver Stone's *Talk Radio* (1988) has attracted comparatively little critical attention. Dwarfed by the budgetary excess, box office success, and controversial nature of Stone's other films, *Talk Radio* is a disturbing little masterpiece of adaptation. Shot in Dallas in just twenty-five days for four million dollars,[1] it shows how creative Stone can be when working on a tight schedule and budget. The easy part was working with literary material which embodied his ideological predispositions. Stone's penchant has been for developing melodramatic themes of apocalyptic conspiracy and violent revenge, for exploring corruption, betrayal, and martyrdom at the heart of the American experience. His literary source had all that but it needed Stone's flamboyant directorial style to manifest it on film.

Stone cowrote the screenplay with New York City performance artist Eric Bogosian. Together they adapted two seemingly incompatible literary properties optioned by producer Edward R. Pressman:[2] Bogosian's avant-garde play, *Talk Radio* (New York: Vintage Books, 1988) and Stephen Singular's nonfiction narrative about a Jewish talk show host in Denver who had been assassinated by neo-Nazis in 1984, *Talked to Death: The Life and Murder of Alan Berg* (New York: Beech Tree Books, 1987). The collaboration produced a screenplay which is a skillfully provocative fusion of fiction and fact, satire and docudrama, black-humorist absurdity and social realism, biography, and melodrama.

Initially, the screenplay's coauthorship was contentious. Bogosian, who had starred as the play's protagonist (Barry Champlain)

147

in productions at the Portland Center for the Visual Arts in Oregon
and at Joseph Papp's New York Shakespeare Festival, was doubly
invested in his material as a playwright and actor. His protection-
ist attitude toward his dramatic work and his inexperience as a
screenwriter provoked angry, specific instructions from Stone. As a
veteran screenwriter and as the director whose reputation would
rest upon the adaptation, Stone was more willing to re-create the
material as film. As he said, "I'm not there to interpret a play. . . .
I was there to make a movie. I didn't see Barry Champlain as this
mythic figure I had to transpose like fragile china that might
break."[3]

In addition to the different objectives of the screenplay's co-
authors and the obvious tonal and stylistic incompatibility of their
sources, both literary properties must have seemed cinematically
unpromising. Bogosian's play was set entirely inside a radio-sta-
tion broadcast booth and relied primarily on a single performer
responding to disembodied voices. It was plotless talk within a
spare, confining mise-en-scène. Singular's nonfiction narrative presented problems, too. Its plot was bifurcated into parallel accounts
of Berg's rise to media celebrity and the evolution of the Aryan
Nation's organization which assassinated him. It offered the opposite challenge of sorting through a multitude of peripheral scenes,
characters, events, and issues.

In making *Talk Radio*, then, Oliver Stone was faced with three
major artistic problems:

- creating a coherent narrative structure from no more than a
  situation in Bogosian's play and nothing less than a sprawling
  postmortem in Singular's narrative;

- giving visual interest to material that was so heavily verbal
  that it was more suitable for radio than cinema;

- and making an unusually static, stage-bound, single-actor
  showcase into the kind of highly kinetic melodrama favored
  by Hollywood.

Before Stone became available to direct *Talk Radio* the project
was discussed with Adrian Lyne, William Friedkin, Sidney Lument,
and Alan Parker, among others. But according to producer, Pressman, these men did not know how to adapt the material or did not

want Bogosian to act in the film.[4] Stone did. He not only persuaded Bogosian to participate in the dismantling of his play but also directed him in a virtuoso acting performance. That performance was perfectly compatible with the structure and tone of a story recreated for the cinematic presentation of Stone's favorite themes.

It is Stone's fidelity to his own talent and to the storytelling resources of his own medium rather than those of its two literary sources which make his version of *Talk Radio* such a dynamic adaptation.

Bogosian's play is primarily black humor. During the course of one evening's two-hour talk show, Barry Champlain engages in a sadomasochistic "festival of exchanged cruelties"[5] with a succession of terrifyingly amusing callers including ethnocentric paranoids and would-be intellectuals, flatterers and insult artists, macho child abusers, drug-crazed adolescents, anti-Semites and homophobes, racists and rapists, lonely widows and pregnant girls, the seduced and the abandoned. During this pastiche of fragmented conversations the protagonist invents various personas and stories as well as crafting segues between callers so that the play has little more coherence than an oral collage of attitudes and poses, stories and theories, raw emotions and dialects seemingly under extemporaneous construction. Barry Champlain begins the evening as a crusader ("I have a job to do and I'm gonna do it"), gradually discovers that his listeners are turning him into their savior ("The only thing you believe in is me. . . . I'm not God"), and finally, not knowing what to say, lapses into exasperated silence—forty-five seconds of dead air time. This evening of fragmented talk is interrupted by a succession of commercial messages for constipation and sleeplessness which help amplify what callers have illustrated—the citizenry's decline into self-serving delusion, paranoiac absurdity, and conspiratorial nightmare. To add to the confusion, the play's headlong, two-hour rush into verbal combat is further fragmented by three expository oral snapshots of Barry—one each by his sound engineer, producer, and station manager. Like other examples of black humor and theater of the absurd, Bogosian's play lacks a linear narrative because that is simply one more way of illustrating its theme of cultural disintegration. But while that strategy may work in live theater, it is extremely risky in popular film.

While the play's badly flawed, self-tortured, verbally combative protagonist and its theme of American degeneracy must have appealed to Stone, its structure presented a considerable challenge to film adaptation. Barry Champlain seemed less a character than a succession of personas, and there was no one tangible for him to play off of. As remedy, Stone drew on Singular's characterization of Berg, particularly Berg's dependency upon his ex-wife and his concern over ratings in order to enhance his celebrity status during contract negotiations with the station. Such details gave Stone a way to define Barry Champlain's tangled motives as crusader and self-promoter more clearly, to humanize him[6] into a more sympathetic figure for martyrdom and to provide him with some antagonists who are physically present in the studio setting.

Moreover, by making Barry Champlain more like Alan Berg, Stone could derive the film's plot from Singular's narrative. This journalistic account of the Aryan Nation's conspiracy to assassinate Alan Berg, became the clear narrative line of action suitable for a melodramatic Hollywood thriller. So Richard Corliss oversimplifies when he claims "basically, Stone bought the rights to an assassination and gave himself a big finish.[7]

In Stone's film, the protagonist embodies a more complex and familiar American tragedy, a male driven to prove his manhood by sacrificing love for power. First, in pursuit of celebrity status Barry drives his wife to divorce him; then he seduces her into returning, only to destroy a renewed relationship by humiliating her on the air. Similarly, he is willing to sacrifice any personal relationship (like that with his current lover/producer, his radio engineer, or his studio boss) to maintain the image of a tough-talking, crusading, macho shock jock. Second, in his attempt to gain ratings high enough to impress a potential sponsor into syndicating his show, Barry outrages his white supremacist listeners who suspect that he and his sponsors are part of a Jewish conspiracy to control America. Then, whey they can't intimidate him into silence, they assassinate him.

As David Sanjek has pointed out, such behavior is typical of Stone's protagonists; they tend to be narcissistic masculine artists whose self-obsessions result in making them martyred patriarchs of dysfunctional families.[8] Stone's revisionist characterization of Bogosian's Barry Champlain enables him to reiterate his familiar vision of corrupt American institutions. In the film version of *Talk Radio* the corruption becomes multileveled and interconnected—

familial, societal, and spiritual: A man sacrifices his marriage for business success; commercial radio finds so much profit in the entertainment value of verbal abuse that it incites civil disorder and criminal action; fundamentalist Christianity becomes perverted into paranoid enthnocentrism.

Despite the initial antagonism, Stone's collaboration with Bogosian produced a coherent screenplay in which plot emerged from character and led to a pervasive sense of corruption, betrayal, and revenge. Moreover, despite its melodramatic tone, the plot takes on a tragic dimension. In one sense the assassination is really suicide. As Barry says, "Maybe free speech isn't really free after all; its sort of like Russian roulette." When Barry is gunned down in the parking lot after his Monday night show, during which he invites his listeners to "hit me with your best shot," he has in a sense already killed himself by sacrificing his personal integrity for a sham public image of a truth-telling crusader for reform.

Stone's use of this material from Berg's life allows him to transform a static play into a dynamic film. First of all, Barry's concerns with his ex-wife, his boss, and his potential syndication sponsor become ways of releasing him from the broadcast-booth-bound conflict with his callers and into other areas of the radio station and the nation itself. By including scenes in a sports arena, Barry's apartment, a car, a park, the studio parking lot and (in flashback) a clothing store, another radio station, and Barry's former home, Stone opens the play up just enough to give us a glimpse into a city populated by fools and hucksters, the deluded and the dangerous. And not only does Stone give Bogosian as an actor a greater variety of settings within which to move in developing Champlain's character, he exacts a frenetic performance from him in the booth itself. Burdened by a host a interrelated and compounding worries, Bogosian's film version of Champlain puts on a set of headphones and a portable microphone and abandons his console to pace like a predatory animal inside a large glass cage or to circle like a tornado which the lead-in weather report has warned about. So even when the film's protagonist is confined, he is moving, and he can see a host of antagonists arrayed against him just outside the walls of his glass broadcast house.

Moreover, given the static nature of the material, the frenetically moving camera that is part of Stone's directorial signature is not gratuitous but functional. The hand-held shots while Barry paces around the console expounding on "the gripe theory of history" suggest not only his own psychological instability as personal and professional pressures mount against him but also the instability of a nation of callers who want to blame others for their problems rather than accepting personal responsibility. Similarly, several shot sequences feature a camera which tracks Barry in a circle, becoming a provocatively ambiguous motif. It allows us to see Barry's complexities from all sides; it visually illustrates Barry talking in circles without fixed position or belief; it creates the impression that Barry is surrounded. Most important, the camera is almost always tracking through the scene both on and off the air. As the show opens, it explores the mise-en-scène of the studio while Barry remains a disembodied voice; after the show concludes, it lurks in the parking lot and stalks ominously toward him; it probes the city's skyline and looks through the studio window. Consequently there is an eerie sense that someone is waiting to attack. If it is not the fascist Big Brother that his freaked-out studio guest, Kent alludes to, it might be one of the alliance of anti-Semites who threaten Barry over the radio and through the mail. The camera movement does much to enhance these threats, making *Talk Radio* in the words of David Denby "one of the most complete expressions of paranoia ever put on film."[9]

While Stone's hyperactive camera makes the static literary property into a moving picture, his use of the mise-en-scène transforms a talky script into a visually exciting and thematically coherent thriller. By shooting much of the film from the medium to the extreme close-up range, Stone forces us into uncomfortable intimacy with the prickly, tortured, shock-jock protagonist and those closest to him whom he wounds by his verbal assaults. This close-shot range also calls our attention to all the glossy studio gadgetry which makes mass communication possible. The mean-spirited, uncivil talk which this wondrous technology facilitates seems a mockery of the community-enhancing ideal Barry professes to serve when he refers to his show as "the last neighborhood in America." Stone emphasizes this by including three prominent visual motifs in extreme closeup:

· an "on-air" red light featured when particularly threatening callers are ranting which seems to flash both a warning and a plea to stop;

· the phone line call buttons which enable Barry to stay in control by functioning as kill switches for cutting callers off;

· and the smoke from Barry's cigarettes and those of Kent (a disturbed guest who threatens to take over the show), and from the revolver of Barry's assassin the parking lot.

Together these comprise a sort of visual matrix associating aggressive verbal behavior with heat and death in general and the Nazi holocaust and Barry's show, "Night Talk," in particular. As Barry's ex-wife puts it, he is "going down in flames." To make the comparison even sharper, when Barry is listening to Chet's anti-Semitic threats, he lights a cigarette. The lighter's flame is exaggerated by an extreme close-up and the amplified sound of a gas jet which we are invited to associate with concentration-camp crematoria as the camera tracks across brick walls divided by barlike shadows.

Over-the-shoulder shots of Barry from angles behind Deitz (who will make the decision whether to syndicate the show), Kent (who has perpetrated an embarrassing hoax on Barry and in his outrageousness nearly replaces him as the celebrity host), and the assassin (who stalks him in the parking lot after the show), all visually convey threats to Barry's livelihood, self-image, and life. When combined with the oblique angle shots after the syndication plan is put on hold and the overexposed shots when Barry's marital infidelity is discovered or when he lies dying of bullet wounds, *Talk Radio* assumes a nightmarish look.

Additionally, Stone's design of the radio station, the lighting, and the location contribute to the adaptation's creepy, paranoid atmosphere. The broadcast booth is circular and enclosed in glass. Its circularity makes Barry's circular pacing and the camera's circular tracking seem natural, not contrived. At the same time it reinforces interconnected themes: Barry talks circles around his callers; he has no fixed ideological position; what goes around comes around so that Barry, as one caller says, "reaps what he sows"; and just as Barry replaced an earlier talk show host named Jeff, Kent declares himself to be "the new toastmaster" after Barry's death. Moreover, Stone opens and closes the film with similar long take, aerial shots of the city's skyline while a radio broadcast plays, so that visually the film describes a circle. The opening broadcasts a tornado alert; the closing is an oral epitaph for the murdered Barry by his callers. The atmosphere of inescapable disaster is unremitting.

Inside the studio itself, Stone's use of low-key lighting through the circular glass creates reflections of characters which overlay shots of them. Consequently, Barry seems to be under intense scrutiny. His antagonists' images literally cast shadows over him. Moreover, we are invited to reflect upon the broadcast medium's confusion between image and essence. How much of what Barry presents is who he really is and how much is only an image that he projects? Is talk radio a public service offering an authentic crusade against America's cultural disintegration or merely verbal abuse which panders to a nation's basest interest in demeaning entertainment? Additionally, Stone's change of location from Bogosian's Cleveland or Berg's Denver to Dallas, America's premiere city of assassination, helps stamp his own signature on the material. The Dallas location makes all those images in the glass seem like apparitions in a haunted landscape of America's worst nightmare. Stone released *Talk Radio* on the twenty-fifth anniversary of President Kennedy's assassination in Dallas and two years later returned there to make *JFK*.

Finally, *Talk Radio*'s paranoid, messianic, apocalyptic vision of America is given visceral immediacy by articulating it in sexual terms. This is by now a familiar Stone strategy, one which not only literally panders to his mass audience but also seems to arise naturally from his penchant for masculine characters whose macho exploits in Vietnam, on Wall Street, or on rock music's concert stage seemed fueled by excess testosterone.

In *Talk Radio* Barry Champlain describes himself to his audience as "the man you love to love," but in fact his show's theme song is George Thoroughgood's "Bad to the Bone." At one point while simultaneously soul kissing his wife and offering her the job of producing his new show, Barry says ambiguously, "Wanta do it?" When she replies that all the tension would destroy their marriage, he replies, "Fuck our marriage, this is the show!" Announcing on air that Night Talk is about to be nationally syndicated by Metro Media, Barry characterizes it as an opportunity for "Dallas to have verbal intercourse with the rest of the country." Later explaining to his spaced-out adolescent guest, Kent, what a live microphone is, Barry informs him "you speak into it, and it penetrates their minds." Even the shots of microphone and antenna tower seem like phallic symbols for Barry, whom one caller describes as "a prick in the conscience of America."

This sexual conceit becomes more sharply focused when a rapist calls the show and forces Barry to admit "I'm your buddy, John." Indeed he is. Both men are filled with rage, have a compulsion to display their power by abusing others, blame their victims, and deserve, as Barry finally confesses, "to hang."

Night Talk's sound engineer underlines this sexual metaphor by wondering aloud if someone has put too much testosterone in Barry's coffee, and by way of paying his last respects to the dead shock jock, says, "Whenever you threatened him over the air, man, he'd stick it right back in your face. It was like his dick was flappin' in the wing, and he liked to see if he could get an erection." Even Barry's assassin defines the penalty for the abusive verbal intercourse which Barry has forced upon his callers by shouting, "Die, fucker!"

Stone uses this controlling metaphor to impart additional coherence to his vision of contemporary America in the process of disintegration. An obsession with sex as recreation, entertainment, and an expression of power which dominates, hurts, or humiliates weaker members of the body politic becomes a sort of symptom of a more pervasive social disease.

Stone's hyperkinetic films are filled with angry male patriots disappointed by the failure of American culture to live up to its wondrous promise, men inclined to reinvent themselves as powerful masculine redeemers, given to violent means of punishing those who fall below their high expectations, troubled martyrs overwhelmed by the corruption they unmask in others who conspire against them or succumb to the evil they find within themselves. His adaptation of *Talk Radio* not only bears this signature more clearly than some of his other work but also justifies it aesthetically. There are two reasons for this: First, the talky and static nature of the title source material required his flamboyant directorial style in order to be made suitable for cinematic presentation. Second, as a screenwriter, Stone was extracting his film's constituent parts from two apparently incompatible literary properties, so the thematic concerns guiding his choices become unmistakable.

Notes

1. Peter Blauner, "Word of Mouth," *New York*, 12 December 1988, 56; James Riordan, *Stone: The Controversies, Excesses, and Exploits of a Radical Filmmaker* (New York: Hyperion, 1995), 226.

2. Blauner, "Word," 55.

3. Blauner, "Word," 56.

4. Blauner, "Word," 56.

5. Tom O'Brien, "In the Line of Fire," *Commonweal*, 13 January 1989, 21.

6. Richard Porton, "Talk Radio," *Cineaste* 17, no. 2 (1989): 54.

7. Richard Corliss, "Who Cares?", *Film Comment* 25, no. 1 (January–February 1989): 70.

8. David Sanjek, "The Hysterical Imagination: The Horror Films of Oliver Stone," *Post Script* 12, no. 1 (Fall 1992): 48, 51, 54.

9. David Denby, "Raging Bull," *New York*, 12 December 1988, 112.

Chapter 7

Born on the
Fourth of July

Oliver Stone's Film Adaptation of *Born on the Fourth of July:* Redefining Masculine Heroism

Don Kunz

Ron Kovic's *Born on the Fourth of July*, published during America's bicentennial, is a bitterly ironic birthday present to his country. An inverted success story, Kovic's autobiography is "an extended attack upon the American society and American myths which in Kovic's view compelled him to go to Vietnam and to be permanently disabled."[1] The author conceives of himself as the all-American boy—literally born on the Fourth of July—a "Yankee Doodle Dandy" who wholeheartedly embraced small-town and working-class values like hard work, competition, sacrifice, and duty. These components of heroic manhood are summed up in his declaration that "all his life he'd wanted to be a winner . . . to be the very best."[2] The baseball field, the television set, and the movie house of small-town America made Kovic a true believer in this manly heroic ideal, and especially that version of it contained in war movies like *The Sands of Iwo Jima* and *To Hell and Back*. These films updated the American frontier myth: the archetypal American male as virtuous warrior heroically establishing civilization amid savagery. Kovic enlisted in the Marines and fought in Vietnam trying to fulfill that patriotic myth. His quest carried him into what John Hellman has called "a nightmare version of the landscapes of previous American myths," a place where American assumptions and values were inverted.[3]

Like others of his generation, Kovic discovered that the savagery he committed in Vietnam was not validated by civilization's

159

progress, that he had become the enemy of the population he came to save, that he was the successor not to his "own mythic forebearers but rather to the Europeans against whom those forebearers defined themselves."[4] Kovic's story dramatizes his failure to be an American hero and the failure of his generation to establish Kennedy's "new frontier" by reenacting outside continental boundaries the traditional story which encodes America's understanding of its place in geography and history. Beginning and ending with the wound which paralyzed him in Vietnam, Kovic's cyclical narrative emphasizes an unjustifiable loss which is at once personal and national.

Oliver Stone's cinematic adaptation of the book (with Kovic as screenplay coauthor), while faithful to the original is, nonetheless, more coherently focused and positively concluded. To those ends, new characters, episodes, and dialogue are added; the protagonist's development is clarified by a chronologically structured plot, and the theme is highlighted by an extended sexual trope. These alterations for the film emphasize Kovic's story as an escape from a spuriously defined masculinity underlying America's fundamental values and myths. On the whole, the film constitutes a more profound and comprehensive "attack on the authoritarian macho mentality that led us into Vietnam. . . ."[5] This sharper focus is maintained by a screenplay which restructures the original autobiography's bifurcated chronology into a three-act, linear narrative: the formation of Kovic's heroic masculine ideal in small-town America, its deformation in Vietnam service, then its reformation in the antiwar movement. Additionally, casting Tom Cruise in Kovic's role guaranteed an audience for this iconoclastic theme and clarified that theme by trading on Cruise's all-American-boy image. As Stone said, "We wanted to show America, and Tom, and through Tom, Ron, being put in a wheelchair, losing their potency. We wanted to show America being forced to redefine its concept of heroism."[6]

Understanding the cinematic reconstruction of Kovic's story begins with the adapters' decision to dwell on Kovic's war wound more as impotence than as paralysis. As Tom Cruise noted in an interview for *Playboy*, "With *Born*, I could feel the script in my balls."[7] Certainly in the adaptation, Kovic's "outrage at losing his potency is more graphic and real to us than anything else."[8] Moreover, because Kovic's impotence is made synecdochic, the cinematic version takes on not just more poignancy and drama but more thematic richness than the printed text. In the film the Vietnam veteran's physical emasculation symbolizes psychological, political, and spiritual impotence as well—all ironic consequences of seeking manhood through duty to God and country. Although Hollywood film typically has made Vietnam War wounds "marks of equivocation, disillusion, and rage with war itself,"[9] *Born on the Fourth of July* focuses on the one wound feared more than death itself, a living death. What is, in effect, the protagonist's castration makes terrifyingly concrete the Vietnam War's eradication of the American patriot's most basic means of establishing his identity and bequeathing a legacy of that self.

The film's retelling of Kovic's war story in sexual terms is so methodically developed as to constitute an elaborate objective correlative: specifically, the screenplay's alteration of love and lust interests for Kovic (Donna and the Mexican prostitutes); the expansion of Kovic's mother's role; and the frequency of explicit reference in vernacular dialogue to various and numerous sexually charged activities to allegorize America's Vietnam experience as an act of love perverted into obscenity.

In sum, the film partially fictionalizes Kovic's nonfiction narrative, taking license with some biographical and historical facts in the interest of articulating more significant and moving conceptual truths about America's Vietnam involvement. The Stone/Kovic film of *Born on the Fourth of July* becomes the story of all America's boys who were seduced into the Vietnam War trying to fulfill their culture's myth of heroic manhood, who then were handicapped by confusing rules of engagement abroad and opposition to the war at home, and who were finally repatriated by joining the fight for peace. The film becomes the story of America's Vietnam soldier who, in a sense, died fighting an emasculating war in a foreign country and returned to be resurrected by fighting another for remasculinization within his own country. Thus, the cinematic retelling gives Kovic's personal odyssey great resonance, voicing the profound and multifaceted consequences of the Vietnam conflict while at the same time clarifying them and intensifying their emotional impact.

The film begins with the adult Kovic remembering his childhood as a masculine proving ground. A long shot tracks at a low angle on sun-dappled trees, gradually craning up and tilting down to a bird's-eye view of Ron Kovic as a boy in a World War II American army helmet. Meanwhile the mature Kovic's off-camera voice speaks for a generation as he recalls, "It was a long time ago. . . . We turned the woods into a battlefield and dreamed that someday we would become men." The ensuing scene of prepubescent boys reenacting their fathers' combat experiences undercuts that aspiration dramatically as surely as the stature-diminishing camera angle does perceptually: Young Kovic is ambushed, ending up on his back, covered with dirt, another boy kneeling over him firing a toy pistol and shouting, "You're dead, Ronnie Kovic, and you know it," while Kovic shakes his head and tries to rise from his premature burial.

From a high-angle close-up of young Kovic denying the death of his dream of becoming a man, Stone jumps to a completely black screen and then to a metaphorical match cut—a high-angle close-up of a pinwheeling firecracker exploding in the grass at a Fourth of July parade. This opening scene and its transition offer a condensed preview of the film's narrative structure and paradoxical theme. It is the dramatic and visual equivalent of the poetic epigraph to Kovic's book:

> *I am the living death*
> *the memorial day on wheels*
> *I am your yankee doodle dandy*
> *your John Wayne come home*
> *your fourth of July firecracker*
> *exploding in the grave*[10]

Just as the film's opening prefigures the archetypal American boy's emasculation and death, its concluding scene confirms his remasculinization and resurrection. This scene depicts Kovic's most triumphant moment when he wheels himself out to address the 1976 Democratic National Convention as an antiwar spokesman. To emphasize this theme, Stone intercuts Kovic's slow-motion progress toward the microphone with predominantly peaceful short duration shots from Kovic's youth—the family gathered around the television set in the living room, a kiss at the high school prom, a Little League game-winning home run, as well as the war game. In other words, the film defines a man whose vision of himself has been shaped by more than dreams and nightmares of war. In fact, Kovic tells a reporter behind the scenes that "just lately I've felt like I'm home, like we're home," and, as he moves toward a national audience to say what he has learned, he is bathed in an intensely bright light from above.

Growing up in the small town of Massapequa, New York, Kovic is told what it means to be a man, and he remains a true believer even though his faith is sometimes contradicted by childhood experience. The nation's heroic ideal of manhood is taught in the home and the school, over the airwaves and in the community's public celebrations. To become a man one must seek out physical competition and through clean living, hard work, and self-sacrifice rise above suffering to attain victory confirmed by the applause of the crowd. The young Kovic acts out this scenario in ritualistic play: war games in the woods, Little League baseball, and high school wrestling. When the war game concludes with Kovic being declared a dead loser, he simply denies that result. Hitting a game-winning home run in a Little League game, being held aloft and carried victorious from the field by his teammates to the accompaniment of wild cheering led by his father confirms for him the validity of this dream of manhood. As a child he has emulated the exploits of his hero, Mickey Mantle, and seems to have earned the New York Yankees cap he receives as a birthday present on the Fourth of July. In the cultural mythos, Mickey Mantle, John Wayne, and later John Kennedy are young Kovic's true fathers, more real than his own who is merely a supermarket clerk. As Hellman notes, Vietnam-era protagonists typically reject the father as a false parent associated with a failed present and identify with American heroic archetypes in an attempt to fulfill the mythic past by which the ideal American male defines himself.[11]

But Kovic's faith in heroic manhood is tested as a member of the high school wrestling team. His coach articulates the destructive implications lurking within America's patriarchal definition of its ideal citizen: to be a winner, others must be losers; to live fully, others must die; to be a man, others must be women. As the coach drives his boys mercilessly, he teaches them to fear compassion and failure as feminizing: "I want you to kill. . . . Come on, ladies. You got to suffer. The price of victory is sacrifice."

As a boy at home, Kovic hears the same doctrine of sacrifice used to define patriotism in President Kennedy's televised inaugural speech exhorting a new generation of Americans to whom the torch has been passed to "bear any burden, pay any price" in establishing the "new frontier." As Kovic's devout Roman Catholic mother listens to Kennedy, she tells Ron of her dream: "You were speaking to a large crowd, just like him, and you were saying great things." When as an adolescent, Kovic arrives home late from wrestling practice and refuses food in order to make his weight classification for the conference championship, his mother construes that sacrifice not just as manly or patriotic, but blessed.

However, as the coach's worst epithet, "ladies," suggests, this definition of heroic manhood in the service of God and country is a patriarchal ideal involving sexual domination and repression. When Kovic's mother finds a *Playboy* magazine in his room, she lashes out at him for "filthy, impure thoughts" and tells him "God is going to punish you." She demands he remove the magazine from the home and go to confession. Although Kovic is admired by women while growing up, he is taught to avoid their corrupting influence in order to become a man. When he is kissed by Donna, a young girl at the Fourth of July fireworks, he doesn't know if he likes it and abruptly tries to impress her by doing push-ups. Later, at the baseball game and the wrestling match, Donna, like his mother, can only adore Kovic from the stands in the company of presumably lesser males. The blessed warrior hero may seek the approval of women but must remain separate from them to avoid confusion about what he is. By adding Donna's role and expanding the mother's, the screenplay places new emphasis on the destructive nature of the heroic masculine ideal young Kovic inherits.

Despite pure thoughts, hard work, and self-sacrifice, Kovic fails to measure up to his ideal as an adolescent. While the book celebrates its attainment when he wins a Christmas wrestling tournament, the film depicts him as a loser. In the final seconds of his match for the conference championship, he struggles futilely against being pinned beneath a superior male, a position of humiliating defeat while family and friends urge him to do the impossible: to fight harder. As Kovic lies on his back, the humiliated and isolated victim of all he has been taught, listening to the outrage of the hometown crowd whose creed is threatened by his failure, Stone's camera work recalls and builds on the conclusion of the war game in the woods: close-up of Kovic being counted out by the referee, a high-angle medium shot of Kovic prostrate on the mat crying, and a slow zoom-in for a close-up of his face registering a defeat which this time he cannot deny before an impartial judge and sympathetic witnesses. It seems a metaphorical preview of America's Vietnam experience. Again the screen fades to black.

Although Kovic's dream of heroic manhood is nearly buried by this public mortification, that dream is resurrected in the next scene. With the screen dark as a grave, Stone initiates a sound overlap like the door of a burial crypt being opened; simultaneously he raises the light level to reveal two Marines marching into Kovic's high school auditorium on a recruiting visit. Speaking in a deep voice reminiscent of John Wayne, Sergeant Hayes confirms that there is still a place where boys can become men by fulfilling the American myth of the heroic warrior with a mission: "Just try thirteen weeks of hell at Parris Island, South Carolina. You'll find out if you really are a man. We have never lost a war. We have always come when our country has called us."

Childhood and adolescent experience seems to have shaken Kovic's faith in this cultural ideal, but his failure to live up to it in the war game or the wrestling arena only motivates him to accept a presumably more authentic, mature test of masculinity on the battlefield. It will take the Vietnam experience to disabuse Kovic and many of his generation of this anachronistic, naively arrogant, destructive definition of heroic manhood—to, as Stone would have it, emasculate them.

Earlier Stone's undercutting of the heroic view of masculinity which contributes to war is previewed in the Fourth of July parade which a young Ron Kovic views from atop his father's shoulders. During the celebration he comes face-to-face with the disabled veterans of America's previous wars: a man with no arms and a grief-stricken face unmollified by the crowd's cheers; a paralyzed Marine sergeant (played by the real Kovic) in a wheelchair who flinches at exploding firecrackers. The idea that sacrifice may be inglorious and that celebrating sacrifice may wound rather than heal lurks within the parade like a nightmare within the communal dream. But if the prepubescent Kovic is sobered by the horror of manly sacrifice at the parade, he is intoxicated again by his own heroic potential when he ferociously unwraps a birthday present from Donna, a real Yankees baseball cap. When another boy steals the cap, Kovic is not confused about what he should do: rather than staying with Donna, he chases the boy, pursuing the symbol of heroic stature which he intends to earn.

He does, however, feel confusion between the myth of the hero-

ic warrior and his attraction to Donna, an attraction he experiences
on the night of the high school prom when he stays home to pack
for boot camp. Although he tells his parents he loves his country
and is willing to die for it, in his room he confesses to God, "I'm
so confused. Sometimes I think I just wanna stay here in Massapequa and never leave. But I gotta go." Torn between love of
country, which he has been taught to feel, and love for Donna,
which he has come naturally to feel, he prays to make the right
decision. Then, as if receiving divine guidance, he rushes through
rain-soaked streets to the prom where he asks Donna to dance with
him, kisses her lovingly, and clings to her tightly. As an adolescent awakening to his own repressed sexuality, Kovic feels sorrow
at having to sacrifice his personal desires for conventional masculine obligations. Perhaps he imagines he can return to reclaim what
he gives up, but the war will make that impossible.

The romantic prom scene poses an alternative to the dream of
masculine identity achieved through war—maturing heterosexual
love. Kovic's confusion of these two dreams of becoming a man is
conveyed visually by Stone's establishing shot in-country. Fading
from the scene of Kovic dancing with Donna to an eerie pink
screen penetrated at the left edge by the silhouette of an erect
column, the camera cranes down to a long shot of American soldiers marching toward us silhouetted against the dawn. A white
subtitle identifies the location as the Cua Viet River, 1967. As the
shot develops, our perception of the dark image on the left changes from phallic blade to war-ravaged tree in a barren but perverse-
ly beautiful wasteland. The dead and limbless trunk on the real
battlefield comments ironically on the sun-dappled living trees of
the Massapequa woods where Kovic played war as a boy. The dead
tree also suggests comparison to the soldiers who share its shad-
owy ambiguity as creative or destructive forces. And, finally, the
tree anticipates the soldiers' fates as amputees, burnouts, or those
killed in action. Juxtaposed to the dream of love, the dream of
war is a nightmare.

Kovic's war experience is dramatized and filmed to emphasize
his confusion about what is manly, patriotic, and righteous.
Instructed by his lieutenant, Sergeant Kovic stares hard at a Vietnamese village and tries to confirm that he sees VC with rifles.
A point-of-view shot indicates he does not, but when pressed
by the lieutenant, Kovic sees what he is told to see, just as if he
were back home and being spoken to by his elders. Although he

instructs his squad to hold their fire, they do not. Kovic excuses the firing to his lieutenant as "a possible accidental discharge, sir." When Kovic leads a small detachment in to survey the damage, he discovers only mutilated women and children. Shocked and distraught that Marines under his command have killed those they sought to protect, Kovic tries to repair the irreparable when, suddenly, NVA troops overrun the village, reinforcing powerfully, once again, the ambiguity that faced American soldiers in Vietnam. His lieutenant pulls him away from the innocent victims, repeatedly telling Kovic the slaughter is not his fault and forcing him to retreat. Falling back, Kovic is blinded by the sun and fires three rounds into the silhouette of a soldier emerging over the crest of a dune above him; the soldier is one of his own Marines, Corporal Wilson, whose safety he had guaranteed just prior to the battle.

Stone films Kovic's failure to fulfill America's myth of the heroic warrior so as to intensify his and the audience's confusion and shock. First, inside one village hooch, as the soldiers realize what they have done, Stone uses a hand-held camera, zip pans, and a series of quick cuts before the content curve. The effect is a physically felt destabilization of the soldiers' sense of who they are and what their mission has been. It is the visual equivalent of one Marine's incredulous, "Motherfucker, we wasted them." Second, when Kovic accidentally shoots Corporal Wilson, Stone photographs it from Kovic's point of view in slow and then in fast motion. The scene concludes with a slow zoom from a long to a full shot of Kovic on his hands and knees silhouetted against a pink sunset. Consequently, Stone makes us share Kovic's sudden panic at feeling overrun, his gradual realization of his mistake, and his frantic confirmation of having murdered a fellow patriot. Finally, in the color and shadow of the Cua-Viet-River establishing shot which introduced Vietnam as the authentic test of heroic manhood, we witness Kovic's grief at having failed.

Although Kovic is willing to accept responsibility and make amends for the "accidental discharges" which have murdered Vietnamese civilians and a fellow Marine, his commanding officers will not permit him to do so. His lieutenant will not let Kovic risk his life by treating a dying baby and absolves him of blame. Similarly, Kovic's repeated attempts to confess shooting Corporal Wilson are denied by his executive officer who threatens him with violence.

Guilt thus compels Kovic to find his own penance, once again victimizing himself by acting out the myth of the heroic warrior. In January 1968 near the DMZ he has his chance. As American infantry sweep through an open field, Sergeant Kovic's black machine gunner introduces the redemptive mission with a string of thematically appropriate profanity: "I'm gonna kill me some motherfuckin' gooks. . . . This must be hell. . . . Where the motherfuckin' devil?" As they are ambushed and Kovic is literally shot in his Achilles' heel, he reacts in similarly realistic, if offensive, language: "Son of a bitch! Fuck, man!" Despite his wound, Kovic rises again and, as he later describes it, plays "John Fuckin' Wayne" by recklessly exposing himself to fire. This time Stone shows Kovic's paralyzing second wound in slow motion, complete with blood spray and a death-rattling gurgle, intercut by a sharply contrastive, almost subliminally short flashback to the childhood war game. The black medic who evacuates the nearly dead Kovic under fire chants the final commentary on this scene like a perverted litany: "Motherfucker, motherfucker, motherfucker."

Each of these monologues seems designed to do more than merely illustrate that soldiers talk dirty. The characters' sexually charged profanity works in concert with the film's images to elaborate upon the theme of emasculation. For example, the wound which concludes Kovic's participation in the Vietnam War is graphically depicted as a bloody penetration which serves as incremental repetition of the two earlier scenes ending in flat-on-the-back submission and failure, one concluding the war game and one the wrestling match. Ironically, the child's dream of becoming a man, which his culture has promoted, has unmanned him. Very subtly, Stone's realistic dialogue suggests his meaning at another, deeper level. The confusion of righteousness, patriotism, and manliness (which constitutes the most comprehensive version of the American male's dream of heroism turned nightmare) is amply illustrated in the language and imagery of sexual taboo to create an elaborate objective correlative for Kovic's war experience. They seem designed to shock the film's audience into feeling as well as apprehending the destruction of America's heroic masculine ideal in Vietnam.

Kovic's emasculation in Vietnam nearly kills him. He is given the last rites of the Roman Catholic Church by a chaplain in a field hospital but refuses to actually die. Evacuated back to the States and consigned to a living death as a castrated loser in what Stone pictures as a patriarchal culture intolerant of anything less than clearly winning—either the war or the peace—he begins a long, slow process of trying to resurrect himself as a man.

In the Bronx Veterans Hospital, physicians tell Kovic what he has lost is irretrievable: he will never walk; he will never have children. Initially, Kovic refuses to accept what the war has made of him. In a dream he rises from his wheelchair, walks, and then runs from his fellow disabled veterans in the hospital. But in actuality, he only drags himself around the hospital on crutches. "Walking from midchest. *Semper Fi*, Motherfucker. It can be done," he exclaims proudly before falling to fracture one of his legs and end forever the dream of holding himself erect and walking again.

Meanwhile the hospital staff mock what Stone portrays as Kovic's naively heroic attitude. As the orderly extracts an enema tube from Kovic, he jokes, "My man, Kovic, it's the Fourth of July," then makes a popping sound with a finger inside his cheek. Kovic's physical therapist, Willie, tells him, "You so gung ho you don't know shit about what's goin' on in this country. It's a revolution goin' on. If you aren't part of the solution, you part of the problem." When Kovic calls out to his nurse (appropriately enough named Washington) that he is tired of lying in his own waste and he wants her to treat him like a human being because he fought for his country, she replies, "Don't you raise your voice to me, Mr. Kovic." Finally, an orderly tells Kovic that he doesn't "give a shit about Vietnam; you can take Vietnam and shove it. . . ." Again, this speech is more than merely talking dirty. The excremental language in these hospital scenes suggests metaphorically that Kovic slowly is being purged of his notion that he is a man because he made a heroic sacrifice for which his country is grateful. This is a lesson which he is taught primarily by black men and women, who are other victims, Stone implies, of American patriarchal domination. Kovic's physical wound compels him to share their weakness and dependency. Although he remains prowar even in the VA hospital, it is there that he experiences how it feels to be helpless, like a woman or boy, in a society dominated by the kind of macho man he has dreamed of being. Ultimately, this combination of physical and psychic wounding forces Kovic to begin to question his attitude toward the war and to redefine what it means to be a man in America.

Back in Massapequa, Kovic's confidence that his sacrifice has been worthwhile is further undercut in Stone's film. At a Fourth of July parade welcoming him home as a hero, he witnesses that the war itself has come home. Along the street some spectators smile and give him a thumbs-up sign, but others shake their heads in disbelief or give him the finger. Thus, Kovic's secret knowledge that he is no hero is given public expression by some hometown Americans. The smoky parade route itself literally becomes a battlefield between marchers and spectators, mirroring the Vietnam veteran's own internal turmoil. Later, during the celebration, Kovic has a flashback so realistic that he is unable to complete his speech echoing the clichés of the World War II veteran who precedes him. And that evening Kovic confesses to his fellow veteran and best childhood friend, Timmy, that his failure to meet the test of manhood in Vietnam has compromised his beliefs. "I made terrible mistakes. I was castrated that day because I was so stupid. . . . I'd give everything I believe in to be whole again."

In the autobiography, Kovic's rehabilitation includes attending college, but in the film he visits Donna at Syracuse University; this change develops the film's link between physical and political impotence. Discovering that Donna has become an antiwar activist, Kovic sees that renewing his love for her is as impossible as climbing the stairs to her dormitory in his wheelchair. Then, at an antiwar demonstration on campus, he realizes that the country to which he has returned has changed as much as the girl he planned to come back to and love forever: he witnesses a black veteran throw away medals won in Vietnam; he is clubbed by a policeman while in his wheelchair; and he is forcibly separated from Donna as the war at home escalates. This new episode demonstrates Kovic's discovery that being a disabled Vietnam veteran is no protection against being regarded a traitor merely for exercising his right of free assembly; it confirms his political impotence.

Returning to Massapequa, Kovic is so obsessed with grieving for what he has lost that he can find no way to recover. Coming home drunk one night, he quarrels bitterly with his mother. This amplified scene dramatizes the clearest and most emotionally charged connection between physical, political, and spiritual impotence that is the consequence of the American soldier's Vietnam service. In an interview for *American Film* Ron Kovic noted that it was "the most difficult scene in the movie—for all of us, not just myself, for all the actors and actresses."[12] In the scene, Kovic removes the crucifix from the living room wall and tells his mother bluntly that he is a nonbeliever, that America's holy war against communism in Vietnam was all a lie, that he killed women and children, and that she is to blame because of what she taught him. This dramatic confrontation is couched in language clearly calculated to shock an audience into feeling as well as understanding the humiliation, pain, and outrage of the Vietnam veteran who is in every conceivable sense of the word disabled precisely because he attempted to fulfill his country's ideal of heroic manhood. "Stone has never been a feel-good director, has never shrunk from assaulting the sensibilities of his audiences. He likes to make them squirm before the bad and the ugly, forcing them to look when they'd prefer to avert their eyes."[13] Here the film's perhaps most painfully protracted and offensive dialogue defines Kovic's—and by extension, America's Vietnam involvement as an ideal-shattering obscenity. Targeting the political, religious, and sexual sensibilities of his viewers, Stone in this scene clearly means to drive home his point that Kovic's loss represents the loss of all purpose and belief. In rage, Kovic tells his mother that she needs help with her God and her dreams, that all is a lie, and that God is as dead as Kovic's dead legs, as dead as his dead sex organs. This furious and accusatory exchange between Kovic and his mother results in her expelling him from the house.

Ironically, Kovic's banishment from home is the familial equivalent of the "my country, love it or leave it" ultimatum repeatedly directed at war protesters. When Kovic's father puts him to bed that night he asks his son what he wants. Kovic replies, "I want to be a man again," then asks, "Who's gonna love me?" In the film adaptation, then, Kovic's losing the love of his girlfriend and his mother is the immediate dramatic equivalent of having lost the love of his country. Tragically, he has become an object of pity or contempt in seeking the approval of others in ways those others prescribed. In the film, as in the book, Kovic goes into self-imposed exile in Mexico in an attempt to recover a manhood which will allow him to be loved. Again, this quest is articulated in sexual terms.

South of the border, he meets a legion of Vietnam veterans who, like Kovic, are self-banished from their mother country. Stone's visual introduction of this sequence suggests that this exile is a doomed search, one equivalent to that for manhood in Vietnam. Stone begins with a flashback to the pink sky and dunes along the beach where Kovic unintentionally helped murder women and children and accidentally shot Corporal Wilson; then, following a match-cut to another beach, the camera tracks and pans to a complex of thatched huts identified as Villa Dulce, Mexico, 1970. Here veterans are drinking, playing poker, and fondling prostitutes: acting out the grown-up, peace-time version of the debilitating macho definition of manhood they accepted when they went to war. As Kovic enters the group, another veteran refers to them all reductively and intentionally, offensively remarking, "Just what we need around here, another limp dick." A burnout named Charlie introduces Kovic to the scene, implying that sexual activity can still console the impotent Vietnam veteran and purge him of bitterness. His advice for dealing with Mexican prostitutes seems a black humorist foreshadowing of Kovic's rehabilitative triumph as the veterans' antiwar spokesman at the 1976 Democratic National Convention: "If you don't have it in the hips, you better have it in the lips."

Briefly, Kovic is able to convince himself that he is still a man by consorting with whores, but that too is a lie, a trick which grows increasingly obvious. Vietnam flashbacks prevent Kovic from sustaining the illusion of potency, and eventually the prostitutes openly laugh at Charlie who thought he had found paradise in a whorehouse. When Kovic accompanies Charlie, searching for a new paradise where they might be regarded as men again, Charlie becomes so abusive that the driver abandons both veterans in their wheelchairs in a desert. This scene, added by Stone, illustrates the futility of the Vietnam veteran's attempt to regain his manhood in exile. Nearly inarticulate by this time, the two ex-patriot veterans argue in sexual and scatological obscenities who is the better man as measured by the Vietnam experience:

Charlie: Fuck 'em. Fuck the Mexicans. Fuck the gooks. Fuck 'em
           all. . . . You ever have to kill little gook babies? I'll bet
           you was never ordered to kill little gook babies.

Kovic: Leave me the fuck alone. Maybe I killed more babies
           than you did.

Charlie: You ever look at yourself in a mirror? You better than
           us? You a hero? Shit, Kovic, you wasn't even there.

As the argument develops, the two circle one another in their wheelchairs. Moving closer and closer until they stare into each other's face as if into a mirror, they drag one another down and roll over and over fighting to exhaustion in an orgy of self-destruction. This time Kovic's wrestling match has no referee, no spectators, no winner. It is a *reductio ad absurdum* of the notion of heroic manhood which first seduced the two combatants into Vietnam. Charlie is what Kovic will become unless he can answer the question he asked when abandoned in the desert: "How are we gonna get out of here?"

Kovic does go home again: rescued from the desert by an anonymous good Samaritan, the wounded veteran repatriates himself (and symbolically other veterans) by apprehending new ways to be a man. In a scene added to the film, Kovic goes to Venus, Georgia, Corporal Wilson's hometown. Stopping in the cemetery at Wilson's grave is like visiting his own tomb. As Kovic approaches, Stone's camera gives a slow-motion point-of-view shot tracking in to a close-up of the headstone, then a reverse-angle close-up of Kovic. While this visual is held in a long take, there is a voice-over flashback of Kovic's prebattle conversation reassuring Wilson and his postbattle conversation angering the executive officer who did not allow him to take responsibility for Wilson's death. In effect, Kovic is visiting the grave of his own buried manhood. He resurrects himself when he goes to Wilson's home to confess.

The Wilsons' living room is a war shrine filled with mementos of the family's long history of patriotic combat. Mr. Wilson describes his son's glorious funeral and Colonel Moore's letter indicating how Wilson distinguished himself in the fight and died quickly. But a close-up of the wall clock indicates time has run out for these anachronistic clichés of heroic manhood. It is the mother who admits, "Of course, we never really knew what happened." As Kovic confesses to Wilson's family, he experiences a Vietnam flashback in black and white. His grief-wracked, tear-stained, eyewitness account drains all the color from their illusion of American boys as heroic warriors. Kovic strips away the lies that make it easier for parents to sacrifice their sons: they killed babies; he wasn't Wilson's friend because they didn't talk to new guys much; the battle was confusing, crazy; by accident, he killed Wilson who had fallen behind in the retreat.

The women of the family acknowledge his confession. Wilson's widow tells Kovic that she can never forgive him but perhaps God can. Wilson's mother says simply, "We understand the pain that you been goin' through, Ron." Wilson's father sits in stunned silence, his family's notion, his country's notion of heroic manhood called into doubt by what Kovic experienced in Vietnam.

But Kovic is remasculinized, repatriated, and resurrected by his confession, as Stone's camera work and editing suggest. Kovic's departure from Wilsons' home is captured in a crane shot which slowly rises above Wilsons' front yard littered with generations of cast-off junk and up through brown autumn leaves clinging to a tree in the foreground. A sound overlap of the song, "When Johnny Comes Marching Home," begins and continues as a large American flag is superimposed over the tree. This tree is more like the sun-dappled, green-leaved tree of Kovic's youth than the ravaged battlefield tree in Vietnam: this tree is mature, and although dormant, not dead. Rising above the guilt, Kovic has begun the process of regaining his manhood, his patriotism, and his life by coming home to admit the truth of what he did in Vietnam, to take responsibility for it, and to communicate that to fellow Americans who must share that responsibility. What Kovic learned during his exile in Mexico is that "if you don't have it in the hips, you better have it in the lips." Now he sets out to fulfill an alternative, non-violent dream of manhood bequeathed by his mother before the Vietnam War: to speak to a large crowd just like the president and to say great things. The scene which follows literalizes the sound overlap: Vietnam veterans marching home again to protest against the war at the 1972 Republican National Convention in Miami. The camera provides a long shot of the American flag waving, then tilts down to a high angle and zooms in to Kovic in his wheelchair serving as flag bearer in the parade. The flagstaff rests in Kovic's crotch; he and his fellow veterans chant, "One, two, three, four / we don't want your fucking war." The shot defines Vietnam veterans' political activism as regained potency. This metaphor is extended visually as Kovic and two other veterans in wheelchairs break into the convention hall without credentials and disrupt President Nixon's acceptance speech. As Kovic speaks before the cameras, he rises from his wheelchair and holds himself erect with indignation. For thirty seconds the image of Ron Kovic replaces the image of the president on the huge TV monitor in the convention hall. Those Americans who are most supportive of the Vietnam War are forced to listen to the militant casualties of that conflict. A changed Kovic disputes the creed he was taught:

> We were lied to, tricked into going. They say if you don't love America, get out; well, we love America, but I can't begin to tell you how the leadership of this country sickens me. The government is a bunch of corrupt thieves. . . . The truth is they have killed a

whole generation of young Americans. . . . We are never going to let the people of the United States forget this war. We are your Yankee Doodle Dandy come home.

The film makes opposing the war in 1972 the patriotic equivalent of fighting it in 1967. Kovic and his fellow veterans are forced to retreat from the convention hall by security. They are betrayed and attacked by police disguised as fellow veterans. As this scene unfolds outside, Stone crosscuts to inside the convention hall where the president shamelessly lies to the American people. Inside, the huge television monitor displays Nixon's image urging Americans to "give the veterans the respect they deserve" while outside they are being beaten and arrested. When Kovic is assaulted by an undercover policeman who wants to kill him for being a traitor, he is rescued by veterans in a scene resembling his evacuation from Vietnam. But the sense of déjà vu ends there. This time, Kovic's rehabilitation is managed by fellow veterans, not unsympathetic bureaucrats. Within minutes, he is medically evaluated, restored to his wheelchair, receives a situation report, and rallies his troops to retake the hall. At home, the veterans regain self-respect by becoming guerrilla fighters in what Stone pictures as a new American Revolution, attempting to wrest power from an increasingly remote and corrupt political establishment.

Unlike the autobiography, which ends as it began with Kovic's being wounded, the cinematic adaptation concludes in 1976 at the Democratic National Convention in New York City, when veterans speaking through Ron Kovic are depicted as true patriots trying to restore democracy at home rather than impose it abroad. This convention scene opens with a speech by New York's Congressman Dellums on the huge television monitor. Dellums, a black man, describes the Democratic party as returning America to its heritage by reaching out to include rich and poor, white and black, men and women. Joining this cause, Kovic and other Vietnam veterans against the war are resurrected as redemptive heroes: enlightened by the Vietnam experience, they awaken, Stone suggests, fellow citizens to the folly and waste of violently imposing the American frontier myth upon an alien culture. In helping to repatriate other disenfranchised citizens as well as themselves, they exemplify the Vietnam veteran as a reformed warrior hero: one committed less to the conventionally masculine attitude that there are things worth dying for than to the conventionally feminine one that there are things worth living for.[14] Having suffered betrayal, victimization, and loss of esteem by acting as the violent instruments of a patri- archical myth, they have acquired a chastened, matured, broadened conception of what it means to be a man.

In her book *The Remasculinization of America: Gender and the Vietnam War,* Susan Jeffords argues that most Vietnam War litera- ture can be read as favoring a return to traditional roles which serve the interests of patriarchy. Strikingly, Oliver Stone's adapta- tion of Ron Kovic's *Born on the Fourth of July* seems an excep- tion. The film's transformation of a static circular plot into a linear one which emphasizes the protagonist's being forced to redefine his manhood, its expansion of female roles, its addition of uncon- ventionally heroic episodes like the visit to Corporal Wilson's fam- ily, and the address at the 1976 political convention, and its development of an extended sexual trope in both dialogue and image—all provoke reevaluation of the heroic masculine ideal in- herited from America's frontier history. Rather than polarizing tra- ditional gender constructions, this film blurs them; rather than celebrating patriarchical domination over "feminized" others, it expands upon the disastrous consequences of such domination for both sexes; rather than reaffirming the American frontier myth as a license to commit violence abroad, the film redefines the myth as a mission to extend a nonviolent political franchise at home. In these ways, the film version of *Born on the Fourth of July* is revolutionary. Oliver Stone's film, in its troubling language and powerfully evocative cinematography, as well as in its aggressive sexual metaphors, works to incorporate America's painful legacy of Vietnam not only into a mythic past but also into an ameliorat- ed future.

Notes

1. Peter McInerney, "'Straight' and 'Secret' History in Vietnam War Literature," *Contemporary Literature* 22 (1981): 198.

2. Ron Kovic, *Born on the Fourth of July* (New York: Pocket Books, 1977), 186.

3. John Hellman, *American Myth and the Legacy of Vietnam* (New York: Columbia Univ. Press, 1986), 102.

4. Hellman, *American Myth*, 110.

5. David Ansen, "Bringing It All Back Home," Review of *Born on the Fourth of July*, *Newsweek*, 25 December 1989, 74.

6. Paul Chutkow, "Cruise Declares Independence," Review of *Born on the Fourth of July*, *Providence Sunday Journal*, 7 January 1990, sec. H, p. 9.

7. Robert Scheer, "Born on the Fourth of July," *Premiere*, February 1990, 53.

8. Pauline Kael, "Potency." Review of *Born on the Fourth of July*, *New Yorker*, 22 January 1990, 123.

9. Albert Auster and Leonard Quart, *How the War Was Remembered: Hollywood & Vietnam* (New York: Praeger, 1988), 42.

10. Kovic, *Born*, 11.

11. Hellman, *American Myth*, 103–5.

12. Robert Seidenberg, "To Hell and Back," *American Film*, January 1990, 31.

13. Peter Biskind, "Cutter's Way," *Premiere*, February 1990, 63.

14. Susan Jeffords, *The Remasculinization of America: Gender and the Vietnam War* (Bloomington: Ind. Univ. Press, 1989), 74.

Chapter 8

The Doors

"Enough to Base a Movie On?"

Suzanne E. O'Hop

> The movie will begin in five minutes
> The mindless voice announced
> All those unseated will await the next show
> We filed slowly, languidly into the hall
> The auditorium was fast and silent
> As we seated and were darkened
> The voice continued
> The program for this evening is not new
> You've seen this entertainment
> Through and through
> You've seen your birth, your life and death
> You might recall all the rest
> Did you have a good world when you died?
> Enough to base a movie on?

With these words written and spoken by Jim Morrison, Oliver Stone answers this final question with his motion picture tribute to Morrison and his rock group in *The Doors*. In fact, it is more than relevant that Stone chooses this poem to begin his film. His purpose is twofold. One, he automatically establishes the importance of Morrison's poetry as a guiding force in his filmmaking tribute, and two, he validates Morrison's own views on the cinema. Thus, by closely examining Morrison's poetry dealing with film and by coming to an understanding of his poetic visuals, one can begin to understand how and why Stone made this film.

Morrison sees cinema as having evolved in two major ways. The first is as spectacle. He says that "its goal is the creation of a total substitute sensory world" (*L*, 65).[1] This idea plays itself out in film in several ways. The first is, as Morrison indicates, to help us see God in all things and beings. One way that he believes this can be done is by creating a "powerful, infinite mythology" as well as the "illusion of timelessness" (L, 54). He does this by relying on techniques associated with the "shadow play." He, in fact, calls cinema the "contemporary manifestation of an evolving history of shadows, a delight in pictures that move, a belief in magic" (L, 67). Its images are closely entwined with ideas important to Eastern thought—images associated with the spirit and natural world, religious rituals, and celebrations of death. Indeed, Morrison places a great deal of emphasis on death, believing that "the appeal of cinema lies in the fear of death" (L, 54). Why? Morrison makes sense of this by explaining film as a group of dead pictures which are given life through artificial insemination. It is the creation of the images which allows the film to portray a sense of godliness or divine power. This insemination or creation, however, cannot happen without the spectator. It is the spectators' role which allows that "special divinity" (L, 87) of the created images to emerge.

Morrison's idea of the spectators' role in the life-giving impulse of film is closely related to another one of his views—the cinema's role as outlet for the spectators' voyeuristic impulses. He refers to film as a "peep show," calling it an "erotic science" and a "cerebral erection" (L, 65, 87, 52). This peep show of images is able to make a partner of the spectator, and together "life" is given through what Morrison terms "mutual masturbation" (L, 75). Morrison seems to see the cinema as "male," in its role as inseminator, and the spectator as "female," in its role as lifegiver. Obviously, masturbation is a self-gratifying act which has no real function in a life-giving sense, but the mutual stimulation which film and spectator produce together results in an "artificial" life, the re-creation of reality in pictures. Morrison also considers this mutual masturbation to be a "colorful group therapy" (L, 75). The stimulation and subsequent release of cinema creates a kind of healing. This, in turn, becomes another important function of film. Morrison ultimately says that the creative or life-producing role of the spectator is a therapeutic one. Therefore, the watching of, and participating in, a film is a catharsis of sorts.

Stone's movie uses many of Morrison's ideas from his poetry. It is clear that Stone was, indeed, influenced by Morrison's work. In fact, some would say that "the director appears to be living vicariously through his hero; he wants to be Morrison, to be the Morrison of filmmakers."[2] Certainly it is appropriate for Stone to be influenced by a man who, like him, "experienced the world in literary and visual contexts."[3] Stone remembers Vietnam as being the experience which first made him start "thinking in visual terms."[4] It is more than a coincidence that while there Stone also first heard the music and, more importantly, the lyrics of *The Doors*. He described this experience as "a giant epic poem, Homer reciting the Iliad."[5] And, while Stone saw Morrison's lyrics in poetic and visual terms, Morrison, according to Ray Manzarek, made a concerted effort to see his lyrics in cinematic terms:

> He had always thought of music in cinematic terms because it evoked images and existed in vibrations . . . he was hearing cinematic poetry. Poetry that created images in the mind—pictures. The combination of the cinematic aspects of poetry and the cinematic aspects of music was a concept of unlimited potential.[6]

Morrison could not escape his thoughts on film, and they permeated his music and his poetry.

This combination of the literary and the visual which became important to Stone in Vietnam surely influenced him when he returned from the war. He, in fact, describes his first few attempts at films as "kind of abstract poems."[7] And, like Morrison who, according to his biographers, "wanted to make you feel his poems—in fact he wanted to flood your senses with imagery so strong that the meaning singed your psyche like an exposed nerve straight to the heart," Stone's films have come to be described in much the same way. The combination of "an aural, visual, and psychological journey" became both Morrison's and Stone's credo for their art. Thus, the aim of Morrison's poetry and Stone's films is: "To imply and suggest and elicit a reaction from the listener's whole body rather than just his mind . . . to deliver people from the limited ways in which they see and feel."[8] Clearly, there are many connections between Stone's film work and Morrison's literary efforts.

It is important to look at Stone's views on Morrison's life. He voraciously read all of Morrison's poetry before writing his screenplay. And, like Morrison's description of film in his poetic manifesto, Stone creates a powerful mythology in his portrayal of Jim. He does this by structuring his film around many of the images and themes found in Morrison's conception of the shadow play.

Stone refers to Morrison's images, cataloging some of them as snakes, fire, earth, death, fear, eros, sexuality."[9] These conceptions, as well as a heavy reliance on the use of shadows, play pivotal roles in Stone's creation of Morrison. A special importance is also placed on death in this film. Stone reminds us that Morrison wrote about it all over his poetry and music . . . He was half in love with death;"[10] therefore, it is not surprising that death is a prevalent theme in Stone's film.

Stone knows that he is mythmaking. In response to the potential criticism that he expected for his film, he said, "They don't understand it will not be the real Jim on film—it will be my poem to Jim. It's my vision, my fictional poem."[11] And, it is, after all, the poetry that lasts, according to Stone. With this in mind, Stone's use of Morrison's poetry to guide his filmmaking is no surprise, for his intent seems to be to not only mythologize Morrison, but to make a film that lasts.

Stone pays no less attention to the spectators' role in the film than Morrison does in his poetry about cinema. Stone, in fact, helps his spectators to participate in Morrison's journey by a kind of voyeurism similar to that already described. His mutual masturbation, however, takes a bit of a different format. He helps his spectators to experience his vision and take part in the creation of his images by reconstructing a hallucinogenic trip in order to assist his audience's mind "expansion and contraction"[12] which he, himself, found through drug use. Morrison, interestingly enough, described in his poetry the effects of such drugs in the language of a cinematic experience:

> the event in which either is introduced into a roomful of people through air vents makes the chemical an actor . . . The people consider themselves audience, while they perform for each other, and the gas acts out poems of its own through the medium of the human body (L, 74).

Morrison illustrates the participatory nature of drug use in much the same way as he describes the quasi-sexual experience of film. He goes on to confirm that the purpose of drug use is virtually the same as the sexual ethos of the cinema:

> the aim of this happening is to cure boredom, wash the eyes, make childlike reconnections with the stream of life. Its lowest, wildest

aim for purgation of perception. The happening attempts to engage all the senses (*L*, 74).

Likewise, Stone believes that "the act of imagination, the act of seeing beyond yourself, stepping outside your ordinary, small, mundane life, living a larger life" through drug use and the cinema "will make your life so much more joyous, less painful . . . allow escape and freedom."[13]

The use of drugs which create a vision in the mind was not only vital to the 1960s, but also played a crucial role for many visionaries over the centuries. Stone realizes this and he knew that re-creating such an effect would surely help his viewers to experience his work and to elicit a powerful response from them. This, after all, was his ultimate goal in his filmmaking. He wanted his audience to "share . . . completely cross the barrier," be "empathetic in the Greek sense of the word."[14] Therefore, he structures this movie "as a hallucinatory ritual journey,"[15] one in which Stone "wants to sweep us up in the frenzied spirit of stoned excess, pull us into the psychedelic spiral of Morrison's dance, inside his freaky abandon, to capture us—make us feel—the hallucinatory rapture of the period."[16] By eliciting such a powerful response amongst his viewers, Stone succeeds in performing a cathartic ritual for the spectator. Such a ritual manifests itself in several ways in this film.

One of the most effective ways that Stone evokes the disorienting effects of drugs is through inventive camera work. He uses a swooping handheld camera, odd angles, dreamy soft-focus sequences, jolting camera motions, strobe lighting, and distorting lenses. The use of the subjective point of view also adds to the effect. In addition, Stone saturates the senses by incorporating any extended musical sequence with the use of flashbacks and/or hallucinations. Furthermore, Stone's work relies heavily on the use of "a kaleidoscope of fire and color, reds, blues and black, creating an operatic opulence."[17]

This reliance on color, coupled with his use of visual motifs, plays a crucial role in not only re-creating the sensual experience of drugs associated with the participatory voyeuristic impulse, but also helping to establish the principles that Morrison set forth in his ideas of film as spectacle. Morrison's own use of LSD "centered around primal symbols" like those associated with the shadow play.[18] These symbols include earth, sky (and its associations with the sun), and underworld (and its associations with the moon and water). Each of these symbols suggests a specific color as well. The earth is associated with browns, the sky with whites and yellows, and the underworld with blues. Stone clearly uses these specific images and colors to mythologize Morrison as well as to punctuate the hallucinatory aspects of his life. In this way, Stone and the audience can give life to the man. Yet, it is only through his death that Stone can give life to Morrison via a film resurrection. It is then appropriate that images of death would pervade Stone's film as it did Morrison's poetry. Stone portrays these death images in three specific scenes, and he emphasizes the visual quality of death with the color red. Morrison was, indeed, interested in the traditional or primal symbols. He, in fact, begins his poem "Science of Night" with the words "Earth Air Fire Water / Mother Father Sons & Daughters" (*W*, 172). Stone relies on these symbols which revolve around Morrison's conceptions of the ancient tradition of the Eastern shadow play. Stone not only uses these specific images, but he also relies heavily on the use of shadows in his imagery. In the first scene alone, Stone's screenplay reveals a frequent use of shadows: "shadow a grand piano," "camera moves tentatively along the shadows," and "camera reveals James Douglas Morrison—27, poet, buried in the shadows" (*S*, 1).[19] In much the same way, Stone's screen direction and subsequent imagery reflects Morrison's ideas or visions dredged right out of his poetry.

The first example of an extensive use of Morrison's lyrics as scene direction occurs with the opening desert scene which is pinpointed as a pivotal moment in young Jim's life. Stone's establishment of this scene provides an overview of the desert where two dirt roads—what Morrison's poetry calls "the veins of highways" (*W*, 26)—meet and cross each other. Morrison's poetry describes this particular detail: "The crossroads / a place where ghosts / reside to whispers into / the ear of travellers & / interest them in their fate" (*W*, 46). We know that this "crossroads" implies the fate of young Jim.

Stone tints this particular scene brown. This choice reflects the earthiness of the images which Morrison implies. He describes the way that "the female land / was bright, all swelling to degree / most comfortless & guarding" (*W*, 159) and Stone picks up on this visual and directs that the "blinding desert be so barren, so hot it stings to look at" (*S*, 2) as well as suggesting that the old Chevrolet wind through the landscape beneath a brewing storm.

Morrison then recounts his famous life-changing experience in which he, as a very young child, saw "Indians scattered on dawn's / Hiway bleeding / Ghosts crowd the young child's / fragile egg shell mind" (*W*, 139). Stone sees this in his screenplay:

> The boy's eyes going back to the Indian man looking at him . . . then to the dying opened body bleeding out its guts on the asphalt . . . the dying man's face, twisted, moaning, amazing eyes at the point of death—they settle on Jim.

Finally, this scene concludes with Stone's direction that, from young Jim's receding point of view, he is "looking back through the rear window, terrified, his first view of death. The bodies, the sense of doom overlaying the land—a child's worst nightmare" (*S*, 3). This visual comes directly from Morrison's own poetic images which describe not only the "wayward backward glance," (*L*, 141) but also "The child given in to night / Mare, while the grown / Man fears his fear" (*W*, 151). Thus, Morrison and then Stone establish the imprint of this childhood tragedy on the grown man's life by emphasizing the ominous nature of the earth and its mysteries. Stone continues his visual exploration of the primal symbols of life and death.

The next important visual stems from Morrison's interest in the sky. Two of Stone's scenes in particular suggest this fascination through a heavy emphasis on the color white and sun-drenched images. Stone opens up the important scene in which Morrison and Manzarek formulate the idea of a band by first using a wide-angle vertical shot of the sky and then a reverse-angle, bird's-eye view of the beach. We find that the scene cuts from a white screen to "a vertiginous drift above a crowded beach and finds Jim and Ray through a series of perceptible dissolves—a druggy sunny movement."[20] Morrison often reflects this feel in his poetry, using such terms as "crisp hot whiteness," (*L*, 26) while Stone's work is characterized as "white hot, lapped in honey gold."[21]

In another important scene which capitalizes on the use of the sky and the sun, Stone takes his spectators on a peyote trip in the desert. This scene opens with a car driving through the desert once again. Stone describes it as a dented red Chevrolet which fishtails out onto the desert, whereas Morrison evokes a similar feeling when he writes, "The car a craft / in wretched / SPACE / Sudden movements" (*W*, 41). Stone then calls for the group of young people to be "laughing in a circle somewhere on the edge of a precipice in deep canyons and magnificent rocks and cacti" (*S*, 29). He is guided by Morrison's words, "the boundless galaxies of dust / cactus spines, beads / bleach stones," while he details the sound of "Laughter & young voice / in the mountains" (*L*, 139,103).

Stone's next image is a deep-focus shot of what he calls in his screenplay "a bird of prey in the sky" (*S*, 32). It is certainly no coincidence that Morrison wrote a poem called "Bird of Prey" in which he imagines a bird "flying high in the summer sky" (*W*, 139). The camera then jump-cuts to a sun-drenched, medium close-up of Jim with his eyes closed, as he tentatively opens them like "a prisoner / blinks in the sun" (*W*, 6). Then, his close-up fades into a distorted, diffused one which gives him the appearance of being "Clothed in sunlight / restless in wanting / dying of fever" (*W*, 45). Stone then cuts to a low-angle shot of the huddle formed by the members of *The Doors*. He describes their chanting as "rising and falling like a collective breath," (*S*, 30) whereas Morrison, comparing the band to a tribe, develops a similar image which spotlights the importance of "Ceremonies . . . To reassert Tribal needs . . . a call to worship, uniting . . . a longing for family" (*W*, 14).

Stone intercuts all of this scene with various shots of the sky and the sun. He portrays the storminess of the sky by showing flashes of high-contrast light moving in between fast-moving clouds, panning the desert dunes, spreading sand through the air, rising the sun to a red halo, and finally diffusing it to blackness. All of these visual decisions come directly out of Morrison's work as he writes of how "the clouds flow by / & tell a story," "the climate alters like a / visible dance" and "the sun, an orange skull / whispers quietly, becomes an / island, & is gone" (*L*, 131).

Lastly, Jim wanders from the desert to the cave where he encounters the shaman and, more importantly, the shaman's eye with its vision of Jim's future. As he walks toward the shaman's cave, we see Pamela's outline dancing on the dunes, and Morrison's poetry should echo in our ears: "We have been metamorphosised from a mad / body dancing on hillsides to a pair of eyes / staring in the dark" as a "young woman is left on the desert" (*L*, 29, 108).

As Jim enters the cave and comes face to face with the shaman, he has now entered the realm of death in his mind. In the first of three death scenes, Jim and the spectator are lured by the white-faced man who comes to represent death to Jim during the space of the film. Morrison's poetry seems to recollect how this figure enticed him by "luring the Traveller / Mighty Voyager / Curious . . . The grave grinning / Indians of night / The eyes of night / . . . into the blood bath" (*W*, 43). Stone refers to this place as the "rock palace." Morrison's poetry recollects a similar "palace" which "is burning" and asks us to "bask in the warm hot coals" of the place (*W*, 11). Stone has once again saturated his film in the fiery colors and ideas of Morrison's words.

Stone continues to use Morrison's poetry for his scene direction. He calls for,

A gallery of ancient Indian Petroglyphs surround[ing] him on all sides. Curious oblong figures, buffalo, sacred deer and bear, creatures of the hunt; hunters and their weapons, rain clouds, masked deities proclaiming the answers to the Mysteries, the story of creation . . . staring at him from the wall (*S*, 33).

Morrison also envisions such an image in his own poetry when he tells us that he "received an Aztec wall / of vision" where "secrets [were] unveiled in the scarred chalk wall" (*W*, 140). Upon receiving the visions from the cave and preparing to meet death, Jim "closed [his] eyes, prepared to go / a gentle wind informed [him] so / and bathed [his] skin in ether glow" (*W*, 77).

In this scene, the image of the shaman's ominous eye is also an important one. Stone's camera cross-cuts between Jim and the shaman's eye until the camera zooms to an extreme close-up on the Indian's eye, closer and closer until we can see Jim's figure reflected in the eyeball. The zoom-in continues to focus on Jim's figure in the shaman's eye until the camera pulls back to reveal Jim singing on stage. Morrison's own words seem to reflect Stone's shot making: "The eye looks vulgar / Inside its ugly shell / Come out in the open / In all of your Brilliance" (*L*, 24). Truly, Morrison does "come out in all his brilliance" from the "vulgar eye" when Stone directs our attention to Jim's famous antics on stage in the next scene. It is important to remember that while these antics eventually lead to the man's death, they also provided a forum for his life force through his words and music.

As Morrison enters the cave it is significant that a woman marks his entrance into this underworld associated with both his life and death. Morrison's underworld, in fact, often associates itself with the feminine. He compares the womb to a mysterious, dark, and rather foreboding tomb. He writes: "Night time women / Wondrous

sacraments of doubt / Sprang sullen in bursts / of fear & guilt / in
the womb's pit hole / below / The belt of the beast" (*W*, 29). Often, these images are accompanied by symbols of the moon and
water as well as the color blue. Stone picks up on these associations, and like Morrison arranges his visuals around scenes
with women, for he believes that once you are tired of life and
are ready for death, you really want "to go back to the womb."[22]
These "night time" women are Pamela Courson and Patricia Kennealy.

The first of these scenes is one in which Morrison and Courson
spend time together getting to know each other. Stone shows Jim
"letting" himself into Pamela's house, watching her, and then gently waking her up as Morrison's words first echo: "She looked so
sad in sleep / Like a friendly hand / just out of reach / A candle
stranded on a beach" (*W*, 62) and then "Awake! / Shake dreams
from your hair, my pretty child / my sweet one" (Morrison from
the soundtrack to *The Doors*).

Stone then cuts to Pam and Jim walking along the darkened
"byways on a clear California night" (*S*, 13) as the camera tilts
down at damp buildings and reflects various images of the alley
life where dogs roam among trash cans. Stone directs the dog-like
coyote to "lurk under the sickly light of a streetlamp, pulling its
head from an overstuffed garbage can, looking back at them" (*S*,
13). Here, we are reminded of Morrison's lyrics which depict "the
midnight street" where "the walls" are "wet . . . glint & sleek"
(*W*, 109). He then tells of the sleeping city where the "children /
roam with animal gangs / They seem to speak / to their friends /
the dogs" (*L*, 127).

In the next scene Stone pans the beach at night while Pam and
Jim "like children race down by its side," (*S*, 13) chase the tide,
and dance under a blue/black moonlit sky. Similarly, Morrison's
lyrics draw the picture of "A vast radiant beach / And a cool jew-
eled moon" where couples "race down by its quiet side / . . . like
soft mad children" and "Under the moon / Beneath the stars / They
reel & dance" (*W*, 136, 137). Lastly, Stone places Jim and Pam on
a Venice rooftop where they recline as the moon peaks from clouds
and the palm trees appear silvery in the distance. In this scene,
Morrison begins to think of Pam as his muse for both his poetry
and music. Indeed, his own words reflect this belief as he, comparing Pamela's influence to the moon's influence, writes, "At night
the moon became / a woman's face / I met the Spirit of Music"

(*W*, 36). Stone concludes the scene with them watching "the placenta of evening stars / from the deck on their backs" (*W*, 25). This underworld which Stone presents is more the nurturing side of the womb rather than the terrifying aspects of the unknown. Yet, he does not fail to present the other side of the story with Patricia Kennealy and Morrison.

The "under" side of the underworld is portrayed by Stone through Jim's relationship with Patricia. Here too, it remains clear that Stone develops many of his visuals right out of Morrison's words. For instance, Stone directs that there be "Rain, rain, rain . . . pelting the large windows [of Patricia's loft] as we glide to Jim fucking Patricia Kennealy madly in the twisted sheets" (*S*, 53). Morrison, himself, couples the rain and sex when he writes, "When they see the union of rain / and earth, they see it in an erotic sense, as / copulation" and then foreshadows the rest of the scene with his image of a "love affair of chemicals and stars" (*L*, 85). The apartment is decorated in this same mystical motif as "A hut, lighted by candle" and Patricia is portrayed as "Magician / Female prophet / Sorceress" (*L*, 110). Stone places "books, intellectualabilia, skulls, candles, globes of the world" (*S*, 53) all around the set to further emphasize the occult aspects of this relationship.

After a failed attempt at sex, the camera follows Jim as he wanders around the apartment and picks up an ancient volume of witchcraft off the bookshelf. He begins to read, "history in blackened / books, charcoal sentence" and this book can be further described by "leaves of gold / old books in ruined / Temples / The pages break like ash" (*W*, 48, 75). Patricia walks through "Shiny blackness / so totally naked" and after doing some cocaine, they drink from silver and gold goblets and raise "full glasses held aloft / & spilled to the moon" (*W*, 59, 79). Both Jim and Patricia begin to crawl around like two animals and we see Patricia from Jim's point of view as his "eyes took a trip / to dig the chick / Crouch'd like a cat" (*W*, 79) and the camera cuts to an extreme close-up of blood dripping onto a pile of cocaine or "lunging with blooded sickness on the snow" (*L*, 135). After cutting each other with a knife, each "drinks / red victory" (*W*, 47) and then the scene dissolves to a swirling, ritualistic dance in front of the large windows which reflect the storminess of the external and internal worlds of this surreal underworld. Morrison's poetry continues to assist Stone's direction as the dancing can be described as "Wasps, poised in the window / Excellent dancers / detached" while they "whirl'd, in / the warm aquarium"-like room (*L*, 105).

The occultlike aspects of the underworld with their associations of both life and death are emphasized in another important scene entitled "Limbo." In Limbo, a place between heaven and hell, a person cannot make positive changes in his/her life—paralysis is experienced. This is where Morrison is living in his mind in this second death scene; he cannot change the path he has taken. He is moving closer and closer to a physical and spiritual death. In fact, this concert sequence, in which Morrison sings "Five to One," is described by one critic as "swimming in gouts of fire, awash in a blaze of red, almost resembling something out of Bosch's hell,"[23] and Stone actually calls for "a Dantean look" in his screenplay.

Stone continues to explore Morrison's shamanistic characteristics in this scene. We are reminded of Morrison's words when we examine Stone's staging of this scene. Morrison tells his readers that,

> In the séance, the shaman led. A sensuous panic, deliberately evoked through drugs, chants, dancing, hurls the shaman into trance. Changed voice, convulsive movement. He acts like a madman . . . mediated between man and spirit-world . . . formed the crux of the religious life of the tribe (*L*, 71).

Stone evokes this sentiment: he orders "Jim, mind totally gone into his trance, spreading his arms like wings, hopping from one foot to the other like a shaman around his microphone, whirling, yelling out great rewards for the tribe," to do a "ghost dance around the microphone, Indian style, one foot, resurrecting the dead, the power of the circle" (*S*, 90, 87).

Stone extends the theme of shamanism by dissolving the ghost of the old Indian shaman on stage with Jim. This "old man appears & / moves in tired dance" while the audience or "the scattered dead / gently stir" (*W*, 75). The call to resurrection is heard by his stirring audience—and for Stone's—but Morrison cannot hear this call and, instead, is slowly taken in by death. Stone shows the downward spiral of Morrison in this scene by interspersing "a montage of hallucinatory insanity" (*S*, 87). While the movie audience participates in the celebratory ritual of the concert, they also watch silently as Morrison's poetry asks, "Does the house burn? So be it / Smoke drifts thru these chambers / Murders occur in a bedroom" (*W*, 102) as Stone shows Jim intentionally setting fire to his house while Pamela is locked inside in a closet. This self-destructive behavior continues as Stone cross-cuts between the concert and the Wicca marriage ceremony of Patricia and Jim and then to a drug-induced drive through the streets of L.A. which ends in a collision with a police car. Morrison maintains this "crash" course to death, and Stone takes his spectators along for the ride.

As Stone portrays Morrison's radicalism, it is hard not to recall Morrison's and Stone's opinions on excess. While Morrison said, "I believe in excess," Stone explains this personal and professional credo by remarking, "Through excess I lead, I live, a larger life. I inflate my life, and by inflating my life I live more of my life; therefore, I know the world more. I have more experience of the world. I die a more experienced man."[24] It is then fitting that Stone films right up to the actual scene of Morrison's death.

In one shot, Stone uses a point-of-view shot to show an agitated Pamela awakening and moving toward the bathroom where Jim's body is. As she gets closer, Stone continues his use of the point-of-view shot by approaching the bathroom door and then focusing on the light shining around its perimeters. In addition, Stone makes use of the figure of death once again by using a full shot of the white-faced man retreating away from the bathroom and looking back down the hall, presumably at Pam and the audience. Here, Morrison's words should echo into our ears: "Thru the sudden light / Thru the room / A ghost precedes us / A shadow follows us" (*W*, 33). Indeed, the ghost of death has visited Jim as Pamela enters the bathroom and sees his body. Stone calls for Jim's "face floating upward, angelic eyes, . . . a little smile on his face" in death (*S*, 135), and Jim's words, "I hope you went out / Smiling / Like a child / Into the cool remnant / of a dream," (*W*, 130) reverberate in our minds. Stone hopes that he did go out smiling, that "he enjoyed it as it happened because he was in love with the death experience. He wanted to experience it, and he did."[25]

Stone's cinematic re-creation of Morrison's film-school experience shows Ray Manzarek, upon seeing Morrison's own film project, proclaim, "It's great! It's nonlinear! It's poetry! It's everything Goddard stands for." If we accept these criteria, more of the same could be claimed for Stone's cinematic achievement. He has created "a substitute sensory world" in his movie *The Doors*. Furthermore, his cinemagraphic style seems to be signed by Morrison's own ideas and visual poetics. Yet, Stone knows that he cannot bring Morrison back to life without the audience. By allowing us to participate in Morrison's hallucinations, we are exposed to the driving force of his creativity. And by experiencing Morrison's death, Stone allows both Jim and his audience "to be nascent again."[26]

Yet, as Stone takes leave of us and our newly "informed senses," it is Morrison's poetry which continues on its journey toward immortality. Stone's film echoes Morrison's vision by giving life to the poet and raising him to the level of shaman by awakening a '90s audience to the man's life and work. And, while Stone closes his film with Morrison's "Last words out, Last words out," we know that this filmmaker's homage to Morrison and his poetry has allowed him to continue speaking to us years after his death.

Notes

1. Unless otherwise noted, quotations from Jim Morrison's works are cited in the text with the abbreviations listed below:

   L: *The Lords and the New Creatures* (New York: Simon and Schuster, 1969).

   W: *Wilderness: The Lost Writings of Jim Morrison* (New York: Villard Books, 1988).

2. Hal Hinson, "*Doors:* The Time to Hesitate is Now," *Washington Post*, 1 March 1991, sec. B, p. 1.

3. Jerry Hopkins, "Mr. Mojo Rises," *American Film* 15 (October 1990): 38.

4. Hilary De Vries, "Riders on the Storm," *Los Angeles Times*, 24 February 1991, 13.

5. Russel Miller, "Riders on the Storm," *Sunday Times Magazine* (Los Angeles), 24 February 1991, 18.

6. James Riordan and Jerry Prochnicky, *Break on Through: The Life and Death of Jim Morrison* (New York: William Morrow and Co., Inc., 1991), 75.

7. De Vries, "Riders," 13.

8. Riordan and Prochnicky, *Break*, 437, 111, 497.

9. De Vries, "Riders," 11.

10. Miller, "Riders," 18.

11. Miller, "Riders," 23.

12. David Breskin, ed., *Inner Views: Filmmakers in Conversation* (New York: Faber and Faber, 1992), 113.

13. Breskin, *Inner*, 122.

14. Breskin, *Inner*, 121.

15. Stuart Klawans, "The Doors," *The Nation* 252 (25 March 1991): 390.

16. Hinson, "Doors," sec. B, p. 1.

17. Paul Chutkow, "Oliver Stone and *The Doors:* Obsession Meets the Obsessed," *New York Times*, 24 February 1991, sec. 2, 1.

18. Riordan and Prochnicky, *Break*, 194.

19. Quotations from Oliver Stone's screenplay *The Doors* (Hollywood: Script City, 1990) will be cited in the text with the abbreviation: *S.*

20. Robert Horton, "Riders on the Storm," *Film Comment* 27 (May–June 1991): 60.

21. Michael Wilmington, "Sex, Drugs, and The Doors," *Los Angeles Times*, 1 March 1991, sec. F, p. 1.

22. Breskin, *Inner*, 131.

23. Wilmington, "Sex," sec. F, p. 1.

24. Breskin, *Inner*, 133.

25. Breskin, *Inner*, 143.

26. Breskin, *Inner*, 131.

Chapter 9

JFK

JFK: Historical Fact/Historical Film

Robert A. Rosenstone

To those of us interested in historical films, the fuss in the media over *JFK* feels familiar. Complaints that the film bends and twists history; accusations that director Oliver Stone willfully mixes fact and fiction, fails to delineate clearly between evidence and specu- lation, creates characters who never existed and incidents that nev- er occurred—these are the sorts of charges made every time a historical film on a sensitive subject appears. With *JFK* the con- troversy is particularly heated because of both the topic and its treatment. The film hits us with a double whammy: one of Amer- ica's most popular directors not only explores our recent history's most touchy subject but does so in a bravura motion picture that (maybe it's a triple whammy) also takes a highly critical stance toward major branches of the American government.

Complaints over the misuse of history in film seem to be based on two notions: first, that a historical film is no more than a piece of written history transferred to the screen and thus subject to the same rules of historical practice; and, second, that a fact is a fact and history is little more than an organized compilation of such facts. We who write history should find these assertions question- able. At the least, we have to be aware that "facts" never stand alone but are always called forth (or constituted) by the work in which they then become embedded. In order to evaluate the way in which any work of history—including the motion picture—uses facts (or data) to evoke the past, we must investigate the aims, forms, and possibilities of the kind of historical project in which those data appear.

All this is to say something simple but important: a film is not a book. To judge the contribution of a work like *JFK*, we must try to understand just what it is a historical film can do.

As a dramatic motion picture, *JFK* comes to us in a form that has been virtually unexplored by people interested in the study of past events. Neither historians nor filmmakers have given much thought to the most basic questions about the possibilities and standards of history when it is represented in the visual media. Evaluations of historical films in essays and reviews are always made on an individual basis. Certainly, the historical profession has no agreed-upon way to answer any of the following questions: What kind of historical knowledge or understanding can a historical film provide? How can we situate it in relation to written history? What are its responsibilities to the historical fact? What can it tell us about the past that the written word cannot?

Such questions are too broad to answer here, but they are good to keep in mind as we think about *JFK*. My aim in what follows is to deal less with the contributions and shortcomings of the film than to approach it as part of a tradition. I want to situate *JFK* as both a certain kind of film and a certain kind of historical film. Placed in this context, the factual "errors" (if one wants to call them that) of the work will appear to be less the fault of the filmmaker than a condition of the medium and the kind of movie he has chosen to make. The contributions (if one wants to call them that) of the film, on the other hand, are in large measure its own. They derive less from the form of the film than from the way that form has been put to use.

There is no single way to do history on film. The traditional division into the dramatic work and the documentary is increasingly irrelevant as recent films (*JFK* included) often blur the distinction between the two. My own research has suggested that history on film comes in a number of different forms. *JFK*, despite the many documentary elements it contains, belongs to what is certainly the most popular type of film, the Hollywood—or mainstream—drama. This sort of film is marked, as cinema scholars have shown, by a number of characteristics, the chief being its desire to make us believe that what we see in the theater is true. To this end, the mainstream film uses a specific film language, a self-effacing, seamless language of shot, editing, and sound designed to make the screen seem no more than a window onto unmediated reality.

Along with "realism," four other elements are crucial to understanding the mainstream historical film:

- Hollywood history is delivered in a story with a beginning,
  middle, and an end, a story with a moral message and one
  usually embodied in a progressive view of history.

- This story is closed, completed, and, ultimately, simple. Alternative versions of the past are not shown; the *Rashomon*
  approach is never used in such works.

- History is a story of individuals, usually, heroic individuals
  who do unusual things for the good of others, if not all humankind (ultimately, the audience).

- Historical issues are personalized, emotionalized, and dramatized, for film appeals to our feelings as a way of adding to
  our knowledge or affecting our beliefs.

Such elements go a long way toward explaining the shape of
JFK. The story is not that of President Kennedy but of Jim Garrison, the heroic, embattled, incorruptible investigator who wishes
to make sense of Kennedy's assassination and its apparent cover-
up, not just for himself but for his country and its traditions—that
is, for the audience, for us. More than almost any other historical
film, this one swamps us with information. Some of it, in the black-
and-white flashbacks that illustrate the stages of the investigation,
is tentative or contradictory. So much is thrown at us that, on a
single viewing, the viewer has difficulty absorbing all the details
of events discussed and shown. Yet, even if contradictions do exist, the main line of the story is closed and completed, and the
moral message is clear: the assassination was the result of a conspiracy that involved agencies and officials of the U.S. government,
the aim of the assassination was to get rid of a president who
wished to curb the military and end the cold war, and the "fascist"
groups responsible for the assassination and the subsequent cover-
up are a clear and continuing threat to what little is left of American democracy.

Put simply, if the conventions of the mainstream historical film
make it difficult for such works to create a past that stays within
the norms by which we judge written history, certain other factors
make it impossible. It is not just that most of the data by which

we know the past comes from the realm of words and that the filmmaker is always involved in a good deal of translation from one medium to another, attempting to find a visual equivalent for written evidence. It is also that the mainstream historical film is shot through with fiction or invention from the smallest detail to largest event. (Historians do not, of course, approve of fiction, aside from the underlying fiction that the past itself can be truly told in neat, linear stories.) Invention occurs for at least two reasons: the requirements of dramatic structure and the need of the camera to fill out the specifics of historical scenes.

Drama demands the invention of incidents and characters because historical events rarely occur with the kind of shape, order, and intensity that will keep an audience in its seats. Inventions move the story forward, keep emotions high, and order complex series of events into plausible structures that will fit within filmic time constraints. When *JFK* creates a fascist, homosexual prisoner named Willie O'Keefe to give Garrison evidence that Clay Shaw was involved with Lee Harvey Oswald, or invents a Deep Throat character in Washington (played by Donald Sutherland) to help Garrison make sense of all the evidence he has gathered by providing a theory to hold it all together, one can see that Oliver Stone is doing no more than finding a plausible, dramatic way of summarizing evidence that comes from too many sources to depict on the screen.

Invention due to the demands of the camera may be a subtler factor, but it is no less significant in shaping the historical film. Consider, for example, something as simple as the furnishings in a room where a historical character sits—Jim Garrison's office or conference room, or Clay Shaw's apartment. Or think of the clothing that characters wear. Or the words they speak. All such elements have to be approximate rather than literal representations. They say: this is more or less the way Garrison's room looked in 1966, or these are the kinds of clothes a character might well have worn, or these are likely examples of the words he or she spoke.

The same is true of individuals. This is not just a matter of the director making up characters. Even historical people become largely fictional on the screen. The very use of an actor to portray someone is itself a fiction. If the person is an actual historical figure such as Garrison, even if the actor looks like the figure (which is not true in *JFK*, for actor Kevin Costner looks little like the real Garrison, who in turn does not look much like Chief Justice

Earl Warren, the character he portrays), the film on a literal level says what cannot truly be said: not just that this is how the person looked but also that this is how he moved, and walked, and gestured, and this is how he sounded when he spoke.

To analyze a historical film is to see how small fictions—settings and clothing, the look and sound of characters—shade into larger and larger inventions. Even the tiniest sorts of fictions are not unimportant factors. At least, not if history is about the meaning of past events. In a medium in which visual evidence is crucial to understanding, such pervasive fictions are major contributors to the meaning of the film, including its historical meaning. So, too, is that elusive, extrahistorical element, the aura carried by famous actors and actresses. A star like Kevin Costner, fresh from his award-winning *Dances with Wolves,* cannot simply disappear into the character of Garrison. From that film, he carries for many in the audience a strong feeling of the decent, simple, honest American, the war hero who more than a century ago was critical of a certain kind of expansionist militarism in American life.

Like a history book, a historical film—despite Hollywood's desire for "realism"— is not a window onto the past but a construction of a past; like a history book, a film handles evidence from that past within a certain framework of possibilities and a tradition of practice. For neither the writer of history nor the director of a film is historical literalism a possibility. No matter how literalminded a director might be, film cannot do more than point to the events of the past. At best, film can approximate historic moments, the things that were once said and done, but it cannot replicate them. Like the book, film will use evidence to create historical works, but this evidence will always be a highly reduced or concentrated sample; given its limited screen time, the film will never provide more than a fraction of the (traditional) data of a scholarly article on the same topic. Even as a lengthy, three-hour film that includes an unusually, dense barrage of information, *JFK* must often make major points with sparse evidence or invented images. Within the world of the film, the idea that Kennedy was ready to withdraw American troops from Vietnam, for example, rests on the mention of a single memorandum and the testimony of a fictional character. The notion that black Americans loved Kennedy is conveyed by having a single woman say, "He did so much for this country, for colored people."

What I am suggesting is this: the Hollywood historical film will always include images that are at once invented and yet may still be considered true; true in that they symbolize, condense, or summarize larger amounts of data; true in that they carry out the overall meaning of the past that can be verified, documented, or reasonably argued. But, one may ask, how do we know what can be verified, documented, or reasonably argued? How do we know whether Kennedy was about to withdraw troops or whether he was loved by African Americans? Both of these highly debatable points must be answered from outside the film, from the ongoing discourse of history, from the existing body of historical texts, from their data and arguments. This need for outside verification is not unique to film. Any work about the past, be it a piece of written, visual, or oral history, enters a body of preexisting knowledge and debate. To be considered "historical," rather than simply a costume drama that uses the past as an exotic setting for romance and adventure, a film must engage the issues, ideas, data, and arguments of that discourse. Whatever else it does or does not do, *JFK* certainly meets these requirements as a work of history.

The practice of written history is not a single kind of practice. And if that practice is dependent on data, its value and contribution have never been wholly a matter of those data and their accuracy. Certainly, different works of history use data in different ways, and make different sorts of contributions to our understanding. Some works of history may be important chiefly for the data they create and deliver, others for their evocation of people and events of a vanished time and place. Some historical works are noted for their elegance of argument or skill at representation, others for raising new questions about the past or for raising old questions for a new generation.

It is the same with historical films. They come in different forms and they undertake different historical tasks. Some evoke the past, bringing it to life, giving us an intense feel for people, places, and moments long past. This surely is one of the glories of the motion picture. (Who can sit through *JFK* without reliving many of the agonies of the 1950s and 1960s?) But film may do more than evoke: the historical film can be a stimulus to thought, an intervention into history, a way of re-visioning the past. We do not go to the Hollywood historical film for data but for drama, for the way it intensifies the issues of the past, for the way it shows us the world as process, makes us participate in the confusion, multiplicities, and complexities of events long past.

JFK is a film that undertakes more than one historical burden. Because it chooses as its central strategy an investigation of the past, the film has a self-reflexive edge, one that suggests much about the difficulty of any historical undertaking and the near impossibility of arriving at definitite historical truths. More important, perhaps, *JFK* makes an apparently old issue come to life. Indeed, the reaction it has evoked makes it seem like a very successful piece of historical work, not a work that tells us the truth about the past but one that questions the official truths about the past so provocatively that we are forced once again to look to history and consider what these events mean to us today. Like a good historian, Stone begins *JFK* with a preface that contains a thesis. He uses President Dwight Eisenhower's farewell address, with its warning about the possible effect of the military-industrial complex on the future of our country to set the stage for a film that will illustrate the prescience of Ike's words. By doing this, Stone forces us to face the kind of large issue that a more sober historian, mired in a slough of information and worried about the judgments of professional colleagues, might find difficult to raise so sharply: has something gone wrong with America since the early sixties?

Director Oliver Stone has been faulted for thinking that many changes in the United States stem from a single act, the killing of President John Kennedy, but others who are less sanguine about the judgments and actions of Kennedy may take him as a symbol. Certainly, the experience of the film, like that of any important work of history, resonates well beyond the ideas of its creator and speaks to and for those who do not share Stone's strong faith in Kennedy. When assessing *JFK*, one should ask this question: who else in America has dared to raise such historical issues so powerfully (or at all) in a popular medium? If it is part of the burden of the historical work to make us rethink how we got to where we are, and to make us question values that we and our leaders and our nation live by, then, whatever its flaws, *JFK* has to be among the most important works of American history ever to appear on the screen.

The Rhetorical Structure of Oliver Stone's *JFK*

Martin J. Medhurst

Oliver Stone's JFK *is a mythopoetic discourse that functions as cinematic rhetoric. Through the lens of the Adamic myth, the author examines the film as a metaphoric interpretation or parable of the human condition. Members of the viewing audience are invited to participate in this mythic structure by emulating the actions of the protagonist, thus becoming instruments of sociopolitical change.*

> This is why I speak to them in parables, because seeing they do not see, and hearing they do not hear, nor do they understand.
>
> Matthew 13:13

Occasionally a film appears that seems to have it all—famous director and actors, controversial plot, box-office appeal, and important sociopolitical, not to mention rhetorical, implications. *JFK* is such a film. In the grand tradition of *The Birth of a Nation* (1915), director Oliver Stone presents his vision of life in America. Like D. W. Griffith, the cinematic racist, Stone has a unified vision of American life and morals. Unlike Griffith's racist vision, however, Stone brings a radical social and political critique to his films. What Griffith was to the first quarter of the twentieth century, Stone is to the last, the principal chronicler of the spiritual angst of a people. In such films as *Platoon, Wall Street, Born on the Fourth of July,* and *The Doors,* Stone explores the moral and spiritual vacuum that results from the exploitation, commodification, and bureaucratization of individuals by forces beyond their control.

That both Griffith and Stone can be characterized oxymoroni-
cally as brilliantly flawed ought not to distract one from the important task of trying to understand their respective discourses. The
flaws in *JFK*, for example—and by extension in its director—are
well known. The film is said to confuse fact with fiction, distort
history, cook evidence, slander honorable men, substitute speculation for investigation, and foster disrespect for constitutional government. In the words of syndicated columnist (and former history
professor) George Will, *JFK* is "an act of execrable history and
contemptible citizenship by a man of technical skill, scant education and negligible conscience."[1] On the other hand, historian Robert A. Rosenstone has written: "If it is part of the burden of the
historical work to make us rethink how we got to where we are,
and to make us question values that we and our leaders and our
nation live by, then, whatever its flaws, *JFK* has to be among the
most important works of American history ever to appear on the
screen."[2]

Inherent in the judgments rendered by Will and Rosenstone are
assumptions about what constitutes history, assumptions paralleling
contemporary debate over the nature and purposes of rhetoric. For
Will and other traditionalist historians, the writing of history is an
act of discovery. The historian discovers facts, documents, statistics, and other forms of data which then are assimilated into a
coherent whole—an interpretation—that comes as close as possible to approximating "the way it was" or "what actually happened."
An external reality exists and it is the task of historians to re-
create or reanimate that reality through symbolic means. To Rosenstone, however, history is something quite different, not the discovery of what was so much as creating what might have been
and might still be. For Rosenstone's historian the task is not to
reproduce some external reality—as though that were possible—
but rather to create that reality through critical engagement with
the various symbolic constructions of the past. These constructions
are then brought into dialogue with other "histories" in an ever-
swelling chorus of voices. History, to Rosenstone, is nothing more
or less than a rhetorical construction.

History as rhetoric is not, of course, a new idea. Hayden White
notes that "the historian *shapes* his materials, if not in accordance
with . . . a 'framework of preconceived ideas,' then in response to
the imperatives of narrative discourse in general. These imperatives
are *rhetorical* in nature."[3] If on nothing else, the critics of *JFK*

agree that the film embodies a narrative structure designed to portray a particular, perhaps even preconceived, view of recent American history. Stone's *JFK* offers a historical interpretation of the events surrounding the assassination of America's 35th president. But focusing on the assassination is to see the figure rather than the ground; it is to concentrate on the vehicle while missing the tenor. *JFK* is an extended metaphor that must be deconstructed if one is to have eyes that see and ears that hear.

My argument has several parts. First, I contend that the narrative strategy of the film centers on the Adamic myth—both the story of the first Adam who lost Paradise and the second Adam (Christ) who restored the right relationship of humans both to one another and to their Creator. *JFK* is a film about the loss of innocence and humankind's capacity to restore it. Second, I contend that the enactment of the narrative on the screen is an artistic and poetic exemplification of the rhetorical action demanded of the viewer. The actions undertaken by the protagonist, Jim Garrison, are not merely elements of the plot, but are *exempla* or models for action that viewers are invited to emulate. Third, I contend that by emulating the actions of the protagonist, audience members can reconstitute themselves as autonomous individuals, spiritually and politically awake citizens of the *polis* who are equipped for transcending the profane world into which they have fallen, capable of understanding the system of oppression under which they live, and able to construct new realities and new histories to dwell within.

To develop my arguments, I will adopt White's three-part schema for analyzing how interpretation enters into historiography: "aesthetically (in the choice of a narrative strategy), epistemologically (in the choice of an explanatory paradigm), and ethically (in the choice of a strategy by which the ideological implications of a given representation can be drawn for the comprehension of current social problems)."[4] By examining the narrative strategy, explanatory paradigm, and ideological implications of the film, I will show how the rhetorical power of *JFK* is derived and how that power is employed in pursing an ideological agenda. In so doing, I will be conducting a close reading of the internal rhetorical structure of the film, a mode of analysis that understands rhetorical action to take place within a text as well as between a text and an audience.[5]

Narrative Strategy

JFK uses the Adamic myth as the superstructure upon which the narrative elements are arrayed. Such myths, both biblical and extrabiblical, have long been used by rhetorical analysts to explicate the persuasive power of cinematic and televisual narratives. The myth of the original Adam is the story of the human race's fall from Paradise. Created innocent, Adam falls as a result of a conspiracy between Eve and the Serpent. Adam's fall has dire consequences for all his posterity who dwell in darkness until a second Adam arrives to bring light and life. In the second Adam humankind is restored to its original state of innocence through a spiritual rebirth. The narrative strategy of *JFK* follows this mythic pattern.[5]

As portrayed in the film, John F. Kennedy is a new man on the political scene. He is young, vibrant, and possessed by a desire to bring justice and peace to the world. But through a conspiracy between people close to him—the military, the CIA, and the FBI—the young president is felled in a hail of bullets. His death changes the world forever. Gone is the desire for peace and the pursuit of justice. Gone is the spirit of cooperation and détente. The death of President John Kennedy plunges the world into darkness, a darkness from which it has yet to emerge. Yet there exists hope. That hope is embodied in a second Kennedy, a man who also believes in truth and justice and who, through his investigation of the assassination, will resurrect the spirit that was stolen from the American people on 22 November 1963. New Orleans District Attorney Jim Garrison is the second Kennedy. By bringing to light that which has been hidden—the "secret murder at the heart of the American dream"—Garrison is the vanguard of the resurrection, of those who will bring back to life the spirit and ideals of John F. Kennedy. By emulating Garrison, by pursuing the truth, members of the viewing audience can help to resurrect peace and freedom, and bring light out of darkness. This is the mythic superstructure upon which the individual elements of the narrative are based.

Several dialectical pairs power the narrative: past/present, interior/exterior, appearance/truth, sleeping/waking, concealed/revealed, sight/blindness, and possible/impossible. The opening segment of the film is situated firmly in the past. From the opening frames of Dwight Eisenhower delivering his famous warning about the "military-industrial complex" to shots of John Kennedy on the campaign trail, Martin Luther King, Malcolm X, Adlai Stevenson, Fidel Castro, Allen Dulles, J. Edgar Hoover, and Nikita Khrushchev, the viewer is taken on a whirlwind tour of the imagery of 1950s and early 1960s America. As Kennedy is seen and heard delivering his American University address, the director cuts away to the more distant past—an even younger Jack Kennedy enjoying friends and family, having fun, reveling in life. As the collage of imagery ends we hear Kennedy's words: "We all inhabit this small planet. We all breathe the same air. We all cherish our children's future. And we are all mortal." On the word "mortal," the director cuts to a woman's body being dumped alongside a deserted roadway. Now in the hospital, the woman moans, "They're going to kill Kennedy." Immediately shots of Kennedy's arrival in Dallas and the motorcade that will take him to his death start to be intercut with the woman's pleas for help. "Call somebody and stop them," she wails; but it is too late. There is a cut to black, then silence. Viewers hear the sound of a rifle being cocked. A shot rings out.

In this opening segment, viewers are immersed in the imagery of the past. Some of the shots are documentary footage, some recreations, some still photographs. Some are in black and white, some color.[6] The filmmaker locates his story among the real, inviting the viewer to remember the events of 22 November 1963. By first establishing the historicity of the subject matter, Stone creates a presumption in the minds of his viewers that what they are seeing is grounded in the people and events portrayed. The imagery of Kennedy intercut with the various figures and events of his time function metonymically to suggest an association between people and events, an association never argued or explained, but merely left as a suggestion or hypothesis in the viewer's memory. That this technique was consciously adopted by the filmmaker is clear from the diary of the film's cinematographer, Robert Richardson, who wrote: "Utilize the opening documentary material to establish a concrete foundation of factual reality. Let the audience move through the material, never doubting its authenticity. Using this as a basis, move away whenever the desire to accomplish the concrete arises."[7] Having laid a foundation of "factual reality," Stone then moves away with a cut to the office of New Orleans District Attorney Jim Garrison.

The central portion of the narrative follows Garrison's pursuit of Kennedy's assassins. From the moment that Garrison and his assistant D.A. go to Napoleon's Bar to watch the televised reports on the assassination until the end of the film, the media, particularly television, are ever-present. Everything appears to be revealed by the televised reports, but as the film unfolds, it soon becomes clear that the media, directly or indirectly, are being used to conceal the truth about the assassination. Garrison, like the American public generally, initially believes the mediated reports. Even after he has interviewed alleged conspirator David Ferrie and had him bound over for questioning, he still accepts the decision of the FBI—which he learns about by watching television—that Ferrie had no connection with Oswald. "They must know something we don't," says Garrison, in the first of several instances of dramatic irony.

Also in the film's second segment the viewer is introduced to W. Guy Bannister, the former FBI agent who, along with his friend Jack Martin, is drinking in a bar when the news of Kennedy's death is announced. Bannister immediately is established as an enemy of Kennedy's, as he loudly exclaims, "I don't see anybody crying for all those thousands of Cubans that bastard condemned to death and torture," and proposes a toast, "Here's to the New Frontier—Camelot in smithereens," as he pours his drink on the floor. As Bannister and Martin drunkenly stagger back to their office, Bannister suddenly turns surly, wondering out loud about his associate's "loyalty." When Martin says "I've *seen* enough here this summer already to write a book," Bannister pulls out his revolver and pistol-whips him, saying, "You didn't *see* a goddamn thing" (emphasis added). To see—to open one's eyes and look at the evidence—is immediately established as a dangerous thing to do. Sight is to become a central metaphor throughout the rest of the film, as first Garrison and then the audience members come to "see" the truth.

Three years elapse between the second and third segments. The third opens with Garrison on a plane with Russell Long, U.S. senator from Louisiana. The conversation turns to Kennedy's assassination and Long, after expressing his doubts about the Warren Commission findings exclaims, "One pristine bullet? That dog don't hunt." This experience sends Garrison back to the twenty-six-volume report of the Warren Commission. As he reads, he becomes increasingly suspicious until he finally blurts out in disgust, "It's one of the sloppiest, most disorganized investigations I've ever *seen*" (emphasis added). By examining the evidence, Garrison is starting to see, starting to understand that what he and others have meekly accepted as truth may not be true at all. As Garrison stays up late into the night to study the report—and in the process begins to neglect his wife and children—viewers see on the screen the imagery that runs through Garrison's mind as he reads the words on the page. When Liz Garrison finally becomes exasperated with her husband's increasingly compulsive behavior ("These books have gotten to your mind"), he bluntly tells her, "I've been sleeping for three years." Garrison's on-screen awakening is paralleled by the awakening of the audience. Like Garrison, the viewer is becoming increasingly skeptical of the official version of events.

That Garrison's awakening from three years of sleep is meant to echo Christ's resurrection after three days in the earth is clear from the many references to Sunday—the day of resurrection—throughout the film. When Garrison first starts to investigate Oswald's link to New Orleans, he tells his investigators to meet him "Sunday at 11:00." After his three-year sleep, Garrison meets with his assistants, Bill and Lou, at "7:30 Sunday morning." To make sure that the imagery cannot be missed, Stone has New Orleans businessman Clay Shaw meet with Garrison on "Easter Sunday." As Garrison awakens from his slumber, so too does the audience.

As Garrison takes his assistants Bill and Lou on a walking tour of downtown New Orleans, he shows them how appearances can be deceiving. The address of Guy Bannister's old office, 531 Lafayette Street, is shown to be the same building as 544 Camp Street, the address that appeared on pro-Castro leaflets distributed by Oswald. Buildings that appear nondescript to the naked eye are actually shells for such organizations as the CIA, the Office of Naval Intelligence, and the FBI. The dialectic between appearance and truth comes into sharp relief. When Garrison announces to his two aides that he is going back into the Kennedy case, Bill says, "Good lord, *wake me up, I* must be dreaming." Garrison replies, "No, you're *awake* Bill, and I'm deadly serious" (emphasis added). The dialectic of sleeping and awakening, the central opposition in the film, is starting to be revealed.

As a first step, Garrison locates Jack Martin and persuades him to disclose what he had seen at Guy Bannister's office during the summer of 1963. Martin reveals that Bannister's office was a front for gunrunning Cuban exiles and that Ferrie, Shaw, and Oswald were all part of the operation. Admitting his own blindness to what was happening around him, he says of the Cubans, "I confess, they all *look* the same to me" (emphasis added). Finally, he reveals the truth that "they were all working for the CIA." For the first time, Garrison's hypothesis about government involvement in Kennedy's assassination is confirmed by an outside source.

Martin's revelations lead Garrison to Dean Andrews, the lawyer whom Clay Shaw hired to represent Oswald. "Dino" Andrews first denies everything, then confesses, "If I give you the name of the big enchilada, then it's bon voyage Dino." Throughout the conversation, Andrews blows cigarette smoke. The smoke is part of the sight/blindness dialectic, as the act of blowing smoke is set off against the effort to smoke them out. Throughout the film, smoke and smoking is ubiquitous. Not only do most of the antagonists smoke (Ferrie, Shaw, O'Keefe, Andrews, generals, FBI agents), so too do the protagonists (Garrison, Bill, Lou, Susie, and Liz Garrison). Oswald, who is represented as a patsy in the film, has smoke in his face by David Ferrie. Even Judge Haggerty smokes in the courtroom, as does Clay Shaw's defense attorney. The implications of the imagery seem clear: the truth is shrouded in a fog of smoke, coming from all directions. and a clear view will not easily be obtained.

Whereas Andrews denies everything, Willie O'Keefe, a male prostitute serving time in the Angola State Penitentiary, is more than willing to reveal everything. He immediately tells Garrison, "I've got nothing to hide." What he reveals about his relationships with Ferrie and Shaw is to the majority of heterosexual viewers, a nightmare of sexual debauchery and perverted relationships. In the most shocking dialogue of the film, O'Keefe informs the crusading district attorney, "You're a goddamn liberal, Mr. Garrison. You don't know shit because you've never been fucked in the ass." This language, along with the imagery of O'Keefe's homosexual escapades with Ferrie and Shaw, clearly has shock value, but like the rest of the film, these scenes must be interpreted metaphorically.

While it is doubtless true that "Stone caters to the sense of distrust that most of the film's viewers feel toward homosexuals," it is a mistake to conclude that "a homosexual primal horde slays the young father-king."[8] The homosexual imagery is introduced not primarily because Shaw and Ferrie were homosexuals, but rather because homosexuality serves as a synecdoche for the assassination plot and its aftermath. All of the beliefs and images associated, rightly or wrongly, with homosexuals in the 1950s and early 1960s are drawn upon as parts representing a larger whole. The homosexual is seen as closeted, hidden, secretive, self-centered, sterile, and willing to go to great lengths to satisfy the will-to-power, erotic power over the other. Thus homosexuality stands synecdochically for the fascist *coup d'état* that secretly has taken power over the people to serve its own selfish ends, resulting in the sterility and sense of impotence that has stalked the land since 1963. Homosexuality is the vehicle; fascism is the tenor. Thus, read figuratively, to be "fucked in the ass" is the equivalent of knowing the reality of fascism, a reality which liberals refuse to see, perhaps because it is so antithetical to what they have been taught about the "right" ordering of government and the presumed power of constitutional checks and balances.

Explanatory Paradigm

The dialectical pairs of sight/blindness, appearance/truth, and interior/exterior point to the central mechanism by which Garrison—and through him the audience—come to knowledge. To be able to "see" is to come to know the truth. But such knowledge is a function of mind, not of physical sight. It is produced internally as the result of cognitive operations that do not depend upon simple one-to-one correspondences between events, objects, and people as they exist in the world of sensory impressions. Indeed the world of the senses is explicitly rejected as a source of knowledge. When Garrison tells his investigators, "We're through the looking glass here, people—white is black and black is white." The world experienced by the senses is not to be trusted.

Garrison's conclusion that the world is not as it appears to be follows a review of the investigation's status by Assistant D.A. Susie Cox. She informs the group that key witnesses have died mysteriously, that Oswald's tax returns are still classified, that despite his seemingly procommunist sympathies Oswald was stationed at a top-secret military base in Japan, and that even after defecting to the Soviet Union, Oswald had no difficulty reentering the United States, even bringing his Russian wife with him. Through the technique of accumulating instance after instance of incredible occurrences, Garrison's team comes to share his beliefs about the unreliability of the world as it appears to the naked eye. So, too, does the viewing audience. As Garrison finishes saying "and black is white," the director cuts to the black-and-white photograph of Oswald holding the murder weapon, a photograph that has been systematically constructed by an unknown conspirator to make it appear as though the weapon and Oswald belong together.

If the exterior sensate world cannot be trusted, then one must use the interior world of the mind to form ideas or hypotheses about the nature of the real. To come to know what is really going on, one must be a seeker after truth. Garrison fills this role as he doggedly pursues witnesses that the Warren Commission either has overlooked or whose testimony the commission has misconstrued, perhaps intentionally. Even during this process, Garrison is portrayed as coming to his conclusions only with great difficulty. When Julia Ann Mercer reports that her statements to the FBI have been "altered," Garrison replies, "As a former FBI man, it is difficult to accept this."

The theme of knowing the truth pervades the film. Jack Ruby says, "If I am eliminated, there won't be any way of knowing any bit of the truth with regard to my situation." Truth lies within individual minds and it is only through probing those minds that the ultimate truth will be discovered. The film, with its flashbacks into the memories of its characters and its visual explorations of potential or speculative truths, functions like a Socratic dialogue where mind encounters mind, ideas are probed, turned, examined, and rejected, until finally only one conclusion is left. As Ruby makes his plea to Earl Warren (ironically played by the real-life Jim Garrison), light reflects off Warren's glasses just as it had earlier reflected off Garrison's spectacles. The platonic overtones are unmistakable. We live in a world of reflections, where only shadows of the truth are known. Reflections, if accepted as true knowledge, will never lead to the truth. One must take off the glasses that blind—as Garrison does at the end of the film—and engage in an act of mind, of cognitive and intellectual reconstruction.

The dialectical movements of the mind, as exemplified in Garrison and his group of investigators, lead to one conclusion: "they" did it. A high-level government conspiracy is the explanatory paradigm in *JFK*. It is the conclusion that Garrison and the viewing audience necessarily reach after having "thought"—through visual imagery and memories—about the possibilities. The conclusion of the film and of its hero is quite simply that the views articulated in the Warren Commission Report are impossible to believe and that the only rational conclusion is that a conspiracy was responsible for President Kennnedy's assassination.

This conclusion is present even from the film's opening frames. The initial montage of people and events is edited in such a way as to conspire to form a mental impression—that all of these people and events have something to do with one another. As one writer aptly notes, "The montage is the message in *JFK*."[9] Shot composition, framing, editing, lighting, and sound all conspire to compel the viewer to consider a government-led conspiracy as the answer to Kennedy's killer. As the film progresses, the conclusion is bolstered by testimony from various characters, starting with Jack Martin's assertion that "they" were all CIA, to Jack Ruby's prediction that "a whole new form of government is going to take over this country." By the time Garrison finally discovers the true identity of Clay Bertrand (aka Clay Shaw), both he and the viewer already have become convinced of the reality of a conspiracy.

Garrison brings Bertrand/Shaw to his office on Easter Sunday. As the one—and to date only—person brought to trial in connection with the Kennedy assassination, Shaw represents one of the keys to resurrection, the possibility that the truth may yet be known and the spirit of John F. Kennedy returned to the land. Though Shaw denies any knowledge of or involvement with Ferrie, Oswald, or the assassination plot, the viewer recognizes that his internal thoughts are the precise opposite of what he is saying. That Garrison is to be understood as the second Kennedy is clear from the editing. When Shaw professes his admiration for Kennedy, he notes that the late president had "a wife of impeccable taste." Immediately the director cuts to Liz Garrison waiting at the restaurant for her husband. Jackie Kennedy and Liz Garrison are cinematically linked just as Jack Kennedy and Jim Garrison are conceptually linked. If Kennedy was the prototype, the first Adam, then Garrison is the second Adam, the one through whom redemption is to come.

Garrison recognizes that Shaw is lying and that he is not what he claims to be. "One may smile and be a villain," Garrison tells his aides, emphasizing, once again, the dialectic between appearance and truth. On the exterior, Shaw is a respectable businessman; on the interior, he is a fascist conspirator in the murder of President Kennedy. As the viewing audience comes to identify more and more with Garrison's quest for the truth, it becomes increasingly leery of all appearances. Television newscasts, for example, now start to seem part of the conspiracy as they criticize Garrison's handling of the investigation. Can what the media report now be any more accurate than what they had reported in the hours following Kennedy's assassination? Slowly but inexorably the viewer is led to the conclusion that no external source can be trusted.

Conspiracy as explanatory paradigm is affirmed once and for all in the clandestine meeting of Garrison and his associates with David Ferrie. Ferrie, who had tried to remain aloof from the investigation, now finds that his connection with the assassination plot has been revealed by the media. What he has concealed earlier in the film, he now reveals. When it is suggested to him that he might once have been affiliated with the CIA, Ferrie responds, "You make it sound like some remote fuckin' experience in ancient history. Man, you don't leave the agency." The dialectic between past and present, between what "history" teaches and what we now are is affirmed. That we do not know ourselves because we do not know our true history is suggested by Ferrie when he says, "The fuckin' shooters don't even know. Don't you get it? . . . It's a mystery, wrapped in a riddle, inside of an enigma." History continues to conspire against us by the very fact that we are ignorant of our past. Like a classical tragic hero, we are fated to roam the world blind and in ignorance until the moment of discovery opens our eyes to the truth. While conspiracy drives the explanatory paradigm (those dialectical devices in the film that bring us to a state of knowledge), it is the military-industrial complex that accounts for the film's ideological implications (how artistic choices invite viewers to adopt a particular slant on what they should believe and do with respect to their own government's actions).

Ideological Implications

If a conspiracy masterminded by the CIA explains who killed Kennedy, then the military-industrial complex's desire for wealth and power accounts for the why of the assassination. Garrison travels to Washington, D.C., to meet with the secretive Mr. X. There he learns that the entire plot was carried out by the "black ops" component of the Pentagon and their friends in the military-industrial complex. Mr. X, who externally appears to be just like any other visitor to the Lincoln Memorial, turns out to have vital information stored inside his memory. After recounting his involvement in black ops from the end of World War II through the Bay of Pigs, Mr. X details the extraordinary story of how he was sent to the North Pole during the time when his unit normally would have been preparing extra protection for President Kennedy's trip to Dallas. He recounts how he became suspicious about the nature of the assassination and then tells an intellectually overwhelmed Garrrison what it all means. As X speaks, Garrison takes off his glasses. No longer will he—or we—be blinded by mere reflections of the truth.

Mr. X wastes no time in coming to the point. "The organizing principle of any society, Mr. Garrison, is for war," he explains. "The authority of the state over its people resides in its war powers. And Kennedy wanted to end the cold war in his second term. . . And he set out to withdraw from Vietnam." Those with a vested interest in war, Mr. X says, acted in line with those interests. The assassination of John Kennedy was a necessary act of self-preservation to those who profited from the cold war and who stood to make even more profits from a shooting war in Vietnam. In his final analysis it is the capitalist economic structure and the fascist police state that killed President Kennedy. References to Bell Helicopter, General Dynamics, and the Chase Manhattan Bank interlace with shots of generals and admirals complaining about Kennedy having his hand on "the chicken switch."

Having heard all that Mr. X is willing to tell, Garrison makes a pilgrimage to Kennedy's grave in Arlington National Cemetery. With the eternal flame to light the way and the sight of a black man with his young son to remind him of the hope that has been lost, Garrison returns to New Orleans. When his wife accuses him of having "changed," Garrison replies, "Well, of course, I've changed. My eyes have opened. And once they're open, believe me, what used to look normal seems insane." When he asks her, "Can't you *see*?" she replies "I don't want to *see*" (emphasis added). Herein lies the ethical nexus of the film. Will Liz, and by implication all those in the audience whose eyes have been closed, choose to wake up and see, or will they "go hide somewhere"? Garrison shows himself willing to do whatever it takes—even to making the ultimate sacrifice of himself and his family—to uncover the truth. When his assistant Bill Broussard questions the ability of such sinister and unseen forces to murder Kennedy, Garrison tells him, "Alls [sic] it takes is one Judas, Bill."

As Garrison prepares for the Clay Shaw trial, he learns of the assassination of Robert F. Kennedy. Liz is sleeping. He wakes her up and tells her what has happened. Suddenly, she understands. "You were right. It hasn't ended," she says, and for the first time in the film we see them start to make love. In this one scene is condensed the whole of the filmmaker's vision. Stone wants the viewer to wake up, cast off the blinders of disbelief and fear, and reestablish a proper relationship, a relationship based on openness, trust, and oneness of vision rather than on secretiveness, coercion, division, and hate.

As the Shaw trial begins, Liz and her eldest child enter the courtroom. Their eyes have been opened. They believe in Jim Garrison and his mission. That the mission is likely to fail is signaled from the outset when the judge arrives at the bench smoking a cigarette. Nevertheless, Garrison makes an impassioned plea to the jury after having shown them the Zapruder film of the assassination. "We've all become Hamlets in our country," he contends, "children of a slain father-leader whose killers still possess the throne. The ghost of John F. Kennedy confronts us with the secret murder at the heart of the American dream. He forces on us the appalling questions: Of what is our Constitution made? What is our citizenship, and more, our lives, worth?" Garrison warns the jury about the "ascendancy of invisible government in the United States" and instructs them that "when it smells like it, feels like it, and looks like it, you call it what it is—fascism."

The final summation is directed to the viewers as much as to the jury. Returning to his belief that truth is an act of mind, Garrison reminds the jurors that "Individual human beings have to create justice." Justice, like the history within which it operates, is something made by humans. Sounding like such cinematic sociopolitical reformers as Mr. Smith *(Mr. Smith Goes to Washington)*, Tom Joad *(The Grapes of Wrath)*, and John Doe *(Meet John Doe)*, Jim Garrison, tired and with voice breaking, pleads with the jury to remember that "you the people . . . represent the hope of humanity against government power." "In discharging your duty," he instructs them, "'Ask not what your country can do for you; ask what you can do for your country.'" Looking directly into the camera, Garrison tells the viewers, "It's up to you."

Implications and Conclusions

Peter Collier is correct when he notes that *JFK* "is only super-ficially about the death of a President. Its real subject is the fas-cist state we have been living in for the last twenty-eight years."[10] Stone's film is explicitly ideological, seeking to relate past to present through an extended metaphorical treatment of the Kennedy assassination. The filmmaker's narrative strategy and explanatory paradigm are powerful weapons in his quest to make the audience "see." The use of an archetypal mythic pattern, conspiratorial log-ic, and an explicitly ideological stance have caused some critics to label *JFK* "propaganda;" others have been less charitable in their descriptions.[11] While *JFK* certainly uses many of the techniques of cinematic and televisual propaganda, it is doubtful whether the label is heuristic in helping to understand either the film's appeal or its potential effects on the viewing audience.

Propagandistic or not, *JFK* is best considered a piece of cine-matic rhetoric whose primary means of persuasion are the ambigu-ities of history and the dialectical tensions that are part of the human condition. Stone's film is an artistic wake-up call to those having ears to hear and eyes to see. Clearly not everyone will understand, and even among those who do, not all will believe. But this is the nature of any rhetorical situation. And it is as a response to a rhetorical situation that one ultimately should judge *JFK*. Viewed as such, two questions arise: what is the nature of the situation Stone seeks to address? and, is his response a fitting one?[12]

The situation can be summarized as follows. Thirty years after John Kennedy's assassination, more than half of the American pub-lic disbelieves the conclusions of the Warren Commission.[13] In those three decades, Americans have experienced wars, riots, re-cessions, more assassination attempts, the dissolution of the tradi-tional family, the breakdown of social mores, an epidemic of drugs and violence, and the loss of respect for and trust in governmental leaders. Most centrally, many Americans no longer believe that they control their own lives. Unseen forces—economic, social, politi-cal, even spiritual—seem to control the individual. Clearly some-thing is amiss.

The Kennedy assassination stands synecdochically for this loss of direction and identity. In it is condensed the horror, violence, powerlessness, and sense of betrayal felt by millions of American citizens. It is a mark in time, an absence that constitutes a presence that we cannot escape. As such the assassination is more than just a historical event; it is a mythical moment that conjures images of what was and memories of what might have been. That thirty years after the event commercial films, television documentaries, and best-selling books on the assassination still fire the popular imagination is eloquent testimony to the centrality of the assassination in American cultural consciousness. President John Kennedy's death really did change the way many Americans felt about themselves, their social political institutions, and their country.

But is Oliver Stone's film a fitting response to this state of affairs? Certainly no single rhetorical response, be it film, speech, play, or any other form of symbolic inducement, could completely satisfy the multitude of exigencies in such a complex situation. And Stone has seemingly gone out of his way to invite viewer skepticism with his penchant for conspiracy theories and his conscious decision to integrate fact and fiction in ways that those familiar with the evidence surrounding the assassination could not help but recognize and question. The film is far from an encompassing, much less a perfect, response to the situation. Even so, a single response can be directional, perhaps even propaedeutic to other responses. Evaluated in this light, *JFK* seems to be fitting if only because it provides a clarion call to involvement on the part of the U.S. citizenry.

Beyond that, the film has had a discernible effect on the willingness of governmental leaders to declassify documents pertaining to the Kennedy assassination.[14] Elected leaders have felt the force of an outraged citizenry, an outrage provoked, in part, by *JFK* and the many books about the Kennedy assassination that have appeared on the bestseller lists.[15] One concrete result of this outrage was the "President John F. Kennedy Assassination Records Collection Act of 1992," signed into law on 26 October 1992 by President George Bush. This bill established "an independent commission to review government records and release all except those that greatly compromise national security or a person's privacy."[16] Upon signing the bill, President Bush remarked, "S. 3006 will help put to rest the doubts and suspicions about the assassination of President Kennedy. I sign the bill in the hope that it will assist in healing the wounds inflicted on our nation almost three decades ago."[17]

Effective as the film was in motivating governmental action, it must be remembered that Stone is not so much concerned with the Kennedy assassination per se as with the type of governmental system that holds sway in America. His radical vision, according to one critic, "manifests the ambitions of the mid-seventies, New Left, which saw the Kennedy assassination as a means of mobilizing an issue-oriented population into a radical critique of the American political economy."[18] The film seems less successful on this level if only because it is the product of the same economy it critiques. A $40 million extravaganza produced by the Time-Warner Corporation and marketed with all the savvy of Madison Avenue is hardly the stuff of radical politics, unless black really has become white.

A related problem is the inherent contradiction that lies at the heart of the film. On the one hand the film functions as "revisionist history" as it winnows, selects, adapts, and constructs the story of the assassination plot.[19] Such an approach to history is clearly informed by the view, shared by Rosenstone and others, that history is created, not discovered ready-made. History is a rhetorical construction of the historian or historical filmmaker. On the other hand, however, the film features an epistemological position holding that there is only one truth and that it is absolute and unchanging. Furthermore, within the *diegesis* of the film, Stone purports to know what the truth is and assumes the task as a cinematic rhetorician of convincing the audience of that truth—America is in the grip of fascism. Alternative truths are never really explored in *JFK* (critical comparisons with *Rashomon* notwithstanding) even though there are as many different truths as there are writers about the assassination. Indeed, many basic and widely accepted facts are simply ignored in the film.[20] Thus a basic contradiction appears between Stone's theory of history, which is relativistic, and his theory of truth, which is absolute, at least as those theories take on concrete expression within the cinematic world. Since history is his rhetorical means and truth, his rhetorical end, one might expect a greater degree of consistency. But this is a problem shared by all who call themselves rhetoricians, for the burden of rhetoric is to be forever bound by the contingencies of history and the ambiguities of substance, but called upon to transform appearance into truth and ambiguity into understanding.

JFK is not only a mythic discourse about "America's drift toward covert government,"[21] it is also a parable about our humanity. Born into a history of our own creation, we humans continue to scribble—to make our marks—in an effort to discover th truth about ourselves.[22] What we find, however, is that our pen is not the first to have touched the page. We are born into a story already told. Our choices are circumscribed: accept the story as told or tell another; dwell in history as written or create alternate histories. The moral of the parable, and of the film, is this: we are not only symbol-creators, but symbol-created. In this sense the story we tell can be none other than our own. In the telling we are constantly making and remaking ourselves. If, therefore, we do not like tht denouement of our narrative, we have only to continue making our marks until the story is more to our liking.

Oliver Stone has told a story. It now takes its place along with the many other accounts of the Kennedy assassination. But Stone's story is different. It is not about what happened on 29 November 1963, but about how the events of that day and their interpretations have shaped whom we have become.[23] While we may never know the whole truth about the Kennedy assassination, we can begin to know ourselves. And that is a knowledge most useful and necessary.

Notes

1.   Quoted in James Petras, "The Discrediting of the Fifth Estate: The Press Attacks on *JFK*," *Cineaste* 19, no. 1 (1992): 15.

2.   Robert A. Rosenstone, "*JFK*: Historical Fact/Historical Film," *American Historical Review* 97, no. 2 (April 1992): 511.

3.   Hayden White, *Tropics of Discourse: Essays in Cultural Criticism* (Baltimore, Md.: Johns Hopkins Univ. Press), 102.

4.   White, *Tropics*, 70.

5.   For a fuller discussion see Northrup Frye, *The Anatomy of Criticism: Four Essays* (Princeton, N.J.: Princeton Univ. Press), 131–242.

6.   The array of cinematic techniques employed includes "16 mm, home movies shot in 8 mm (and re-creations of same), still photographs, diagrams in close-up, photographs of a miniature model of the shooting site, black-and-white drama, and, of course, the usual color Hollywood movie that weaves through it all. Images are slowed and frozen, processed, cropped, and distorted. Often these different frame sizes, textures, and colors hurtle in fragments under, and intercut with, a spoken conversation or a reading of a report." See Pat Dowell, "Last Year at Nuremberg: The Cinematic Strategies of *JFK*," *Cineaste* 19, no. 1 (1992): 10.

7. Bob Fisher, "The Whys and Hows of *JFK*," *American Cinematographer* 73, no. 2: (February 1992): 45.

8. Roy Grundmann and Cynthia Lucia, "Gays, Women and an Abstinent Hero: The Sexual Politics of *JFK*," *Cineaste* 19, no. 1 (1992): 21; Michael Rogin, "*JFK:* The Movie," *American Historical Review* 97, no. 2 (1992): 503.

9. Dowell, "Last Year," 9.

10. Peter Collier, "Ollie Uber Alles: Oliver Stone's Triumph of the Will," *The American Spectator* 25, no. 4 (1992): 28.

11. Kenneth Auchincloss, "Twisted History," *Newsweek*, 23 December 1991, 47; Collier, "Ollie," 29.

12. For a fuller discussion of criteria see Lloyd F. Bitzer, "The Rhetorical Situation," *Philosophy and Rhetoric* 1, no. 1 (1968): 1–18.

13. Auchincloss, "Twisted," 46.

14. Adam Clymer, "Bill Would Open Kennedy Death Files," *New York Times*, 27 March 1992, sec. A, p. 16; Elaine Sciolino, "C.I.A. Director Announces Plan for More Access to Agency Files," *New York Times*, 22 February 1992, p. 9; Virginia Cope, "Senate Votes for Release of Secret JFK Files," *Congressional Quarterly Weekly Report* 50, no. 31 (1 August 1992): 2250.

15. Examples include the following two books used as the basis for Stone's film: Jim Garrison, *On the Trail of the Assassins: My Investigation and Prosecution of the Murder of President Kennedy* (New York: Sheridan Square Press, 1990); Jim Marrs, *Crossfire: The Plot that Killed Kennedy* (New York: Carroll and Graf Publishers, 1989).

16. Beth Donovan, "JFK Disclosures Cleared by Hill," *Congressional Quarterly Weekly* Report 50, no. 39 (3 October 1992): 3018.

17. "President John F. Kennedy Assassination Records Collection Act of 1992," *Weekly Compilation of Presidential Documents* 28 (27 October 1992): 2134–35.

18. Christopher Sharrett, "Debunking the Official History: The Conspiracy Theory in *JFK*," *Cineaste* 19, no. 1 (1992): 13.

19. Jorge Carreon, "Conspiracy?", *The National College Newspaper*, February 1992, p. 12.

20. Alexander Cockburn, "John and Oliver's Bogus Adventure," *Sight and Sound* 1, no. 10 (1992): 22–24; Jacob Cohen, "Yes, Oswald Alone Killed Kennedy," *Commentary* 23, no. 6 (1992): 32–40; Thomas W. Hazlett, "Oliver Stone's Brain Is Missing," *Reason* 23, no. 58 (April 1992): 58; Anthony Lewis, "*JFK*," *New York Times*, 9 January 1992, p. 23; George Lardner Jr., "On the Set: Dallas in Wonderland," *Washington Post*, 19 May 1991, sec. D, p. 1, 4; Jon Margolis, "*JFK* Movie and Book Attempt to Rewrite History," *Chicago Tribune*, 14 May 1991, p. 19; David Gates, "Bottom Line: How Crazy Is It?," *Newsweek*, 23 December 1991, 52–54.

21. David Ansen, "A Troublemaker for Our Times," *Newsweek*, 23 December 1991, 50.

22. As I have noted elsewhere: "Mankind's marks in time—paintings, books, photos, architecture, film—are all necessary. None, however, is sufficient as a basis for action. Before humans can act, they must discover the truth that lies beneath the image. . . . This is the task of the artist. To slow down the world. To create marks in time. And to invite the audience to imagine and thus create a truth not yet in existence." See Martin J. Medhurst, "*Hiroshima, Mon Amour:* From Iconography to Rhetoric, *Quarterly Journal of Speech* 68, no. 4 (1982): 370.

23. For a fuller discussion of this thesis see Barbie Zelizer, *Covering the Body: The Kennedy Assassination, the Media, and the Shaping of Collective Memory* (Chicago: Univ. of Chicago Press, 1992).

JFK: The Lesson and Legacy of Vietnam

Jim Welsh

Even most of his enemies and detractors would probably admit that Oliver Stone is one of the most gifted filmmakers of his generation, as well as the most controversial. Stone firmly established his directing credentials with *Platoon* (1986), arguably the best film treating Vietnam as a mythic quest, followed by *Born on the Fourth of July* (1989), adapted from Ron Kovic's autobiography, a raw and disturbing narrative demonstrating the human cost of combat. *Heaven and Earth* (1993) offered closure for a trilogy of films that treated the problem of the Vietnam War, but this trilogy is actually a tetralogy since *JFK* (1991) also probes the question: "Why were we in Vietnam?"

Stone knows how to disturb viewers, as was evident in *Natural Born Killers* (1994), a brutal and violent spectacle of two youngsters on a killing spree, which Stone defended as an exposé of the excesses of the media. *Natural Born Killers* became a frequent target for Senator Robert Dole and the Republican Right, inspiring far more controversy than Stone's later *Nixon* (1995), his more subdued and arguably most effective excursion into political biography.

The director has specialized in the cinema of alienation, but, shocking as *Natural Born Killers* was, *JFK* remains his most controversial film, a film that could have more accurately been titled "The Jim Garrison Story." It attempted to challenge and ridicule the findings of the Warren Commission's investigation of the assassination of President John Fitzgerald Kennedy. Along with D. W. Griffith's *The Birth of a Nation* (1915), it became the most controversial American film of the twentieth century.

227

JFK was deemed controversial for its conspiratorial speculation about the Kennedy assassination, but the director's main purpose should be clear to anyone who has followed Oliver Stone's career. He repeatedly has attempted to answer the question: "Why were we in Vietnam?" The implication is that under Kennedy's leadership, we might have avoided the cataclysm of a heavily involved land war in Southeast Asia, even though the first American troops were sent there as advisors under his administration. Stone begins his film with archival footage of President Dwight David Eisenhower's warning to the nation to beware of the "military-industrial complex" that Eisenhower feared might become powerful enough to dictate policy. For Stone, Eisenhower's fears were a reality.

As a consequence of this speculative position, Stone paid the price that political filmmakers must pay in America when their message runs counter to the Establishment: scorn, ridicule, and contempt. Tom Wicker led the attack in the *New York Times* on 15 December 1991, asking in a rhetorical frame: "Does 'JFK' Conspire Against Reason?" Wicker criticized Stone for treating "matters that are wholly speculative as facts and truth, thus rewriting history."[1] His denunciation was paralleled later in the week by Vincent Canby's review on 20 December, headlined "When Everything Amounts to Nothing."[2] On 17 December Stone was attacked in a piece on the Op-Ed page of the *Washington Post,* signed by Warren Commission counsel David W. Belin and former President Gerald R. Ford.[3] Were they trying to protect dark state secrets? Oliver Stone replied with a spirited defense of his film in the *Washington Post* a week later, on 24 December.[4] Both the *Washington Post* and the *New York Times* obviously wanted to destroy Oliver Stone's credibility before *JFK* went into general release. The question is, why? Why was the Establishment so frightened by this movie and its speculations?

JFK looks back at what might be called the crime of the century that occurred in Dallas, Texas, on 22 November 1963, when John Fitzgerald Kennedy was assassinated. Anyone who was alive then will remember that day when the most energetic and youthful president our country had seen since Theodore Roosevelt was cut down in the prime of his life. Kennedy seemed to offer the nation ideals, vision, and purpose. He assembled around him, seemingly like Plato's philosopher-king, a group of advisors who have since been called, for better or worse, "the best and the brightest." He faced down the Soviets during the Cuban Missile Crisis, which

Stone links to the Bay of Pigs fiasco. He brought more class and culture to the White House than any other president in recent memory. He appeared to be sophisticated, cultured, articulate, well informed, and well read. At the Berlin Wall he astonished his audience by addressing them in flawless German: *"Ich bin ein Berliner!"* He was a cosmopolitan citizen of the world. He was possessed of a beautiful wife and beautiful children. Moreover, he was wealthy, a paradigm of the American success myth, and the legend of Camelot was attached to his tenure in office. The nation seemed happy, secure, upbeat, optimistic, and proud.

But Kennedy's "New Frontier" was not to last. Instead, we got Lyndon Johnson, the "Great Society," and a protracted, soul destructive war in Vietnam. By the end of the 1960s the nation was ripped apart by dissent and with Johnson's decision not to run in 1968, the Democrats lost the White House to Richard Nixon, who gave us the legacy of Watergate. Perhaps Kennedy would have done better had he lived. Perhaps he would have had the wisdom not to get embroiled in a civil war in Southeast Asia, at least in the informed opinion of Arthur M. Schlesinger Jr., a respected historian in Kennedy's camp.

Perhaps the assassination was politically motivated. The Warren Commission rushed to judgment to convince the nation that Kennedy was assassinated by one lone gunman, so the government could get on with the the business of waging war. Doubts lingered on, however, about the Warren Commission's "one-man-one-gun" theory. Stone's film shows why people had reason to question the Warren Commission's conclusions. It effectively discredits the "one-man-one-gun" notion and makes the so-called "magic bullet" explanation seem especially ridiculous, regardless of whether one accepts Stone's larger and more general conspiracy theory.

Oliver Stone's skepticism does not represent a peculiar minority opinion. A recent Gallup Poll (quoted by the studio when the film was released) indicated that 73 percent of those Americans polled did not believe the Warren Commission's Report and believed that there was in fact a conspiracy to kill the president. Stone's screenplay, written with Zachary Sklar, follows two sources, Jim Garrison's *On the Trail of the Assassins* and Jim Marrs' *Crossfire: The Plot That Killed Kennedy,* concluding that the assassination was a coup d'état to remove from office a president who the hawks believed was "soft" on Communism. Lyndon Johnson, one of the most savvy and powerful politicians in the Senate before he became vice president, was their man to hold the line against the Communists in Southeast Asia. At first, this may seem as plausible an explanation as that offered by the Warren Commission, or is it? Did Lyndon Johnson remark to his biographer: "If we get involved in that bitch of a war my Great Society will be dead"?

If Stone errs, it is in keying his story to Jim Garrison's crusade to prosecute New Orleans businessman Clay Shaw for conspiracy in the murder. Those old enough to remember these events will recall that this spectacular sideshow, organized by the district attorney of New Orleans and attempting to link Clay Shaw to Lee Harvey Oswald through middleman David Ferrie, eventually fizzled out. Many thought that Garrison was exploiting the trauma of the Kennedy assassination to build his own reputation. Thinking better of Garrison, Stone contends that those responsible for the coup did everything within their power to discredit Garrison, who emerges as the unlikely hero of Stone's film.

The casting of Kevin Costner as Jim Garrison helps to raise the stakes and elevate the district attorney's heroic potential. Tommy Lee Jones plays Clay Shaw as a wealthy, dangerous, powerful, devious homosexual sleaze, and the film generates absolutely no sympathy for him or his lowlife cronies, such as retired FBI agent Guy Bannister (Edward Asner), and, especially, Shaw's henchman David Ferrie (played as a pathetic psychopath by Joe Pesci in the most astonishing supporting role of a thoroughly astonishing film).

Sissy Spacek gives a strong performance as Garrison's wife, who attempts to hold her family together through her husband's ordeal. Gary Oldman (who played Sid Vicious in *Sid and Nancy*) plays Lee Harvey Oswald and seems to be a dead ringer for that loser. The talented supporting cast also includes John Candy, Jack Lemmon, Walter Matthau (as Senator Russell Long), Donald Sutherland (as Garrison's mysterious Washington informant, known only as Mr. X), Kevin Bacon, and Garrison himself, ironically playing Chief Justice Earl Warren.

Despite the attempts to discredit the film, *JFK* was strongly in contention for being the best film of 1991, and was nominated as such by the Motion Picture Academy. There can be absolutely no doubt that it was the most significant film of the year as well as the most contentious. It was overly long but splendidly made, offering a dazzling all-star cast to carry its debatable thesis. What makes it unusual is that, unlike most American movies, it had a thesis, offering an interpretation of one of the most important events in recent American history. Such an interpretation does not necessarily constitute a rewriting of history, as Tom Wicker asserted, but it does force the viewer to think back over a tragic event that surely altered the course of American history during the latter half of our century.

Official Washington was demonstrably upset by Stone's interpretation of history, as evidenced by the number of column inches devoted to the film in the *Washington Post.* On 20 December first-line film critic Rita Kempley at least gave Stone some credit: "Another futile attempt to exorcise the nightmare of Vietnam, *'JFK'* is Stone's best and most emotional film since 'Platoon.'"[5] Favorable comments were hard to find in Washington, however. In an angry and intemperate *ad hominem* attack entitled "Paranoid History" on 26 December, right-wing pundit George F. Will criticized the film as a "travesty," an "act of execrable history and contemptible citizenship by a man of technical skill, scant education and negligible conscience."[6] Pat Dowell, the *Washington* magazine film critic, resigned after her editor, Jack Limpert, refused to publish a brief, laudatory review of *JFK* she had written. As reported by Howard Kurtz in the *Washington Post* on 24 January 1992, Dowell wrote, "I cannot in good conscience keep my job at the price of tailoring my evaluation of a film's merits to fit someone else's idea of political (or cinematic) correctness."[7]

Many objected to Stone's mingling fact with fiction. There was, for example, no secret Washington meeting between Jim Garrison and the mysterious Mr. X. Reviewing the film for *The Guardian* in Britain on 23 January 1992, Derek Malcolm wrote, "It is almost but not quite history as gossip."[8] Charles Bremmer wrote in the *London Times Saturday Review* on 18 January: "Until he tackled *JFK,* Stone was rarely pressed over his argument that artistic licence gave him the right to recast history provided it was done with the intention of sticking to the spiritual truth of his subject." Bremmer concluded by quoting Stone from *Premiere* magazine: "The assassination was America's first coup d'état and it worked."[9]

In Britain Arthur M. Schlesinger Jr., who was interviewed along with Oliver Stone on BBC-1 (17 January 1992), noted, "The premise that Kennedy was moving out of Vietnam was defensible; the conclusion that the CIA or the Joint Chiefs or J. Edgar Hoover were involved in a conspiracy is not," though not all historians would agree with Schlesinger, seen by some as an apologist for the Kennedy administration. Schlesinger objected to the way Stone presents "an extreme hypothesis as literal fact."[10] He conceded that the inquiry was justified, but added that "film is not necessarily the best medium for that inquiry." In fact, that would depend on the intended result. Certainly the American networks were soon reviewing the major conspiracy theories, and ultimately, in the wake of the film, the closed files on the assassination were opened partially because of the renewed controversy. How many films have exercised such influence and produced such results?

As a controversial political filmmaker Oliver Stone may seem unique, but his crusading nature and his tendency to challenge authority and demand answers is not without precedence. His nearest equivalent is Britain's Peter Watkins, whose career and approaches to history parallel Stone's, though Watkins belongs to an older generation and a different tradition. For one thing, Stone began as a purveyor of horror films, whereas Watkins began as a documentary filmmaker. But like Stone, Watkins was challenging conventional notions of history and historical truth from the very beginning of his professional career. In *Culloden* (1964), a history of the Jacobite Uprising in 1745 when the Highland Clans fought for the Scots Pretender to the English throne, Bonnie Prince Charlie, Watkins challenged the conventional techniques of documentary filmmaking and rejected the idea of historical objectivity by seeking out subjective truth and questioning received notions of truth and reality. From a patriotic British perspective the Battle of Culloden was historically significant because it marked the end of civil unrest in the Highlands of Scotland and, as the last battle fought on British soil, it made the ideal of a United Kingdom a reality. However, Watkins was not interested in the official, institutional interpretation of that event, but in the story of the Highlanders, whose clans and culture were destroyed by the invading English army. From their perspective, the battle was a mismatched massacre, followed by a calculated policy of genocide.

Culloden took a revisionist minority position, following the lead of advisor John Prebble's scholarship, representing historical approaches in vogue at midcentury, assimilating facts, statistics, and documents into an apparently coherent whole. Anticipating Stone, Watkins' approach was that of a maverick revisionist, and his film was subversive both in its point of view and in its narrative technique. Using standard documentary techniques, Watkins managed to dramatize and reanimate the past and to reconstruct the event in a way that it might have been presented if twentieth-century television reporters had covered it. The suffering of the clansmen fighting and dying for Bonnie Prince Charlie, whose heroic image is seriously deflated, seemed realistic, but the continuing narrative mediation of Sir Andrew Henderson was an obvious fabrication.

Later, in *The War Game* (1965) Watkins developed his technique in more daring ways, speculating about the effects of a nuclear attack on Britain. Here too, he presented a well-researched aural montage of facts and statistics mixed with the personal reflections of ordinary people caught up in a cataclysm of catastrophic events quite beyond their control. Watkins mediated these events in documentary fashion through a carefully controlled voice-over narration by himself and others. However, the events narrated in *The War Game* were entirely fabricated, whereas the events of *Culloden* had been more like Stone's would become, symbolic constructions arising from informed historical speculation.

So, in *Oliver Stone's America* when Susan Mackey-Kallis talks of Stone presenting the "creation of reality" through the "critical engagement with the various symbolic constructions of the past," brought into a "dialogue with other 'histories' in an ever-swelling chorus of voices,"[11] she might as well be describing his predecessor, Peter Watkins. Watkins was operating in this mode of postmodernist historian twenty years before Stone directed *Salvador* (1986). Consciously, or not, Stone has built on a tradition which Watkins pioneered decades earlier. As a consequence of challenging official versions of history in appealing, technically innovative ways, Stone has provoked controversy and been vilified as Watkins was before.

To summarize, Oliver Stone and Peter Watkins are in many ways parallel talents. Both are passionate moralists representing overtly leftist agendas; have presumed to reshape and reconstruct past events to suit their purposes and political interpretations; have been accused of being polemicists and propagandists; have attempted to document the perceived fragmentation of the postmodern era; have scripted and directed their films; and have won Academy Awards for their direction. Finally, both are obsessively driven filmmakers. They became obsessed with the plight of ordinary citizens caught up in cataclysmic events, Watkins in past and imagined future wars and Stone in the Vietnam war.

As we have seen, in their basic distrust of government and its institutions, Watkins and Stone share a kind of kinship. But Watkins was more uncompromising and in his later career chose to work modestly, making privately funded films that could never achieve wide distribution. In contrast, Stone has managed to work independently within the framework of Hollywood. Consequently, Stone has been far more effective in reaching a large audience. And the larger the audience the fiercer the controversy.

In 1992 Oliver Stone and Zachary Sklar published *JFK: The Book of the Film* (New York: Applause Books), as if to answer the firestorm of adverse publicity the film inspired. This six-hundred-page book included "The Documented Screenplay," "340 Research Notes" compiled by Jane Rusconi, twenty five pages of reprinted "Historical Documents," and a sampling of "The *JFK* Debate," reprinting "97 Reactions and Commentaries" by journalists, politicians, and critics. By publishing the screenplay in this format, Stone seemed to suggest that he had nothing to hide and that he was putting all of his cards on the table.

As if preparing himself for a second firestorm that never quite developed over *Nixon*, which could be considered a sequel to *JFK,* Stone also published the original screenplay written with Stephen J. Rivele and Christopher Wilkinson in *Nixon: An Oliver Stone Film* (Hyperion, 1995). The annotated screenplay, edited by Eric Hamburg, was preceded by an interview with Stone and essays by John Dean, E. Howard Hunt, and Daniel Schorr, among others, and followed by 245 pages of translated Watergate documents and tapes. Both of these oversized books create the impression that Stone is a kind of cinematic historian absolutely determined to document his sources.

Stone has described himself as a mythmaker, and, as such, he tends to confuse fact with fiction to make history his story. "Our film's mythology," Stone told *Premiere* in January 1992, "will replace the Warren Report, as *Gone With the Wind* replaced *Uncle Tom's Cabin,* and was in turn replaced by *Roots* and *The Civil War*."[12] Margaret Mitchell was not exactly writing history, however, but merely ornamenting it, which, to a degree, is what Stone has also done in *JFK.*

In *The Cinema of Oliver Stone*, Norman Kagan has pointed out that the function of myth is "to explain the world and give people hope and faith," claiming that a "true myth" does not simply "give a new version of events," but "renews our hopes and increases our understanding."[13] By this measure, perhaps Stone is not really a mythmaker. In *JFK* he does not educate his audience, other than to demonstrate the flawed findings of the Warren Commission. Beyond this, all he does is to speculate intelligently about the inconsistencies of the Warren Commission Report and to articulate demonic conspiratorial theories. He offers no convincing solutions to the mystery of who shot or ordered the shooting of President Kennedy and altered the course of U.S. history. He has no real evidence to prove any single, specific conspiracy theory.

Yet, Stone claimed *JFK* offered a countermyth to the Warren Commission's version, which, by analogy, becomes merely a bureaucratic myth. Because the first cut of Stone's film was over four hours long, compressing the narrative to the film's final release running time gives it an unreal, hypnotic, and fragmented style in its conspiratorial subtext that makes it resemble *The X-Files* in its treatment of reality. Perhaps this is why Kagan claims that Stone's countermyth "leaves us in the dark, facing a corrupt, evil, frightening mystery."[14]

In her *New York Times* review on 5 January 1992, Janet Maslin objected to the film's flashback montage work and rapid pacing that intercut "real material and simulated scenes" and intermingled "composite characters" with "actual ones."[15] In fact, Stone follows the formula and technique of the typical action-adventure film that is paced rapidly so that the viewer will not have time to puzzle over plot inconsistencies, but since *JFK* seems to be rewriting history, it is understandable that some critics find Stone's methods irresponsible.

The film is at times as wacky as the conspiracy theories it seems to embrace. It will be viewed with skepticism by anyone who lived through the dark days of the autumn of 1963. It will be distracting and confusing even to those who know the details of the assassination and its aftermath, and even more confusing to younger viewers who approach the countermyth as a history lesson. It turns Jim Garrison into a Capraesque hero, reaching for a truth that is beyond his grasp. On the other hand, the film caused many documents concerning the assassination to be declassified, and its speculations became a part of the national debate. The film is nihilistic and perhaps even subversive in that it encourages skepticism and distrust of government, but to the postmodern sensibility, that could be a positive result.

In conclusion, Oliver Stone is neither the first nor the only contemporary leftist filmmaker to have commandeered millions of viewers to his causes, but he may well be the most successful. He has managed to subvert the very infrastructure of Hollywood filmmaking from the inside, and although alienating critics, journalists, and politicians and challenging cherished notions and beliefs, he captured a substantial viewing public, even during the 1980s, when, under Ronald Reagan and George Bush, the country had taken a sharp turn to the Right. His work demonstrates a consistency of vision and a high level of commitment, dedication, and integrity. Stone has taken career-threatening chances and has managed to face down his opponents, powerful Establishment figures from the media and government who have attempted to discredit his work and damage his credibility. His conclusions and his methods may sometimes be flawed and suspect, but his courage is undeniable and daunting.

Notes

1. Tom Wicker, "Does *JFK* Conspire Against Reason," *New York Times,* 15 December 1991, sec. II, 1, 18.

2. Vincent Canby, "When Everything Amounts to Nothing," *New York Times,* 20 December 1991, sec. C, p. 1, 2.

3. Gerald R. Ford and David W. Belin, "Kennedy Assassination: How About the Truth?," *Washington Post,* 17 December 1991, sec. A, p. 21.

4. Oliver Stone, "The JFK Assassination—What About the Evidence?," *Washington Post,* 24 December 1991, sec. A, p. 13.

5. Rita Kempley, "'JFK': History Through a Prism," *Washington Post,* 20 December 1991, sec. D, p. 1, 2.

6. George F. Will, "'JFK': Paranoid History," *Washington Post,* 15 December 1991, sec. A, p. 23.

7. Howard Kurtz, "Film Critic Resigns Over 'JFK' Review," *Washington Post,* 24 January 1992, sec. C, p. 2.

8. Derek Malcolm, "Taking Another Shot at Kennedy," *The Guardian* (London), 23 January 1992, p. 25.

9. Charles Bremner, "Reshooting the President," *The Times Saturday Review* (London), 18 January 1992, p. 12.

10. Arthur M. Schlesinger Jr., interview, British Broadcasting Corporation, 1, 17 January 1992.

11. Susan Mackey-Kallis, *Oliver Stone's America: "Dreaming the Myth Outward"* (Boulder, Colo.: Westview Press, 1996), 23.

12. Oliver Stone, "Oliver Stone Talks Back," *Premiere* 5, no. 5 (January 1992): 66–72

13. Norman Kagan, *The Cinema of Oliver Stone* (New York: Continuum, 1995), 201.

14. Kagan, *Cinema*, 201.

15. Janet Maslin, "Oliver Stone Manipulates His Puppet," *New York Times,* 5 January 1992, sec. II, p. 15.

Chapter 10

Heaven and Earth

When Man and Woman Changed Places . . .

Bryan Marinelli

According to some established criticism, films concerning war have traditionally been tales of men and for men. In his article, "'Do You Walk the Walk?': Aspects of Masculinity in Some Vietnam War Films," John Newsinger begins with the definitive statement that "[a]ll war films are tales of masculinity."[1] And, in *The Remasculinization of America*, Susan Jeffords asserts that "the defining feature of American war narratives is that they are a 'man's story' from which women are generally excluded."[2]

Even some of the landmark motion pictures involving war have failed to elude these types of criticism. For instance, both *Platoon* and *Born on the Fourth of July* have been recognized as innovative "mile Stones" in the genre of Vietnam War film. *Platoon* offered what was at the time an unprecedented picture of American soldiers perpetrating baneful crimes upon innocent Vietnamese peasants.[3] And, according to Linda Dittmar and Gene Michaud, *Born on the Fourth of July* was unique in combining combat with protest as well as in bringing taboo political issues to the public arena.[4] But, despite their marked achievements, both of these epics failed to avoid the stigma that Vietnam War films primarily depict," [masculinity] as unable to cope with the problems and dilemmas, the stresses and horrors that confronted it in Vietnam."[5] Even the most noteworthy innovations in the genre have come at no expense to concerns about the shattered masculinity which often propels these motion pictures.

Much like *Platoon* and *Born on the Fourth of July*, *Heaven and Earth*—the third segment of Oliver Stone's Vietnam War trilogy—verges on the deconstruction of criticism surrounding war films. In

Wakeup Cinema, Frank Beaver praises this latest Stone epic by saying that it

> moves the Vietnam story away from a narrowed American perspec-
> tive and close to the lives of the people who endured the confusion
> and tragedy of the war in their own land. In this regard, *Heaven and
> Earth* offers a larger, less provincial consideration of political re-
> alities than previous films on the Vietnam War. And in his sympa-
> thetic treatment of a strong female character, Stone addresses some
> of the criticism labeling him as severely deficient as a balanced
> storyteller.[6]

Stone indeed deserves some credit for his valiant effort to furnish a perspective of the Vietnam War from the erstwhile forlorn view-point of not only a woman, but a Vietnamese woman. Furthermore, although the reproduction of horrifying biographical events in the film is sanitized to some degree (because a reproduction naturally lacks authenticity), the director has produced a commendable, com-pelling reenactment of the gruesome suffering of Le Ly Hayslip (Hiep Thi Le), her family, and her fellow villagers in Ky La, Viet-nam. Finally, what is most provoking is the film's avowal of the Vietnam War's nullification of Le Ly's early lessons of male sov-ereignty—introduced by her mother (Joan Chen)—and the subse-quent reformulation of Le Ly's identity as Phung or "woman warrior."

Yet, while *Heaven and Earth* provides a plethora of opportuni-ties for cultural and feminist analyses, there exists a pervading "masculine subtext," which I will argue is really more of an over-looked primary text, in the film. Since the terms "masculinity" and "femininity" are codependent social constructs, an analysis of gen-der roles at once presupposes the presence of a binary opposition. This general axiom translates into *Heaven and Earth* where the relative strength of Le Ly Hayslip is intensified by the juxtaposi-tion of her character against those of men, particularly her hus-band, Steve Butler (Tommy Lee Jones). It is essential to note that while the other central characters in *Heaven and Earth* parallel their biographical counterparts, Butler is "an amalgam of four dif-ferent men in Hayslip's life." This fact explains why "he's hard to figure out, sometimes tender, sometimes violent, mainly confused about what he wants from his woman and life in general."[7] Stone's fusion of the attributes of four different men into a constructed, volatile ex-soldier is concordant with his directorial custom of inscribing his "signature" upon each one of his features. Furthermore, this virtual invention of a man by Stone exemplifies the fact that notions of manliness and masculinity are social constructs themselves.

A transient digression into Hayslip's relationships with the actual men who constitute the Butler character will be beneficial in uncovering what I see as Stone's ulterior motive in the film. In the second part of her autobiography, *Child of War, Woman of Peace*, Hayslip portrays her first husband, Ed Munro (a World War II veteran, *not* a Vietnam veteran), as a staunch, "middle-aged American civilian construction engineer"[8] who assists her in her exodus from Vietnam. Because her wedlock to Munro is more a marriage of convenience than passion, Le Ly acquiesces to the temptation of an extramarital affair with Dante (Dan) DeParma, an American soldier who has served in "Nam." DeParma professes his love for Le Ly and sustains his overall psychological stability after having finished his tour of duty. However, because he is unable to formally separate from his wife (Tuyet) and because his civilian occupation is to be the brokering of firearms (a career which Le Ly vehemently opposes), they are never married.

Le Ly's second husband, Dennis Hayslip—who abducts their son, Alan, and around whom the abduction of the children in the film is based—never serves in the Vietnam War. However, like Butler, he is emotionally disturbed due to a separation from his first wife and children. The fourth and final lover that Hayslip mentions in *Child of War, Woman of Peace* is Cliff Parry. Initially, Parry obtains Hayslip's trust and sympathy by posing himself as an emasculated soldier, a man who laments his horrific slayings of the Viet Cong and suspected VC sympathizers. In a convincing fit of passion, he discloses several of his abominable war crimes to Le Ly:

> [W]e'd slit their throats like chickens and leave them to die in the jungle. But that wasn't the worst of it. Sometimes we'd torture the target first—not to get information, but just because we hated those bastards so much. We'd cut off their ears or gouge out their eyes. . . .[9]

However, Parry is later discovered to be "a professional swindler—a pathological liar and con man—with a long list of aliases."[10] Unfortunately, this realization is made after he has guilefully ex-

ploited Le Ly's sympathetic disposition in order to solicit her trust
and extort some of her private property.

This biographical information is quite significant. First, Le Ly
Hayslip is never officially married to a veteran of the Vietnam War;
but in the film, Stone has opted to fashion Le Ly's husband as a
Vietnam veteran. Secondly, Oliver Stone, who is also a Vietnam
veteran, has elected to embody the neurotic tendencies of Dennis
Hayslip and Cliff Parry (both nonveterans) in the constructed ex-
soldier, Steve Butler, reveals the director's persistent inclination to
depict the emasculating effects of "Nam" upon the American men
who served. Stone maintains that "the entire movie is framed as
her [Le Ly's] life."[11] However, from the moment we are introduced
to Butler in Da Nang, the film begins to evolve into the epic of a
distraught Vietnam veteran, subsequently overshadowing the saga
of the resilient heroine.

Playing the devil's advocate, Gavin Smith (in his interview with
the director) raises the interesting detail that Stone uses very few
camera shots from Le Ly's point of view in the picture. When in-
terrogated on this point, Stone replies, "You don't need subjective
shots to be subjective . . . it doesn't really make much difference
if you see her coming into a room or you're going into a room
with her. It's an aesthetic that you must choose as a director."
However, in the same interview, Stone informs Smith that he considers the camera to be an actual participant in his films, "not a
recording device."[12] The confident director seems to be contradict-
ing himself. Stone exercises few shots from Le Ly's point of view
which naturally weakens the viewer's perception that the dramati-
zation is entirely her story. The evidence suggests that Stone has
appropriated Hayslip's compelling and critically acclaimed texts as
vehicles to once again exhibit his own personal and political agenda. *Heaven and Earth* is as much about Oliver Stone/Butler as it
is about Le Ly Hayslip.

In addition to incorporating neurotic tendencies into his manu-
factured Vietnam veteran, Stone has exerted a marked degree of
energy in constructing scenes that portray Steve as a sympathetic,
emasculated war hero. The results of this effort have been applaud-
ed by Gavin Smith who states that Jones' role as the tormented
marine is "a rich portrait of a lost soul, layered with tenderness
and violence, vulnerability and self-loathing."[13] Granted, Butler
originally presents himself as a confident, masculine warrior, forcing his way into Le Ly's apartment in Da Nang, providing her and

the children with safe helicopter transport out of An Khe, and emerging from his status as missing in action to swoop Le Ly and the children up into his muscular arms. However, a retrospective view of some of Tommy Lee Jones' early scenes reveals ironic subtleties which suggest that the character has been "unmanned" by his murderous acts, that his machismo is only a mask. Tommy Lee Jones has professed that even when we initially encounter his character, there is a suggestion that the "Nam" experience has ravaged his manhood, that "the things he's done have begun to prey on him. He's a needy man at that point, emotionally and spiritually."[14] He is not the macho, sex-starved grunt in quest of a little "boom boom," as Le Ly calls it; and his interests do not lie in the prostitutes that parade the black market streets of Da Nang. Instead, his choice is the natural and innocent-looking "little peach blossom": "I'm a little too old for hookers. I just wanted to meet you . . . Your friend introduced us and that's all I wanted." It is interesting that Butler repeats the word "wanted" because, as I discuss in the upcoming pages, much of the remainder of the film is concerned with what he wants—namely to regain some sense of manhood through the establishment of patriarchal order after his discovery that success as a soldier is questionable as a basis for masculinity. Subsequently, the needs and tribulations of Le Ly are moved to the margin.

In addition, while Steve's tenacious pursuit of Le Ly into her private, humble abode resembles "breaking and entering," he is motivated by desperation for camaraderie and bears affinity to a lonely, distressed child. His persistent mendicant for Le Ly's companionship implies a search for compassion and the nurturing predilection of a woman. Butler's despondency becomes more apparent later that evening when his distraught psyche manifests itself in a dream, presumably containing unsettling visions of his war experiences. This ominous nightmare originates his mumbling and the respective, frantic waving and kicking of his arms and legs. When the "peach blossom" wakens him, "[h]is eyes pop open—alert, terrified, a brief hint of the demons to come now buried by her smile" (S, 99).[15]

Butler's implied psychological instability becomes palpable later in the film when it reaches a definitive climax. After viciously jackhammering a shotgun to Le Ly's head and threatening to kill her, he breaks down emotionally with a "wracking SOB" and the "vast shaking of his body, a sad, embittered man," and then, in his emotionally tattered state, he divulges the atrocities of an immoral covert operation that continue to afflict his conscience:

> I killed so many over there . . . I was so good at it they reassigned me to the program . . . sometimes three, four a night . . . I was in hell, Ly, pure hell. Maybe I went nuts, maybe I am nuts, who the fuck knows! . . . The more I killed, the more they gave me to kill . . . It's like being eaten inside out by a bellyful of sharks. You gotta keep moving, you gotta keep hitting, 'cause if you stop, the sharks 'll fuckin' eat you alive . . . (*S*, 71-72).

Here it is ironic that doing what he thought would prove his manlihood—acting as a great warrior—becomes the cause of its denial. We see that his success as a killer is haunting him, leading him to question it as a basis for masculinity. The realization that he has not been the quintessential masculine warrior, but simply a butcher, is too much for him; quite frankly, it's hell not being a man. Thus, despite Butler's incisive treatment of his wife throughout their marriage, these particular scenes manipulate the viewer into sympathizing with him.

Steve Butler is much like the Ron Kovic who preceded him in *Born on the Fourth of July*. Both men are victims of a social construct, the masculine ideal that a great soldier signifies a great man. To appropriate Don Kunz's description of Kovic, Butler is "America's Vietnam soldier who, in a sense, died fighting an emasculating war in a foreign country."[16] Although Butler does not suffer the physical emasculation of Ron Kovic, he is likewise handicapped by the atrocities he perpetrated as an American soldier. And, just as for Kovic, the mythological heroic ideal of the American soldier becomes for Butler a psychologically debilitating trauma.

There is, however, a vital constituent differentiating the two infantrymen. Ron Kovic apprehends a new way to be a man by becoming a fighter "in what Stone pictures as a new American Revolution, attempting to wrest power from an increasingly remote and corrupt political establishment."[17] However, Butler's attempts to remasculinize himself prove futile. And, after his private war to remasculinize and reintegrate himself into America fails, he resorts to an internalization of his anguish that culminates in self-destruction.

Butler's attempt to remasculinize and reintegrate on the home front involves engaging in quite a different war than that conducted by Ron Kovic. Rather than attempting to remasculinize as Ron Kovic does, by questioning "his attitude toward the war and [redefining] what it means to be a man in America,"[18] Butler attempts to reestablish himself in America in the more traditional role of the familial patriarch and starts by marrying an Asian woman, stereotypically signified as the embodiment of complacency and servility.

While *Born on the Fourth of July* seems an exception to Susan Jeffords' argument that "most Vietnam War literature can be read as favoring a return to traditional roles which serve the interests of patriarchy,"[19] *Heaven and Earth* does not. There is a snarl in Butler's plan to return to this "traditional role"—that being his ignorance of both Le Ly's former role as a Viet Cong warrior and the extent of her suffering (rape and torture) during the war. When Steve proposes marriage to Le Ly, she cautions him: "I have bad karma." However, he disregards her invocation: "Bad karma? How much can have happened to a pretty girl like you?" Here, he professes his naïveté about the war's eradication of her "would-be passivity," simultaneously marginalizing the impact of the Vietnam War upon innocent Vietnamese civilians. In addition, by casting Le Ly as the stereotypical Asian—lumping her into an all-inclusive category—Butler is recognizing her as simply an object and failing to distinguish her as a complex, female, Vietnamese subject. Once again Steve Butler comes to occupy the center, but only by placing Le Ly and Vietnamese people at the margin.

Le Ly's "would-be passivity" is embodied in the teachings of Le Ly's mother, of which there are several instances in the film. For example, during a dinner scene in Ky La, which includes several of Le Ly's aunts and uncles, Mama argues with Papa concerning their sons whom the Viet Cong have just recruited as freedom fighters. As the argument escalates, Mama affronts Papa in front of the guests, referring to him as a "stupid, selfish man"; Papa then strikes her across the face. Later that evening, Mama, with a glowing red mark on her face, warns Le Ly: "I made your Papa lose face in front of everyone. If you ever do what I just did to a husband, I'll have both your cheeks glowing, one from him and one from me." Despite the abuse she receives, Mama continues to preach the axiom of male sovereignty. But, due to the war experience, Le Ly can never be the stereotypical passive, subservient, Asian woman. In the first place she "was called 'my little mud-flower'—something fragile that blows with the wind and yet it's strong."[20] Secondly, Le Ly has already been partially Americanized by living in the Americanized black market in Da Nang and selling illegal substances—even her body—as a means of survival. Most importantly, she is forced to mature at an early age as a result of being raped, tortured, and witnessing much bloodshed. In short, Le Ly's initiation into adulthood occurs through a process of pain-gain, which is more a male formula for the process of maturity. And, the intestinal fortitude she develops as a result of this male rite of passage is too strong for the patrimonial prison cell which her husband later imposes upon her.

For Butler, who remains ignorant to the lifetime of experience his young wife has lived, Le Ly personifies the stereotypical quiescent Asian woman as opposed to the Americanized Vietnamese "Woman Warrior" into whom she has evolved. Steve's expectations for Le Ly as his matron are evident; for instance, when he proposes marriage, he says "My first wife taught me a real lesson in my life. I'm serious. I need a good Oriental woman like you." Here, Butler is the complex subject with the intricate need for a "good Oriental woman" signifying his exigency for some semblance of male power. Le Ly is merely the compliant object through which he can fulfill his desire.

Other characters in the film also stereotype Le Ly as the "good Oriental woman." Steve's sister, Erma, describes her as being "like a little China doll!" (S, 37). And, during the Thanksgiving dinner scene, the celebration includes Steve's friend Larry's adulation over Steve's choice of the "perfect wife":

[Larry]   Oriental women tell you anything you want, Steve, do anything you want—but if you believe 'em, hey, that's your right man, and I'm the first to take my hat off to you.

[Steve]   Whatcha saying Larry? Oriental women are also very loyal, they . . .

[Larry]   I'm saying more power to you, brother (S, 47).

In addition to the emphasis on loyalty and subservience that stereotypically conjoins marriage to an Asian women, Larry's final comment in this scene suggests that patriarchal power is also enforced by such a union; there is more power *to* Steve.

According to Susan Jeffords, women in Vietnam narratives "fulfill Eve Kosofsky Sedgwick's prescription for the maintenance of masculine power."[21] In her *Between Men: English Literature and*

Male Homosocial Desire, Sedgwick says that "in the presence of a woman who can be seen as pitiable . . . men are able to exchange power and to confirm each other's value."[22] Butler's demeanor toward Le Ly during the initial stages of their marriage connotes his self-perceived dominance in the relationship. After all, Butler (like her real-life first husband, Ed Munro) is Le Ly's ticket out of life on the black-market streets of Da Nang. Furthermore, when they arrive in what for Le Ly is the new world of America, Steve maintains masculine power over his "pitiable" foreign wife by adopting the role of provider and protector, introducing her to the strange but wonderous phenomenon known as the supermarket and ensuring her that food will no longer be a scant commodity. He is her armor against the piercing gaze of a racist supermarket cashier: "They don't understand, Ly, I do. And I'll never let you down. We'll lick 'em together." He is also her aegis from the overtly condescending verbal assaults of Erma:

[Erma] Well, I just want to show her we're being generous. I just want her to be thankful for what she has.

[Steve] Thankful! . . . In Da Nang when we drove by hospitals, past people our bombs had blown to bits, they'd wave, boys without legs would wave to us in our jeeps . . . because they were happy to be alive. So don't expect Ly to do handstands over your goddam turkey, Erma. She knows exactly what she's got, and what she left behind! (*S*, 47).

Finally, Steve promises that he will be the patrimonial breadwinner:

I just got three more years, I'll get out with a good pension. After that, I got a civilian job waiting—big bucks—the two of us. We'll be back in the Far East—Indonesia, Singapore. I'll be making 75 thousand a year. Guaranteed, promised to me (*S*, 42).

All of these scenes accent Butler's self-perceived role as guardian and provider for his immigrant wife. He is a "real man" who can be depended upon for emotional and monetary sustenance in this new, alienating, and hostile environment. However, because of his ignorance to his wife's true identity, Butler's perceived dominance is essentially a mere power construct, much as are gender roles themselves.

In addition to his remasculinization as a patriarch, this marriage
to an Asian woman operates on a deeper symbolic level. Susan
Jeffords' argument in *The Remasculinization of America* serves as
an apropos vantage point for my own assertions due to its insights
into the figurative function of women in Vietnam War narratives.

> Although the feminine is used chiefly to account for failure and to
> provide explanations about the loss of the war, what becomes appar-
> ent is that the feminine is used finally to identify the "enemy"—that
> against which the soldier had to struggle in order to fight and pos-
> sibly win the war in Vietnam, whether the Vietnamese, a difficult
> landscape or the U.S. government itself. . . . Given contemporary
> representations of the Vietnam veteran as emblematic of American
> masculinity itself and the war as a battle for the stability of mascu-
> linity in American culture, the feminine is not merely the enemy of
> soldiers but the enemy of all American men.[23]

For Butler, Le Ly embodies the "enemy" and the Vietnam War itself. His marriage to her is a symbolic endeavor to bring home the
war and attain some sense of the victory that eluded him and all
American soldiers in "Nam." Victory in war entails the surrender
of the enemy. Butler strives for a "surrender" or surrogate type of
victory on the home front by exercising his self-constructed, patriarchal dominance in an attempt to reconstruct Le Ly's identity. As
Jeffords' says, "The real threat of women's inconsistency is that
they confound men's 'powers' by disallowing them a stable basis
for control." Furthermore, she adds that "one of the critical functions of Vietnam representation in contemporary American culture
is to maintain and propagate an image of the feminine as multiple, varying, unpredictable, and, consequently, threatening and
contaminating."[24] Much like the unpredictable Viet Cong soldiers, Le Ly's foreign and hence unpredictable nature poses itself
as a menacing type of guerrilla warfare to Butler. Thus, as the vulnerable male subject, he attempts to exercise control over the
female object through a process of redefinition. By redefining
and Americanizing Le Ly—or shaping the "enemy" into his
desired image—Butler's adversary becomes more predictable, easier to control, and easier to conquer. In the process a role reversal takes place; through his attempts to control Le Ly, Butler in a
sense becomes "feminized"—multiple, unpredictable and, especially, threatening.

One way in which Butler fights to bring about Le Ly's surrender is through his attempt to convert her from her native Buddhist religion to that of the Catholic Church. He poses himself as her savior, her salvation, by doing his utmost to extinguish her worship of the Buddhist Gods that he calls "Heathens." He says that "he's [Budda] a graven image—a golden calf—read the Bible and you'll see. He was just a man. You can't worship just a man!" What Butler implies by this statement is that, since Le Ly worships heathens, she herself is one. His new mission therefore becomes an attempt to "domesticate a savage," to salvage her soul from the damnation that attends idol worship, a noble act for which she will forever be indebted to him. In the process, he can rid his home of the alien and daunting Buddhist shrine, thereby vanquishing a threat to his patriarchal order. Ironically, however, Butler marginalizes Le Ly's religion while simultaneously placing the Catholic faith, which also worships a man, at the center. Upon close examination, it is quite evident that Butler's justification for her conversion is also an empty construct. His "highly intellectual" argument against Buddhism is the persuasive proclamation that "your Buddha don't know shit!" However, it is Butler who "don't know shit." He cannot comprehend his wife nor her beliefs, much like American soldiers who blindly pegged the Viet Cong as "communists" rather than as the revolutionary freedom fighters we see in the film. As in Vietnam, Butler fights a similar "war" on the home front without an extensive understanding of the "enemy." He is motivated only by his blinded masculine quest for victory, a victory that entails remaking his wife/"enemy" into an ineffectual rival.

Another way in which Butler attempts to achieve a surrogate victory is by depriving Le Ly of free enterprise, thereby stunting her ability to achieve any sense of financial liberty. As previously stated, Butler wants to be the patrimonial breadwinner. However, when Le Ly begins to achieve success in the restaurant business, providing most of the financial support for the family, Butler perceives another threat. Just as in the case of his attempts to convert Le Ly religiously, he begins to construct empty arguments to discourage and deprive her of economic prosperity. For instance, when Le Ly asks him what they have to lose by her success, he replies:

What can we lose? I'll tell you: our house, our cars, the school money—everything! What if the potato salad goes bad and everyone gets sick! What if someone falls and breaks . . . They'll sue for everything we got! You don't know Americans like I do. They sue at the drop of a hat. Besides, you're just a dumb immigrant. Lawyers'll skin you alive (S, 61–62).

Of course his arguments are absurd. Even his deterrents to her endeavors are self-centered constructs. Rather than allowing his wife's business some opportunity to reap success, Butler denigrates it from the very start; the restaurant fails before it has even begun. He strives to convince her that without his "proper divine guidance," she stands no chance of survival in the exploitative USA. Furthermore, these arguments reemphasize his desire to maintain her dependence upon him for survival. For Butler, the new "enemy" cannot be allowed any advantage which might threaten his dominance and negate his "victory."

Butler's final attempt to induce Le Ly's surrender involves supplanting her in her role as the matriarch. Susan Jeffords states that

For the male . . . the reproductive process is an alienated one, as his experience is indirect and discontinuous, mediated in its uncertainty by the female. As a result, the male establishes other forms of continuity, and it is these that constitute patriarchy . . . These "artificial" forms of continuity take the form of political systems.[25]

Controlling Le Ly's religion and retarding her business venture are, in essence, part of the "political system" that Butler has developed to maintain his wife's subservience. Jeffords adds that these "artificial forms of continuity" can also take the form of "appropriation of the children through legal control of the mother." Butler first appropriates the children when he says, "They're my sons too. I'm going to take 'em up into the mountains and teach 'em how to hunt and shoot, thank you. They gonna learn what it takes to survive in this world" (S, 69). In other words Steve will assume responsibility for the boys' most formative experience—that is, teaching them the physical means of survival in a man's world. This male survival expedition into the jungle is of course far removed from the home and, concurrently, exclusive of the cogent intestinal fortitude exemplified by the marginalized mother. But, corporal survival is all that Butler can teach his boys because, while he survived the Vietnam War physically, he did not survive it psychically.

Butler's most significant appropriation of the children in the film is his abduction of them from the church. Since, at this point in the film, the "enemy" has denied Butler his utopian patriarchal victory by filing for divorce, he makes his last desperate offensive maneuver by denying the female "enemy" that which is most precious to her. This turn of events parallels the events in Vietnam for, by denying that it lost the Vietnam War, the United States (at least formally) deprived the Vietnamese of their precious victory. Butler's last stand nearly succeeds; when he kidnaps the children, he phones Le Ly and threatens her that if she ever wants to lay eyes on the boys again, she should write a letter to her "bitch lawyer"—dropping the divorce and all charges against him—and that the house and all of their belongings are to be put into his name. By taking legal possession of their property, Butler intends to stymie his wife's insurrection and renew her reliance. With the welfare of her children in mind, Le Ly accedes to the terms of her "surrender": "We make this right. We try. I will go to your church. I try harder. I put the shrine away. I work harder to understand you because I love you, Steve." She is willing to compromise her identity and to pretend to love a man she no longer loves in order to have her children back safely. From the close-up of his face as Le Ly makes her desperate plea, there is a sense of recognition on the part of Butler that his patriarchal utopia has failed, that the callous warfare he has used on his wife has been undeserved, and that his victory is an empty one at best. He realizes that his wife does not love him or need him to survive and that his patriarchal dominance has invariably been a mere mask. He has in essence attempted to push the stronger warrior to the margin, leaving himself the weakened center, a center which eventually implodes because it cannot hold. And, before she can meet his demands for surrender, Butler "meets an unhappy country boy's ending in the pickup, killing himself with one of the guns he's so fond of. It's another case of the war coming home."[26] With the recognition that he has lost yet another war and his masculine authority, there is no other choice for him but self-destruction—a bloody, naked death behind the steering wheel of his van—a symbolic death suggesting that his constructed patriarchal order has failed, that it has literally been exposed as a masquerade.

But even in death, Butler remains at the forefront of the viewer's attention. His graphic demise is a powerful directorial reminder that the Vietnam War has claimed yet another American male victim. We are left with the recognition that social constructs of masculinity (i.e. going to war, ruling the family) are detrimental to the men as well as the women in society, that men often aspire to self-destructive ideals. Finally, if Le Ly is the enemy, she too must take responsibility for Butler's destruction. Her responsibility in the matter further emphasizes her marginalization in the film as a baleful force contributing to the demise of a distraught, emasculated casualty of war.

The evidence suggests that despite Oliver Stone's intentions to silence the critics who label him as misogynist, the director has undercut himself. He has clearly constructed the Butler character to express his own disenchantment with the Vietnam War's effects on American male soldiers. Stone manipulates the viewer into sympathizing with Butler, to excuse his abuses of patriarchal power as the effects of a tattered masculinity. I do not, however, suggest that Stone is misogynist or racist; he has, after all, given us a story of a Vietnamese woman who emerges from war as a stronger individual than her male counterpart. However, *Heaven and Earth* does more to confirm than deny that

> Vietnam representation is only topically "about" the war in Vietnam or America's military strength or political policymaking. Its true subject is the masculine response to changes in gender relations in recent decades, its real battle that of the masculine to dominate and overpower its "enemy"—the feminine.[27]

The screen presence of Jones and the pervasive centeredness of the masculine subtext in the second half of the film suggest that maybe Stone was ill-equipped to reproduce the story of this great woman (and that men are ill-equipped to tell the stories of women in general) because his own interests take precedence. Perhaps a simple reproduction of Hayslip's life without this American GI was not political enough for this award-winning director who persistently makes himself and his political views a substantial component of every film he directs. *Heaven and Earth* is not simply Le Ly Hayslip's story; it is Oliver Stone's partially fictionalized account of a volatile Vietnam veteran's marriage to Le Ly Hayslip. For now at least, war films remain tales of masculinity.

Notes

1. John Newsinger, "'Do You Walk the Walk?': Aspects of Masculinity in Some Vietnam War Films," *You Tarzan: Masculinity, Movies, and Men*, eds. Pat Kirkham and Janet Thumim (New York: St. Martin's Press, 1993), 126.

2. Susan Jeffords, *The Remasculinization of America: Gender and the Vietnam War* (Indianapolis: Indiana Univ. Press, 1989), 49.

3. Newsinger, "Walk," 130.

4. Linda Dittmar and Gene Michaud, Introduction to *From Hanoi to Hollywood*, eds. Dittmar and Michaud (New Brunswick: Rutgers Univ. Press, 1990), 10.

5. Newsinger, "Walk," 126.

6. Frank Beaver, *Oliver Stone: Wakeup Cinema* (New York: Twayne Publishers, 1994), 192.

7. Robert Stone, "Oliver Stone's USA," *New York Review of Books*, 17 February 1994, 24.

8. Le Ly Hayslip, *Child of War, Woman of Peace* (New York: Doubleday, 1993), 3.

9. Hayslip, *Child*, 291.

10. Hayslip, *Child*, 296.

11. Gavin Smith, "Oliver Stone," *Film Comment*, January 1994, 37.

12. Smith, "Oliver," 37.

13. Gavin Smith, "Tommy Lee Jones," *Film Comment*, January 1994, 30.

14. Smith, "Tommy," 31.

15. Quotations from the screenplay will be cited in the text under the following abbreviation:
S: Oliver Stone, *Heaven and Earth: Screenplay* (Hollywood: Ixtlan, 1992).

16. Don Kunz, "Oliver Stone's Film Adaptation of *Born on the Fourth of July:* Redefining Masculine Heroism," *War, Literature and the Arts* 2, no. 2 (Fall 1990): 4.

17. Kunz, "Adaptation," 22.

18. Kunz, "Adaptation," 15.

19. Kunz, "Adaptation," 23.

20. Smith, "Oliver," 28.

21. Jeffords, *Remasculinization*, 64.

22. Eve Kosofsky Sedgwick, *Between Men: English Literature and Male Homosocial Desire* (New York: Columbia Univ. Press, 1985), 160.

23. Jeffords, *Remasculinization*, 155.

24. Jeffords, *Remasculinization*, 67, 160.

25. Jeffords, *Remasculinization*, 107.

26. Stone, "Oliver," 24.

27. Jeffords, *Remasculinization*, 167.

Chapter 11

Natural Born Killers

Natural Born Killers and American Decline

Daniel Green

Although Oliver Stone has generally been recognized as a film-maker interested in interpreting recent American history, most viewers, as well as most critics, probably view him more as a cinematic provocateur than as a serious chronicler of our life and times. This impression is strongly reinforced by, for example, Frank Beaver's *Oliver Stone: Wakeup Cinema* (New York: Twayne Publishers, 1994), a survey of the critical response to Stone's films that aptly captures in its title a widely held perception of Stone as a director more interested in visceral impact than in subtlety or nuance. *JFK*, in particular, seemed to strike many as a distortion of historical events for dramatic effect and has left Stone with the reputation—deserved or not—of being a director willing to play fast and loose with the facts. Missing in the debates Stone's films have provoked is much consideration of the possibility that in presenting his own vision of the past thirty years of American social and political history, Stone is precisely contesting the notion that there is an authoritative record for us to consult in determining these historical facts (and of course that we should defer to its official keepers). A fair and measured analysis of Stone's cinema should ask whether the films, taken as a whole, do present a distorted picture of post-Kennedy America or whether their admitted distortions and embellishments ultimately provide an altogether accurate sense of the tenor of this tumultuous, frequently overwrought period. The present essay will pursue this question as it pertains to all of Stone's films, but with most emphasis on its particular relevance in *Natural Born Killers* (1994), a film that depicts with horrifying force the sorry state to which America has descended in the generation following the Kennedy assassination.

Salvador (1986) seemed to suddenly thrust Oliver Stone forward as a serious filmmaker, even though he had won an Academy Award as a screenwriter for his script of *Midnight Express* in 1979 and had also written the screenplays of several high-profile films in the 1980s, including Brian De Palma's *Scarface* (1983). His previous films as a director, *Seizure* (1974) and *The Hand* (1981), were easily enough dismissed as second-string horror films, but as David Sanjek has correctly suggested, these films do forecast aesthetic strategies and thematic preoccupations that would be important elements in Stone's approach to the later films, beginning with *Salvador*. It would eventually become clear, over the course of his directing career and through interviews he concurrently granted, that Stone had been preparing for his mature work as a filmmaker during the whole period from his return from Vietnam to the making of *Salvador*. He did not suddenly transform himself into a politically conscious writer-director or improvise his critique of cold war-era America to fit audience taste. (Although Stone's films have been popular, their success actually cuts across the grain of mass audience response in the 1980s and 1990s.) Rather, Stone's work has seemed from the first to be both purposeful and considered in seeking to realize an ultimately coherent—albeit defiantly personal—vision of American political and cultural development from the 1960s to the 1990s—despite Sanjek's contention that the horror films are examples of "incoherent texts."[1] While any particular film can be appreciated as a contribution to this overall vision, an understanding of its source and depth should start with *JFK*, actually one of the later films in the series.

The nearly hysterical reaction to Stone's 1992 film, by now almost inseparable from our experience of the film itself, was a clear indication that Stone had touched a raw nerve in American society's feelings about the Kennedy assassination. The nerve was obviously rawest among the opinion class, the reviewers, commentators, and journalists who apparently considered themselves the guardians of the truth about this episode in American history and who reviled both Stone and his film for their alleged derelictions. That *JFK* most raised the ire of journalists may have pleased Oliver Stone indeed, since the target of the film's attack is not so much the gullible American public (most of which doesn't accept the Warren report anyway), nor even those involved in the possible conspiracy against the president (most of whom are now long dead), but those who allowed the Warren Commission version of events to become the official version through their own ineptitude and, more importantly, their willingness to defer to the established view, namely, the American press.

While the film does not include journalists among its cast of characters (aside from the famous clip of Walter Cronkite tearfully reporting Kennedy's death), their very absence from the story Stone is telling is itself worthy of analysis. Much of the criticism of *JFK* has been directed at Stone's use of Jim Garrison as its protagonist. It is disingenuous, to say the least, for journalists to criticize this movie because of the flaws they claim to see in its main character's methods of investigation. Stone is implicitly asking, through his focus on Garrison's admittedly unsuccessful prosecution, why most journalists did not seriously inquire into the assassination at the time and why many have not done so in the years since. If Stone has embellished Garrison's story, presenting his theory of the assassination conspiracy as wider ranging and more cohesive than it really was, such embellishment is necessary only in the vacuum left when the legitimate press has abandoned its responsibility to seek out the truth when it is in question, as it certainly has been for three decades. Anyone considering the debate about the historical accuracy of *JFK* should consider that those demonizing the film with the greatest indignity may need to answer themselves for the largely unexamined account of this important event. As Amos Vogel has commented, "it is to the media's eternal shame that they have launched a concerted attack on Stone's credibility, perpetuating their previous attacks on those refusing to take the single assassin theory seriously. Buttons are once again being pushed to discredit those who raise questions."[2]

In *Natural Born Killers* we shall again see Stone's critique of the media's abandonment of principle and the effect of that abandonment on society's perception of its own reality. In both films Stone is attempting to compensate for the lack of a reliable vantage point on the circumstances of contemporary American life. His account of the Kennedy assassination and its aftermath may be controversial and certainly contentious, but it is also completely thought through, put together audaciously but ingeniously out of the fragments of evidence and shards of speculation offered by skeptics of the Warren Commission over the years. In the final analysis, however, what is required is not that the film's version of the assassination be taken as literally true—nor even necessarily always plausible—but that, in the words of William D.

Romanowski, it provides "an alternative interpretation of the events surrounding the assassination," thereby "demythologizing the Warren Commission's lone gunman theory."[3] The result is to highlight this episode as a turning point in Americans' relationship to their own established institutions. For it is only in the context of Stone's other films that *JFK* can be fully understood. Taken together, the films trace the unraveling of the American social and cultural fabric as it existed before 22 November 1963; in one way or another, each of them dramatizes an episode in our subsequent history that illustrates the gradual dissolution of the ties that bound Americans to the centers of authority and to the ideas and principles such authorities supposedly embodied.

JFK was attacked perhaps most intensely by some left-wing critics who believed that Stone was romanticizing John Kennedy as an essentially progressive president who, had he lived, would have avoided taking the United States into Vietnam, and thus avoided the painful consequences depicted in Stone's other films.[4] According to Alexander Cockburn, for example, "Kennedy had betrayed the hopes of people like Stone before he had even stepped off the inauguration stand."[5] While critics like Cockburn are almost certainly more accurate in their estimation of Kennedy as a progressive political force than Stone's film has it, such a hindsight view does not explain away the desire of many in Stone's generation to believe in him as such a force. The idealism evoked by JFK may have in some respects flowed from a corrupted source, but can those who responded—sincerely, one presumes—to the idealism of the early 1960s really be accused of regressive thinking simply for wondering if its demise was accelerated by those who had the most to lose from its success?

As someone who experienced firsthand the perversion of liberal idealism in Vietnam, Oliver Stone seems entitled to seek out its cause without being accused of bad faith. Moreover, if ultimately Cockburn is charging Stone with sharing some vestiges of Kennedyesque idealism (which to those sufficiently disabused of its progressive potential is hopelessly circumscribed by bourgeois democracy), there may actually be some substance to the charge. It might even be appropriate to call Stone's values conservative, if by the term we mean, for example, those values associated with the young Ron Kovic in *Born on the Fourth of July.*

While *Platoon* is likely to remain Stone's most detailed and coherent account of the Vietnam experience itself, *Born on the*

Fourth of July is the most thorough depiction of the cultural and psychological mileau bracketing the war, so to speak, first encouraging young Americans to believe in the worthiness of the cause and then forcing many (some more painfully than others) to subject those beliefs to deeply searching scrutiny. As the story chronicles this transformation allegorically through the life of Ron Kovic, idealism seems to give way to outrage and disillusionment, even outright rejection of all that America was previously thought to stand for. Yet, as some reviewers pointed out, Kovic's conversion to antiwar activism does not altogether mark a complete break with his former beliefs and attitudes. For one thing, it is certainly possible to conclude that, as Christian Appy put it, "the real motive behind Kovic's antiwar activities is the desire to recover his manhood."[6] Although in Kovic's case manhood is not merely an abstract construction, it cannot be denied that the issue of male identity looms large in Kovic's odyssey, as it does for many of the characters in Stone's films. For another, the film's depiction of Kovic's appearance at the 1976 Democratic convention as the culmination of his journey toward enlightenment seems to suggest something less than outright rejection of the American political system.

Most critics have interpreted the pre-Vietnam section of *Born on the Fourth of July*, set in Kovic's hometown of Massapequa, New York, as an indictment of the cultural assumptions of American life as they solidified in the 1950s and early 1960s. However, while the glorification of the military ethic which led those like Ron Kovic (and Oliver Stone) to find in war a noble calling is clearly condemned, the opening scenes of Fourth of July unity, as well as the later scene showing the family gathered around the television to listen to President Kennedy's inaugural address, leaves a lingering impression that feelings of common purpose and calls for citizen service were not in themselves phony or fraudulent and that Stone finds admirable, *in principle*, Kovic's capacity to respond to such calls. Taken together, *JFK* and *Born on the Fourth of July* suggest that at the core of Stone's survey of "the history of the second half of America's Twentieth Century"[7] is the reformist liberal notion that the war in Vietnam represented a betrayal of America's highest principles, with the disastrous repercussions registered in the post-Vietnam episodes of *Born on the Fourth of July* and in all of the other films in Stone's historical saga. Before criticizing *JFK* for misrepresenting the Kennedy era,

Alexander Cockburn should perhaps have recalled his previously published interview with Stone, in which Stone told him, "More and more, I feel that movies are not reality, but an approximation of reality, and, in some cases, a wish fulfillment."[8]

At first glance, *Natural Born Killers* would seem to be a wish fulfillment only for a sadist—or serial killers like Mickey and Mallory Knox, the film's antihero protagonists. As a portrayal of American cultural deterioration since the Kennedy assassination, however, the film unfolds like a projection of that culture's most self-destructive impulses. If *JFK* depicts that moment when the dream of American virtue begins to darken, *Natural Born Killers* conjures up a nightmarish vision of the corrupt and depraved society America has become over the generation separating our world from that whose passing can be marked by the events of 22 November 1963. Although *Natural Born Killers* is clearly an indictment of '90s America, it takes on added breadth when viewed as part of Stone's overall rendering of American decline, beginning with *Salvador*.

Someone who had seen only *JFK* among Stone's films might logically expect the specifically political corruption of American culture to be his central preoccupation. *Natural Born Killers* makes it clear, however, that Stone finds the broader cultural decline brought on by political malfeasance to be more profound in its significance. Most obviously, the film shows how thoroughly violence has come to seem not merely pervasive. Violence has become a primary way of coming to terms with American life, whether, as with Mickey and Mallory, through its direct indulgence or, as with the media and the public at large that make Mickey and Mallory into national celebrities, through a corresponding fascination with it and those willing to use it. But a careful viewer of all of Stone's previous films would say that the unraveling of the cultural fabric is a theme uniting all of them, at least implicitly, from the initial pull at the threads portrayed in the Vietnam films to the more visible fraying evident in such films as *Talk Radio* and *Wall Street*.

It could be argued that Stone has spent much of his career working with inherently violent genres such as the gangster film and the war film, as well as with characters more prone than most to violent behavior. Even those films whose main character is not explicitly portrayed as violent—*Salvador, The Doors*—nevertheless revolve around personalities clearly on the edge, beset by internal demons always threatening to escape in unpredictable ways. Since Stone seems drawn to figures exuding a kind of frenzied masculinity, one might consider it disingenuous to present in *Natural Born Killers* a "critical" portrayal of violence run amok. Yet Stone seems to have considered this point himself, as his indictment of the contemporary culture of violence extends as well to the way that culture is represented—and perpetuated—by the merchants of visual media. Indeed, although Wayne Gale, host and producer of a *Hard Copy*-type television program and the third major character in *Natural Born Killers*, is a purveyor of trash TV, he allows Oliver Stone to implicate himself and his profession in the social disintegration of America.

The title of Gale's program, *American Maniacs*, is on the one hand an apt indication of the degraded quality of American television, but it also seems a subtle reminder of many of the protagonists of Oliver Stone's movies, in a gesture that might be signaling us to reflect on the sensationalistic and voyeuristic elements in *Natural Born Killers* itself. In addition, the charged, in-your-face style of Gale's video pieces are unmistakably suggestive of Stone's own kinetic style. The film is thus able to increase its own visceral impact by excerpting passages from *American Maniacs*, while at the same time inviting us to notice the congruence of its stylistic features and those characterizing the TV show. One could take this close identification of Wayne Gale, video producer, and Oliver Stone, film director, even a step further. It has frequently been noted (by, among others, the filmmaker himself), that Stone's best work derives from his ability to feel a kinship with his protagonists. Usually this has resulted in the heroizing of the characters, sometimes, as with *JFK*'s Jim Garrison, drawing charges of distortion and misrepresentation. In *Natural Born Killers* the character with whom Stone seems to be implying a connection would have to be Wayne Gale, which not only makes *Natural Born Killers* the most self-reflexive and self-critical of Stone's films, but also finally shifts the story's emphasis away from Mickey and Mallory onto its own process of signification. Ultimately, *Natural Born Killers* strongly implies that its killers are not at all naturally born but are products of the media environment (including Hollywood movies) that has shaped them.

If either of the two "maniacs" in *Natural Born Killers* seems to get sympathetic treatment from Stone it would arguably be Mallory, who is portrayed as being, if anything, more disturbed than

Mickey but who has also more clearly suffered from the degrada-
tions of the culture in which she was raised. A constant criticism
of Stone has been, of course, that he either neglects to include
female characters or relegates them to conventional roles subordinate to the male characters. That Stone has become sensitive to
these charges is evident not just in the Bonnie Parker-type characterization of Mallory in *Natural Born Killers*, but also in his immediately previous film, *Heaven and Earth* (1992), which explicitly
uses a female character as protagonist. One could question how
convincing these female characters ultimately prove to be, but in
both films Stone can be seen struggling to include in his survey of
recent history the experiences of women and the impact on them
of the destructive drift of that history. In *Natural Born Killers*,
Mallory is shown to be the most direct victim of the violent and
depraved society America has become, although she proves equally capable of striking back at that society—even if her behavior
only reinforces that violence is a deep-seated response to the circumstances of American life.

The most vivid illustration of the way Mallory's environment
has conditioned her—and one of the most memorable sequences in
Natural Born Killers—is the flashback to her life at home before
she met Mickey. Presented as a parody of a 1950s situation comedy, this sequence first of all further dramatizes the role of modern
media in desensitizing its audience to the true nature of violence.
As Mallory's ghastly father, played in a frighteningly believable
way by Rodney Dangerfield, shows himself to be a crude and dangerous man, as her mother comes to seem a woman for whom the
term "long-suffering" was invented, as Mallory herself is revealed
to be a victim of father-daughter incest and other physical abuse,
a canned laugh track provides the kind of reassuring presence that
has come to be a defining feature of the sitcom. The effect is to
normalize the behavior of this family and thus implicitly to suggest its pervasiveness among other "happy" American families. The
sequence additionally suggests that if television can't be blamed
for creating the conditions that make a character like Mallory's
father possible, it does help foster an atmosphere in which our
understanding of reality as it is actually experienced gets blunted
by its mediated representations.

Granting that Mallory is fully justified in her rage against these
conditions, even perhaps to the point of finally killing the father,
the film does not therefore justify the murderous rampage on which

Mallory embarks after running off with Mickey. Although glimpses into Mickey's past show him to have been the product of an
abusive upbringing as well, it is easier to accept the characterization of him as a demon, which was first put forward by the Indian
whose dream of a fatal encounter with such a demon unfortunately
seems to come to life during his encounter with Mickey and Mallory. Mickey is clearly in the line of Stone's previous male protagonists, except that in his case, through whatever combination of
circumstance and inclination, he has crossed over the line inhibiting all-out destructiveness. It is perhaps an indication of the wear-
ing away of restraint between the '60s and the '90s that while *The
Doors'* Jim Morrison ultimately expresses his worst impulses mostly
through his own self-destruction, Mickey lashes out directly at
anyone in his way, with little or no concern for the appropriate-
ness of the target. (Stone also parallels Mickey and Morrison in
their encounters with Native American mysticism; Morrison believes himself to be inhabited by an Indian spirit and fancies his
music to be a form of shamanism, while Mickey shows no comprehension of the visionary Indian, who clearly sees through him).
Still, when Mickey accidentally shoots the Indian, he has just awak-
ened from a dream of his childhood, and one could conclude that
finally he too is acting out the unresolved conflicts of a violent
and dehumanizing youth.

The violence perpetrated by Mickey and Mallory, while portrayed in *Natural Born Killers* in all its horrors, eventually is mir-
rored in the institutional brutalities represented by Jack Scagnetti,
the FBI agent who takes on the pursuit of Mickey and Mallory as
a personal crusade, and the prison warden (played by Tommy Lee
Jones) responsible for them after they are caught and convicted.
Because both Mickey and Mallory are determined to be insane, the
warden's own lust for blood is not satisfied and he invites Scagnetti into the prison to murder them covertly. Scagnetti's violent
impulses run at least as deep as the prisoners', while his position
in law enforcement gives him official permission to indulge them
in the name of keeping order and securing society's retribution for
violating it. But Scagnetti carries his own baggage from the past,
as we discover when he tells the warden of being with his mother
on the University of Texas campus the day Charles Whitman
climbed a clock tower and began shooting at passersby, claiming Scagnetti's mother as one of his victims. This explains his
obsession with mass killers like Mickey and Mallory, but also puts

in historical perspective the picture Stone is presenting of America in the '90s as a culture nearly overwhelmed with carnage and mayhem.

Although it might seem that Stone is providing all of his characters with what has come to be called an "abuse excuse," the use of historical context to help explain these characters' behavior should not be taken to either justify or dismiss it. In Scagnetti's case in particular, the origin of his vendetta in the Whitman case points up a connection that is central to both *Natural Born Killers'* implicit argument and the larger lesson to be drawn from all of Stone's films: America in the thirty years after the turmoil and sociopathology of the 1960s continues to see played out the anarchic forces first released at that time. Even so, Jack Scagnetti, as a representative of established authority, must be held to a higher standard of behavior, a standard he clearly fails to meet. Further, Scagnetti suffers in a comparison with the "criminals" he detests in one significant way. If Mickey and Mallory are at all presented as Bonnie-and-Clyde-like '60s outlaws, it is through their obvious devotion to and love for one another. Certainly their expression of that love is to say the least unconventional (although at one point Mickey wonders aloud why the makers of explicit Hollywood films don't "believe in kissing"), but few viewers of *Natural Born Killers* could doubt its intensity. Scagnetti, however, is shown to be a man so thoroughly warped that his moments of intimacy with women apparently include the act of strangling them during sex. His essentially narcissistic relation to the world is perhaps most vividly illustrated in the scene depicting Mickey and Mallory's capture, which Scagnetti has arranged to be videotaped and during which he insists that his self-dramatization not be ruined by failing to take the outlaws alive. In a gesture of self-reflexivity even more disturbing than that which links his film to the practices of Wayne Gale, Stone ends the capture sequence with a tableau that chillingly evokes the famous videotape of the Rodney King beating.

In many ways, this image brings us back directly to *JFK*. If the beginning of the era Stone has chronicled can be seen in the Zapruder film—reenacted by Stone in his own film—then its ugly fulfillment can perhaps be seen in the King video three decades later. Although both events were recorded inadvertently, by the 1990s cameras of all kinds have become so omnipresent that it is hard to imagine an event comparable in significance to the Kennedy assassination not producing its visual reimaging in multiple forms. Reality has become hot-wired, with the result that it is no longer simply influenced by its various representations (as a superficial reading of Mickey and Mallory's story might suggest) but has become dependent on them. In order to give his excessive actions the appearance of heroism, Scagnetti need only tape them and wait for the transformation a simulated reality can effect. (Judging from the verdict they reached, the jurors in the original King trial must have found that videotape similarly transformative.)

Of course, the Zapruder film was shocking because it showed so graphically the deadly consequences of the American propensity for vigilantism (regardless of who actually pulled the trigger in Dallas), directed at a president attempting to appeal to the better side of the American character. The Scagnetti tape, like the King tape, depicts the same inclination to vigilante violence but shows it to be equally characteristic of those in positions of "authority" who directed it at those perceived to be a threat to that authority. Perhaps this officially sanctioned violence inflicted on the likes of Mickey and Mallory could be seen as the cumulative response to the seeming spread of sociopathic behavior that has afflicted American society in the last three decades. Mickey and Mallory have thus become in the minds of the police and the society they're charged with protecting sacrificial stand-ins for the protosociopath, Lee Harvey Oswald. But *Natural Born Killers* nevertheless makes powerfully manifest the degree to which violence in American culture has become largely undifferentiated in its source and mostly undiscriminating in its effect.

In moving from the Kennedy era to the Mickey and Mallory era, Stone seems to be tracing a parallel movement from shattered idealism to utter nihilism. The sheer carnage that ensues during the duo's escape from prison (accompanied by Wayne Gale) at the end of *Natural Born Killers* is perhaps unrivaled in American film. It is dramatically rendered as the logical expression of the philosophy of life espoused by Mickey in his climactic *American Maniacs* interview. Claiming that he is a biologically determined predator, a "natural born killer," Mickey warns us that we must accept his kind as an inevitable part of life. Thus, while the prison riot that concludes the film is shocking in its overwhelming blood and gore, if we are to believe that Mickey Knox is speaking for Oliver Stone, we can expect our civilization to end in nothing else.

But if films like *Born on Fourth of July* and *JFK* do document

Stone's (and the country's) shattered idealism, *Natural Born Kill-ers* cannot be dismissed as simple nihilistic outrage. Certainly both the film's explosive content and its supercharged style imply a high degree of anger on its maker's part about the conditions being dra-matized; nothing prevents us, however, from regarding this anger as in service of the ultimately regenerative vision associated with the satirist. This is not necessarily to suggest that *Natural Born Killers* be taken as a comedy, although in structure the film does not depart much from the plot conventions of the romantic come-dy as described by Northrop Frye and other literary scholars and historians. Readjusting the focus in this way is especially illumi-nating in understanding the film's final image. It projects Mickey and Mallory into a future where they not only continue to be free but have apparently begun a family, which is shown traveling in a Winnebago with Mickey at the wheel in a suitably fatherly fash-ion. One is perhaps first tempted to see this brief scene as a kind of nasty joke that at best reinforces a strain of grotesquely dark humor running fitfully through the film. But the evidence from Stone's previous films should remind us that what animates them is precisely the moralist's disenchantment with the deficiencies of his society.

The concluding glimpse of a peacefully domestic Knox family might then be interpreted less as an ironic gesture than as a sin-cerely rendered portrait of Mickey and Mallory's ultimate ambi-tion. That someone like Wayne Gale can so readily accept Mickey's account of nature red in tooth and claw says much about his and the media's susceptibility to the romance of outlaw violence, and his subsequent death at the hands of the outlaws themselves is bit-terly satirical of that romance. At the same time, this final killing seems to free Mickey and Mallory from the need to live out the outlaw myth any further, as few are likely to see much romance in destruction so wholesale as that which brings their story to a close. With Scagnetti and the warden consigned to their own ignomini-ous deaths, it is as if the cycle of reciprocal violence has at least momentarily been halted and the romantic couple has found the simple happiness they had all along been seeking. But while this happy ending is certainly outrageous and provocative, in fleetingly offering a vision of paradise regained, it should remind us that Stone's chronicle of American decline has always maintained the standard of the country's own high ideals by which to measure its failures. Seen in this context, *Natural Born Killers* makes vividly apparent how thoroughly the New Frontier has become, like the Old, a blood-soaked territory where those professed ideals have become helplessly—but perhaps not hopelessly—compromised and perverted.

Notes

1. David Sanjek, "The Hysterical Imagination: The Horror Films of Oliver Stone," *Post Script* 12, no. 1 (Fall 1992): 54.

2. Amos Vogel, "*JFK:* The Question of Propaganda," *Antioch Review* 50, no. 3 (Summer 1992): 578–79.

3. William D. Romanowski, "Oliver Stone's *JFK:* Commercial Film-making, Cultural History, and Conflict," *Journal of Popular Film and Television* 21, no. 2 (Summer 1992): 64.

4. This objection to Stone's political judgment seems to me to be at the heart of Sanjek's notion that his films are "incoherent." It is difficult to see how Stone's predilection for melodrama and even outright allegory could be the source of ambivalence and obfuscation—as Sanjek argues it is—unless the standard being used is solely ideological.

5. Alexander Cockburn, "John and Oliver's Bogus Adventure," *Sight and Sound* 1, no. 10 (February 1992): 23.

6. Christian Appy, "Vietnam According to Oliver Stone," *Commonweal* 23 (March 1990): 188.

7. Robert Stone, "Oliver Stone's USA," *New York Review of Books*, 17 February 1994, 22.

8. Alexander Cockburn, "Oliver Stone Takes Stock," *American Film* 13 (December 1987): 23.

Chapter 12

Nixon

"Citizen Nixon"—Oliver Stone's Wellesian View of a Failed Public Figure

Frank E. Beaver

The wide-ranging, provocative discussions that followed the release of Oliver Stone's *Nixon* in December 1995 frequently focused on comparisons of this large, complex film with other dramatic and cinematic models. Shakespearean tragedy was one commonly invoked analogue for a drama that seizes upon the public (documented) and private (imagined) lives of a historical figure and explores the "separate" lives for their revelations about human nature.

That the dramatic exploration involves the great (or near-great) public personality who is subject to self-defeating character flaws further affirms the Shakespearean model. The prologue to *Nixon* lays claim to such grand investigative intentions: "This film is an attempt to understand the truth of Richard Nixon, thirty-seventh president of the United States. It is based on numerous public sources and on an incomplete historical record." A biblical quote from Matthew 16:26 follows shortly in the opening titles: "What shall it profit a man if he shall gain the whole world and lose his soul." (This biblical reference to Richard Nixon's own fate is attributed later in the film's text to the 1952 and 1956 presidential candidate Adlai E. Stevenson Jr.)

As a tale of a fallen achiever, a gainer who in the end loses, Oliver Stone's *Nixon* carries archetypal resemblances to the familiar, darkly toned historical tragedies penned by William Shakespeare, i.e., *Julius Caesar, Antony and Cleopatra, Henry V.* In interviews given to the press during the making of the film, as well as after its release, Stone frequently referred to Shakespeare's penchant for reappropriating historical figures as the antiheroic pro-

275

tagonists of drama. According to Stone *Nixon* was approached in the same manner, not as history but as inventive drama with its basis residing in part in annotated biographical/factual record. Stone said he became attracted to Richard M. Nixon as a subject because of the tragic proportions of the man's life: "Richard Nixon is a giant of a tragic figure in the classic Greek and Shakespearean tradition. Humble origins, rising to the top, then crashing down in a heap of hubris. Nixon himself said that he had been to the highest peaks and the lowest valleys. That's great drama."[1]

Even at first glance film critics and cineastes also saw in *Nixon* methodological construction as well as narrative and visual technique that paid homage to Orson Welles' *Citizen Kane*. Welles and Stone alike claimed that their films were attempts to uncover certain truths about public figures of lasting mystery and enigma. The approach in both cases involved a variety of different ways of looking at the subject for *possible* clues/truths rather than absolutes.

In the search for the meaning of the "Rosebud" statement in *Citizen Kane* a mosaic of interviews and nonlinear flashbacks provide a limited, albeit powerful, portrait of a wealthy man who lives out his final years in isolated lonelinesss. Welles' approach is that of an investigative psychological case study based on the assumption that the truth and value (knowability) of any individual's life is subjective at best, and that the clues revealed in any investigation are merely pieces in a larger puzzle. Philosophically, the investigation embodies the very essence of the film, its raison d'être. Welles said, "The point of (*Citizen Kane*), "is not so much the solution of the problem as its presentation."[2]

Oliver Stone argued the approach to *Nixon* on similar philosophical grounds. In a 1 January 1996 television interview with WNET TV's Charlie Rose, Stone said of Richard Nixon: "This is not a man who is geared to let you in. . . . obviously Pat Nixon we thought was the greatest in. . . . But I maintain . . . the wife, Haldeman, nobody got in. Nobody got in finally to the black hole that was Richard Nixon. He remains like Kane had before him an enigma, an enigma."[3]

Inspired by *Citizen Kane*, Stone makes numerous concessions in *Nixon* to the design of Welles' masterpiece. Structurally, both *Kane* and *Nixon* are mosaic, nonlinear treatments of their protagonists' lives. They are investigative studies which combine the public record with private views for their possible character revelations.

Citizen Kane opens with the death of Charles Foster Kane, a fictional representation of the newspaper magnate William Randolph Hearst. Kane dies in the isolated loneliness of Xanadu, the palatial Gothic mansion where the newspaper magnate in his latter years had shielded himself from a world on which he had increasingly and bitterly soured. Dying alone in a stark upstairs bedroom of Xanadu, Kane utters his last word, "Rosebud," as, simultaneously, a glass globe containing a miniature snow scene and held in Kane's large hands is released and crashes on the marble floor.

Immediately a *March of Time*-styled overview of Kane's life appears, recounting the highs and lows of an existence framed by wealth, power, unrealized political ambition, and failed personal relationships. The producers of the newsreel impatiently turn the projector off and the sound grinds to a distorted halt as the last image fades. Dissatisfied with the public record and its "superficiality," a reporter, the character Thompson, is charged with the task of uncovering the meaning behind Kane's final utterance, by interviewing everybody who knew the man: "Rosebud, dead or alive," Thompson is told. "It'll probably turn out to be a very simple thing."

Thompson's investigation launches a series of interviews and flashbacks that together offer glimpses into Kane's hidden personal life: the innocence of childhood cut short by sudden wealth; precocious arrogance as a young newspaper publisher with money to burn; the betrayal of marriage to a prominent socialite in a "love nest" exposé that also destroys all political ambition; the sad realization that neither success nor love can be bought; the final loneliness in Xanadu surrounded by material possessions purchased out of desperation for gratification of any sort.

From the various personal perspectives of those who had been intimately affiliated with Charles Foster Kane, there emerges a portrait of a man encumbered by wealth ("If I hadn't been so rich, I could have been a great person.") and desperate for love but unable to find it because he had no love to give. Jedediah Leland (Joseph Cotten), once Kane's colleague, closest friend, and confidante verbalizes this character flaw for the reporter Thompson: "Love. That's why he did everything. That's why he went into politics. Seems we weren't enough. He wanted all the voters to love him too. Guess all he wanted out of life was love; that's Charlie's story, how he lost it. Y'see, he just didn't have any to give."

Oliver Stone's own investigation into the enigma of Richard

Nixon (what Stone called in press interviews the search for Nixon's "secrets") copycats, sometimes rather obviously, sometimes more indirectly, the *Citizen Kane* model. *Nixon* begins with images projected on a portable screen of a black-and-white 16mm sales-training film. The location is a Watergate conference room—date: 17 June 1972—and the training film is a ruse to cover the final preparations by the electronic surveillance burglars before their arrest within the headquarters of the Democratic National Committee in the Watergate building. The scene concludes with a shot of the projector lens as the training film rattles to an end, the strong beam of projected light reminiscent of the powerful projector light at the conclusion of *Citizen Kane*'s "News-On-the-March" compilation film. The film-within-a-film analogy serves as a self-reflexive tease for the ensuing analysis of the "political death" of Richard M. Nixon as a result of his handling of the illegal Watergate break-ins and subsequent cover-up.

Again reminiscent of the opening of *Citizen Kane*, scene two of *Nixon* begins with a dark, ominous shot of the White House, dated by subtitle as November 1973 and framed through the iron bars of the fence that looks toward the Executive Mansion's facade. This composition not only resembles the opening shot of Xanadu in detail and in tone, but a light in an upstairs room of the White House correlates Richard Nixon's impending political death with Kane's death in a lonely upstairs room of his Gothic mansion.

What is revealed shortly (in scene four) is that the White House light emanates from the Lincoln Sitting Room where Nixon waits to receive General Alexander Haig and audiotapes recorded in the White House pertaining to Watergate and ordered turned over to the Senate Watergate Committee by Judge John Sirica. The tapes hold evidence of Nixon's personal knowledge of the burglary and attempted cover-up, and thus portend the end (death) of his presidency.

The progression of action begun in this November 1973 scene with Nixon confronting the tapes and his fateful demise is resumed in scene nine and does not conclude until very near the film's end when Pat Nixon enters the Lincoln Sitting Room, finds her by-then intoxicated husband, and berates him for failing to burn the evidence that is about to bring him down.

The stretching of this symbolic "death" scene over the course of *Nixon* serves as the framework around which myriad flashback scenes (more than one hundred) are intercut to suggest the ins and outs and highs and lows of Nixon's public career and his personal life.

The flow of imagery in *Nixon* is highly abrupt, evocative, often abstract. A mixed-media approach frequently places the actors portraying their historical counterparts into documentary footage of significant political events. For example, Anthony Hopkins (Nixon) appears opposite the real John F. Kennedy in one of the familiar televised Kennedy-Nixon presidential debates of 1960. Again this evocative rather than realistic approach, the subtle blending of the documentary with the simulated, the abrupt flow of nonlinear incidents, all take their creative cues from *Citizen Kane*. (The "News-On-the March" simulation often places Welles as Kane with familiar world leaders while authentic documentary footage is interspersed with the simulations, e.g, Teddy Roosevelt and his Rough Riders are intercut in actual newsreel footage.)

Lest one fail to recognize the homage Oliver Stone's *Nixon* is paying to Orson Welles' masterpiece, two very obvious replications occur. In depicting the increasingly strained relationship between Nixon and his wife Pat, Stone restages the alienated husband-wife table scene from *Citizen Kane* where Kane and wife Emily, at the conclusion of a brief montage sequence, are shown at opposite ends of a screen-width dining table, silently reading their newspapers. The image conveys through visual language the dissolution of a once-intimate relationship. Similarly, Stone places Richard and Pat Nixon in 1973 at the far ends of a table in the White House dining room. The toll of Watergate has resulted in a distant, icy relationship with Nixon abruptly dismissing his wife from dinner and she departing with: "Dick, sometimes I understand why they hate you."

The "News-On-the-March" compilation overview of Kane's life, which occurs just after his death early in Citizen Kane, is also imitated by Stone and placed in *Nixon* after Nixon's farewell-to-the-press speech ("You won't have Nixon to kick around anymore.") following an unsuccessful bid for the governorship of California in 1962. The newsreel is remarkably similar in tone to the one in *Citizen Kane* because it treats Richard Nixon as political history, someone in the past who is "dead." A voice-over in the *Kane* newsreel summarizes the newspaper magnate's failed political ambitions metaphorically: "In politics always a bridesmaid, never a bride." While Oliver Stone's film doesn't repeat these exact words, the Nixon newsreel writes a similar political obituary.

Reporter (voice-over): "It was a great story of its time and, in California where it started, it has come to a crashing end. It is too bad in a way, because the truth is, we will never know who Richard Nixon really was. And now that he is gone, we never will . . ." The *Nixon* newsreel fades out with the same distorted, interrupted projector sound employed by Welles in *Citizen Kane*. This sound in both instances suggests, appropriately, that the neatly arranged documentary compilations are not yet final accounts of the men whose lives they have so glibly summarized. The search for the truth as to who these public figures really were will continue.

The plotting device which involves the search for some missing object or person as the basis of a film's narrative construction (and the intrigue that the search generates) has been labelled the "MacGuffin." Searching for Rosebud in *Citizen Kane* becomes the MacGuffin that takes reporter Thompson to a variety of Kane acquaintances and in the process brings telling glimpses of an unfulfilled existence. Ironically, the reporter never learns that Rosebud was the sled with which Kane was playing the day he was abruptly removed from his parents' farm in Colorado. The viewer only receives this information when in the concluding shots of the film the sled is tossed into a furnace by workmen clearing Xanadu of a lifetime of clutter. The painted letters "Rosebud" are seen dissolving in heat as the flames engulf the childhood toy.

This final revelation of Kane's deathbed obsession is wide open to psychological analysis. Perhaps the sled is a symbol of lost innocence? Perhaps final knowledge that power and wealth have little meaning for the ultimate value of one's life? Or perhaps an epiphanal moment for the time when one understands the beginning of worldly sin: a symbolic casting out of the Garden of Eden?

Clearly Rosebud represented something that Charles Foster Kane had lost—been deprived of, and had long craved to repossess for whatever reasons. We in fact learn that Kane was on the way to a warehouse to look at the stored possessions (including the sled) from his Colorado homestead when he first encountered Susan Alexander on a street outside a drugstore. Kane speaks of the desire to see these simple objects in a depressed tone that suggests melancholia, one motivational explanation for the ensuing extramarital relationship with the naive, unpolished but attractive Susan Alexander. The launching of the affair will seal Kane's political fate.

Oliver Stone's *Nixon* avoids any overtly recognizable MacGuffin and yet this element can be clearly detected as a significant part of the film's psychoanalytical revelations about Richard Nixon. In detailing Nixon's progress from a simple Whittier, California, childhood to the presidency of the United States, the film's text presents Nixon—on a number of occasions—obsessed with the early deaths of his two brothers, seven-year-old Arthur and 23-year-old Harold. In no uncertain terms *Nixon* proffers that it was the loss of these two brothers (especially the older Harold) which impelled Richard Nixon's parents to send their son away (to law school) and to expect him, as the survivor, "to be strong" and to achieve.

In the same sense that the taking away of the Rosebud sled in *Citizen Kane* represented a moment of ensuing opportunity and later melancholia (ambition and self-defeat), the loss of Arthur and Harold was, according to Oliver Stone's interpretation, recognized by Richard Nixon as similarly significant in a political career fixated on a drive to succeed at all cost, but one paradoxically plagued by self-doubting and melancholia.

Nixon's text has the 37th U.S. president saying in 1973 to H. R. Haldeman that he knew with the death of Robert Kennedy in the Ambassador Hotel in 1968 he'd achieve his goal of winning the White House: "I knew I'd be president. Death paved the way, didn't it? Vietnam. The Kennedys. It cleared a path through the wilderness for me. Over the bodies. . . . four bodies." Haldeman responds: "You mean two . . . two bodies?" Haldeman does not understand the continuity of loss by death that began for Nixon on his childhood farm and which initiated movement toward public achievement and eventual disgrace of "biblical proportions"—a phrase spoken in *Nixon* by Henry Kissinger just before Nixon's resignation. If *Nixon* has its Rosebud, its deathbed obsession for that which was lost, it is rooted as in *Citizen Kane* on a poor, distant farm where fate abruptly intervenes and casts one, biblically, from innocence into an opportunistic world where achievement ends in sad defeat.

Nixon, like *Citizen Kane,* also develops the theme of an individual desperate for love. In the flashback visualizations of those closest to Richard Nixon—wife Pat, H. R. Haldeman, John Mitchell, John Dean, Henry Kissinger, Alexander Haig, Tricia Nixon—there emerges a portrait of a man obsessed by the popularity and easy acceptance of the Kennedy brothers, a man of low self-esteem who is convinced that the public "hates" him, someone who is depicted as not being able to find love because he himself was incapable of imparting love. When Pat Nixon out of personal frustration indicates the desire for a divorce, her husband can only see the request as the result of political defeat, not personal shortcomings. Nixon says to his wife: "They want to drive us apart. To beat us. We can't let them do that. . . . We belong together." Pat responds: "That's what you said the first time we met. You didn't even know me." The implication is that of a relationship initiated and sustained by necessity and political instinct rather than by genuine affection.

Nixon's distancing from his family in favor of a positive public response is addressed directly when Pat, alone with her husband in their White House bedroom, tells him: "I wish . . . you knew how much I love you, that's all. It took me a long time to fall in love with you, Dick. But I did. And it doesn't make you happy. You want them (the voting public) to love you . . ." This accusation mirrors that given to Thompson by Jed Leland in *Citizen Kane:* "Love. That's why he went into politics. Seems we weren't enough. He wanted all the voters to love him too."

Henry Kissinger (Paul Sorvino) is heard reiterating this idea with hypothetical irony after Nixon's fall: "Can you imagine what this man would have been if he had ever been loved?" Jed Leland might have phrased this question similarly: "Don't you wonder what Charlie Kane might have gotten out of life if he'd had any love to give?" Both *Nixon* and *Citizen Kane* give glimpses of powerful American icons seeking to attract and hold people—privately and publicly—but failing to do so for similarly articulated reasons.

In theme, structure, and process *Nixon* bows to *Citizen Kane.* So too do the visual and sound designs chosen by Oliver Stone and his collaborators resemble those that distinguished Orson Welles' film as an innovative, breakthrough work of art. *Nixon* is filled with cinematographic compositions that co-opt the unsettling power of the canted Dutch-angle shot, the haughty effect of extreme low-angle camera positions and the blocking of actors in foreground-background positions so that character interaction can be sustained without editorial fragmentation. An exemplary use of this technique occurs during an early conversation between Nixon (foreground) and Haldeman (background) discussing White House connections to Watergate. Rack focus shifts from sharp to soft-focused images of the two men provide alternating emphases without editing imposition.

Bird's-eye-view shots introduce and dramatize critical scenes, e.g., Nixon's sudden appearance before student protestors outside the Lincoln Memorial. Extreme wide-angle compositions and dark, low-key lighting schemes convey the White House as an increasingly hollow, lonely prison on the order of Xanadu. Bold, expressionistic black-and-white images—often halated and ghostly—are intercut abruptly with color images to suggest varying perspectives and points of view. Montages, encapsulating important historical and personal events, abound. The music for *Nixon* borrows familiar motifs from Bernard Hermann's score for *Citizen Kane*. Liberal use of voice-over narration dramatizes quick-cut visualizations. Sound bursts, silences, and fades underscore *Nixon's* psychological dimensions. Altogether Oliver Stone seeks to reach the eye and the ear with the same sensorial experimentation that helped set *Citizen Kane* apart from traditional cinematic expression.

The extent of Stone's success in reappropriating numerous technical, stylistic, and narrative elements attributable to the genius of Orson Welles is open to debate. Despite very obvious similarities, *Citizen Kane* and *Nixon* remain entirely different films in their accumulative effect. Both are investigative psychodramas presented in nonlinear form and both present dark, sardonic portraits that in their momentary insights are gripping and unforgettable. Yet *Nixon's* portrait emerges organically from intense historical research where every moment of character innuendo and plotting detail has sought some basis of evidentiary origin, derived from meticulous research. *Citizen Kane*, by contrast, uses the biographical record of William Randolph Hearst's life minimally. Welles' study in the end is essentially imaginative whereas Oliver Stone's film exploits in docudrama-like fashion the power of the "remembered" event. *Nixon* electrifies with its historical facsimiles: a stiff Pat Nixon sitting awkwardly by her husband during his famous "Checkers" speech to the nation; the self-pitying "You won't have Nixon to kick around anymore" farewell; a rambling resignation monologue; and a thousand additional images that remind one of photos seen before in history books. One listens to the dialogue of *Nixon* and has the same feeling that it too or something very much like it was once spoken by the historical figures being impersonated on the screen. Stone, of course, in the prologue admits that part of his film is derived from an "incomplete historical record," and yet the ultimate effect of *Nixon*, its power as drama, comes through its overriding aura of creative authenticity, the sense that what one is seeing and hearing may well have been very much like the world being re-created. *Citizen Kane* on the other hand employs its stylistic maneuverings in such a way that history and the man being fictionalized on the screen (William Randolph Hearst) are ultimately unimportant in the story that Welles builds around his screen character, Charles Foster Kane. Therein resides the essential difference in two very dynamic, powerfully crafted films: Stone remains forever committed to history in the tradition of the docudrama; Welles saw history as the basis of a good story and then departed from the record.

Notes

1. Oliver Stone interview by Michael Singer in *Nixon: An Oliver Stone Film*, ed. Eric Hamburg (New York: Hyperion, 1995), xv.

2. Frank E. Beaver, *On Film: A History of the Motion Picture* (New York: McGraw Hill, 1983), 309.

3. Oliver Stone, interview by Charlie Rose, *Charlie Rose transcription #1542*, Public Broadcast System, WNET-TV (New York City), 1 January 1996.

The Director's Filmography

Seizure (Cinerama and American International Pictures, 1974)

Producers: Garrard Glenn and Jeffrey Kapelmann.

Screenplay: Edward Mann and Oliver Stone, based on a story by Oliver Stone.

Photography: Roger Racine.

Music: Lee Gagnon.

Cast: Jonathan Frid, Martine Beswick, Joe Sirola, Christina Pickles, Roger de Koven, Mary Woronov, Herve Villechaize, Richard Cox, Henry Baker, Timothy Ousey, Lucy Bingham, Alexis Kirk, Emil Meola.

Running Time: 93 minutes.

The Hand (Orion Pictures and Warner Brothers, 1981)

Producer: Edward R. Pressman.

Screenplay: Oliver Stone, based on the novel *The Lizard's Tail* by Marc Brandel.

Photography: King Baggot.

Music: James Horner.

Cast: Michael Caine, Andrea Marcovicci, Annie McEnroe, Bruce McGill, Viveca Lindfors, Rosemary Murphy, Mara Hobel, Pat Corley, Bill Marshall, Charles Fletcher.

Running Time: 104 minutes.

Salvador (Hemdale and Virgin Films, 1986)

Producers: Gerald Green and Oliver Stone.

Screenplay: Oliver Stone and Richard Boyle, based on Richard Boyle's unpublished diaries.

Photography: Robert Richardson.

Editor: Claire Simpson.
Music: George Delerue.
Cast: James Woods, James Belushi, Elepedia Carrillo, Michael Murphy, John Savage, Tony Plana, Cynthia Gibb, Colby Chester, Will MacMillan, Jorge Luke, Valerie Wilman, Jose Carlos Ruiz, Juan Gernandez.
Running Time: 122 minutes.

Platoon (Hemdale and Orion Pictures, 1986)

Producer: Arnold Kopelson.
Screenplay: Oliver Stone.
Photography: Robert Richardson.
Editor: Claire Simpson.
Music: George Delerue.
Cast: Tom Berenger, Willem Dafoe, Charlie Sheen, Forrest Whitaker, Francesco Quinn, John C. McGinley, Richard Edson, Kevin Dillon, Reggie Johnson, Keith David, Johnny Depp, David Neidorf, Mark Moses, Chris Pedersen, Corkey Ford, Corey Glover, Bob Orwig.
Running Time: 111 minutes.

Wall Street (Twentieth-Century Fox, 1987)

Producer: Edward R. Pressman.
Screenplay: Oliver Stone and Stanley Weiser.
Photography: Robert Richardson.
Editor: Claire Simpson.
Music: Stewart Copeland.
Cast: Michael Douglas, Charlie Sheen, Daryl Hannah, Martin Sheen, Terence Stamp, James Spader, Sean Young, Millie Perkins, John C. McGinley, Hal Holbrook, Tamara Tunie, Franklin Cover, Sylvia Miles, Sean Stone.
Running Time: 124 minutes.

Talk Radio (Universal Pictures,1988)

Producers: Edward R. Pressman and A. Kitman Ho.
Screenplay: Eric Bogosian and Oliver Stone, based on the play *Talk Radio* by Eric Bogosian and the book *Talked to Death: The Life and Murder of Alan Berg* by Stephen Singular.
Photography: Robert Richardson.
Editor: David Brenner.

Music: Stewart Copeland.
Cast: Eric Bogosian, Ellen Greene, Leslie Hope, Alec Baldwin,
         John C. McGinley, John Pankow, Michael Wincott, Linda
         Atkinson, Robert Trebar, Zach Grenier, Anna Levine,
         Rockets Redglare, Tony Frank, Harlan Jordan.
Running Time: 110 minutes.

Born on the Fourth of July (Universal Pictures, 1989)

Producers: A. Kitman Ho and Oliver Stone
Screenplay: Oliver Stone and Ron Kovic, based on the book *Born
         on the Fourth of July* by Ron Kovic.
Photography: Robert Richardson.
Editors: David Brenner and Joe Hutshing.
Music: John Williams.
Cast: Tom Cruise, Kyra Sedgwick, Caroline Kava, Raymond J.
         Barry, Jerry Levine, Frank Whaley, Willem Dafoe, Tom
         Berenger, Bryan Larkin, Josh Evans, Tony Frank, Jayne
         Hayes.
Running Time: 145 minutes.

The Doors (Tri-Star Pictures, 1991)

Producers: Sasha Harari, Bill Graham, and A. Kitman Ho.
Screenplay: Oliver Stone and J. Randall Johnson, based on the book
         Riders of the Storm by John Densmore and Jim Morrison's
         poetry.
Photography: Robert Richardson.
Editors: David Brenner and Joe Hutshing.
Executive Music Producer: Budd Car.
Cast: Val Kilmer, Meg Ryan, Kevin Dillon, Kyle MacLachlan,
         Frank Whaley, Michael Madsen, Kathleen Quinlan, Micha-
         el Wincott, Dennis Burkley, Josh Evans, Paul Williams,
         Kristina Fulton, Crispin Glover.
Running Time: 141 minutes.

JFK (Warner Brothers, 1991)

Producers: A. Kitman Ho and Oliver Stone.
Screenplay: Oliver Stone and Zachary Sklar, based on the books
         On the Trail of the Assassins by Jim Garrison and *Cross-
         fire: The Plot That Killed Kennedy* by Jim Marrs.
Photography: Robert Richardson.

Editors: Joe Hutshing and Pietro Scalia.
Music: John Williams.
Cast: Kevin Costner, Sissy Spacek, Joe Pesci, Tommy Lee Jones, Gary Oldman, Joe O. Sanders, Laurie Metcalf, Michael Rooker, Jack Lemmon, Walter Matthau, Donald Sutherland, Kevin Bacon, Edward Asner, Brian Doyle-Murray, Jim Garrison.
Running Time: 189 minutes.

Heaven and Earth (Warner Brothers, 1993)

Producers: Oliver Stone, Arnon Milchan, Robert Kline, and A. Kitman Ho.
Screenplay: Oliver Stone, based on the books *The Day Heaven and Earth Changed Places* by Le Ly Hayslip with Jay Wurts and *Child of War, Woman of Peace* by Le Ly Hayslip with James Hayslip.
Photography: Robert Richardson.
Editors: David Brenner and Sally Menke.
Music: Kitaro.
Cast: Hiep Thi Le, Joan Chen, Tommy Lee Jones, Haing S. Ngor, Debbie Reynolds, Dustin Nguyen, Lan Nguyen Calderon, Mai Le Ho, Conchata Ferrell, Vivian Wu, Dale Dye, Liem Whatley, Robert Burke, Michael Paul Chang.
Running Time: 142 minutes.

Natural Born Killers (Warner Brothers, 1994)

Producers: Jane Hamsher, Don Murphy, Clayton Townsend, Aron Milchan, Thom Mount, and Rand Vossler.
Screenplay: David Veloz, Richard Rutowski, and Oliver Stone based on a story by Quentin Tarantino.
Photography: Robert Richardson.
Editors: Hank Corwin and Brian Berdan.
Cast: Woody Harrelson, Juliette Lewis, Robert Downey Jr., Tommy Lee Jones, Rodney Dangerfield.
Running Time: 118 minutes.

Nixon (Hollywood Pictures, Cinergi/ Illusion Entertainment Group, 1995)

Producers: Clayton Townsend, Oliver Stone, and Andrew G. Vjna.
Screenplay: Stephen J. Rivele, Christopher Wilkinson, and Oliver Stone, based on numerous public sources.

Photography: Robert Richardson.
Editors: Hank Corwin and Brian Berdan.
Music: John Williams.
Cast: Anthony Hopkins, Joan Allen, Mary Steenburgen, Powers
         Boothe, David Hyde Pierce, Paul Sorvino, J. T. Walsh,
         James Woods, Ed Harris, Bob Hoskins, E. G. Marshall,
         David Paymer.
Running Time: 191 minutes.

Index

abstractions, 31, 32
Adamic myth, 209, 210, 217
adventure: cultural history of,
   113-22; drugs and, 114-15
Adventurer, The (Zweig), 113
Aeschylus, on suffering, 22
Alexander, Susan, 280
alienation, 86-90
Allen, Woody, 23
All The President's Men, 78
America: as commodity, 136-37;
   decline of, 264, 266, 268, 270-
   71; spirit of, 54-56
American culture, xx; political
   corruption of, 264; violence in,
   269
American dream, 127, 134
American Dream, An (Mailer), 16
American Film, Kovic interview
   in, 170
American Maniacs, 265, 269
Andress, Ursula, 41
Andrews, Dean, 214
Anglocentrism, 86-90
Angus, Ian: on media/reality, 139
Apocalypse Now, 109
appearance/truth, dialectic of, 215
Appy, Christian: on Kovic antiwar
   activities, 263
art, as prostitution, 15-16
Aryan Nation, Berg and, 148, 150
Asner, Edward, 230

Auteur principle, 67
Axelrod, Pauline, 103

Bacon, Kevin, 230
Baker, Henry, 70
Balzac, Honore de, 10, 26
Bannister, W. Guy, 212, 213, 230
Barker, Adam: on Stone, 78
Barnes, Sergeant, xiii, 47, 72,
   110; influence of, 103, 109,
   120;
Taylor and, 116, 118, 119, 120-
   21, 122
Barn of the Naked Dead, 68
Barthes, Roland: on death, 47
Baudrillard, Jean, 139; on
   restoration of the real, 140
Beast With Five Fingers, The, 71
Beaver, Frank, 259; on *Heaven
   and Earth,* 242; on *Nixon,*
   xxvi-xxvii
Belin, David W.: criticism by,
   228
Belushi, James, 86, 99, 103
Berenger, Tom, xiii
Berg, Alan, xii, xiv, 150, 151,
   154
Bertolucci, Bernardo, 51
Bertrand, Clay. *See* Shaw, Clay
Beswick, Martine, 70, 71
*Between Men: English Literature
   and Male Homosocial Desire*

291

Notes on Contributors

Frank E. Beaver is professor and director of graduate studies in the Department of Telecommunication Arts and Film at the University of Michigan. He is the author of *Oliver Stone: Wakeup Cinema* (New York: Twayne Publishers, 1994) and editor for the Twayne Filmmakers Series.

Jack Boozer Jr. is a professor in the Film and Video Program at Georgia State University in Atlanta. He teaches feature screenwriting, film studies, and film and video production.

David Breskin, who lives in San Francisco, is a poet, novelist, and producer of jazz records. His book of poems, *Fresh Kills*, will be published by Cleveland State University in the fall of 1997.

Daniel Green is a professor in the English Department at Pittsburg State University in Kansas where he specializes in film and contemporary American fiction. He has published articles on Woody Allen, Albert Brooks, John Barth, and Stanley Elkin.

Richard Keenan is a contributing editor for *Literature/Film Quarterly* and professor of English at The University of Maryland Eastern Shore, where he teaches courses in English Literature and the relationship between literature and film. He has published widely including essays on Browning, detective fiction, biography, and film.

Don Kunz is professor of English and coordinator of the Film Studies Program at the University of Rhode Island. He has published satire, fiction, and poetry as well as essays on drama, fiction, pedagogy, and film.

Bryan Marinelli is an instructor in the Humanities/Social Science Department at the New England Institute of Technology where he teaches courses in composition, literature, speech communication, and film.

Martin J. Medhurst is professor and associate head in the Department of Speech Communication and Theatre Arts at Texas A&M University.

Suzanne E. O'Hop recently earned her doctorate in film and literature at the University of Rhode Island and is teaching English in Arizona.

Robert A. Rosenstone is professor of History at the California Institute of Technology and a contributing editor of film reviews to the *American Historical Review*. He has published books on the Spanish Civil War, John Reed, and American encounters with the Japanese.

David Sanjek has taught cinema studies at the New School for Social Research and is at work on a manuscript entitled *Grisly Artistry: The American Horror Film*. He works as the Director of Archives for Broadcast Music, Inc. in New York City.

John F. Stone wrote his doctoral dissertation on Oliver Stone. He is a professor in the Communication Department at the University of Wisconsin at Whitewater. He has published articles on rhetorical strategies and film.

Clyde Taylor is a professor in the English Department at Tufts University, an associate editor of *Black Film Review*, and the editor of *Vietnam and Black America: An Anthology of Protest and Resistance* (Garden City, N.Y.: Doubleday Anchor, 1973).

Jim Welsh is a professor in the English Department at Salisbury State University in Salisbury, Maryland, where he teaches cinema studies and edits *Literature/Film Quarterly*. He is the founding president of the Literature/Film Association. His last book was *Peter Watkins: A Guide to References and Resources* (Boston: G. K. Hall, 1986).

Donald Whaley is a professor in the History Department at Salisbury State University in Salisbury, Maryland where he teaches American cultural history. A veteran of the Vietnam War, Whaley edited the special issue on Vietnam War film for *Literature/ Film Quarterly* 20.3 (1992).

About the Editor

Don Kunz is professor of English at the University of Rhode Island where he has served as Director of Graduate Studies in English and Director of the University Honors Program. He is currently Coordinator of the Film Studies Program in the College of Arts and Sciences. Professor Kunz teaches courses in literature, creative writing, and film studies. He is the author of *The Drama of Thomas Shadwell* (Salzburg, Austria: Institut für Englische Sprache und Literatur Universität Salzburg, 1972). He has published satire, fiction, and poetry as well as essays on British drama, American fiction, pedagogy, and American film.